"Several factors make Sitchin's well-referenced works outstandingly different from all others that present this central theme. For one, his linguistic skills, which include not only several modern languages that make it possible for him to consult other scholars' works in their original tongues, but the ancient Sumerian, Egyptian, Hebrew, and other languages of antiquity as well.

"The devotion of thirty years to academic search and personal investigation before publishing resulted in unusual thoroughness, perspective, and modifications where need arose. The author's pursuit of the earliest available texts and artifacts also made possible the wealth of photos and line drawings made for his books from tablets, monuments, murals, pottery, seals, etc. Used generously throughout, they provide vital visual evidence. . . . While the author does not pretend to solve all the puzzles that have kept intensive researchers baffled for well over one hundred years, he has provided some new clues."

—Rosemary Decker, historian and researcher

ZECHARIA SITCHIN
Author of <u>*The 12th Planet*</u>

THE LOST
REALMS

The Fourth
Book of
<u>The Earth Chronicles</u>

BEAR & COMPANY
P U B L I S H I N G
SANTA FE, NEW MEXICO

LIBRARY OF CONGRESS CATALOGING-IN-PUBLICATION DATA

Sitchin, Zecharia.
   The lost realms / Zecharia Sitchin.
      p.   cm. — (The fourth book in the Earth Chronicles)
   Includes bibliographical references and indexes.
   ISBN 0-939680-84-X

   1. Civilization, Ancient—Extraterrestrial influences.
2. Incas—Antiquities. 3. Indians of Central America—
Antiquities. 4. Indians of Mexico—Antiquities. 5. Central
America—Antiquities. 6. Mexico—Antiquities. I. Title. II. Series:
Sitchin, Zecharia. Earth chronicles ; 4.
CB156.S574 1990
972'.01—dc20   89-91927
                                                CIP

The Bear & Company edition of *The Lost Realms* is the first hardcover edition of this book. It was previously published in paperback by Avon in 1990.

Bear & Company, Inc.
Santa Fe, NM 87504-2860

Jacket illustration: Angela C. Werneke © 1990
Design: Angela C. Werneke
Printed in the United States of America by R.R. Donnelley
9 8 7 6 5 4 3 2 1

TABLE OF CONTENTS

FOREWORD

In the annals of Europe the discovery of the New World bears the imprint of *El Dorado*—the relentless search for gold. But little did the conquistadores realize that they were only replaying a search, on Earth and in these new lands, that had taken place eons earlier!

Buried under the records and tales of avarice, plunder, and wanton destruction that the newly found riches had triggered, there is also evidence in the chronicles of that time of how bewildered the Europeans had been to come upon civilizations that were so akin to those of the Old World: kingdoms and royal courts, cities and sacred precincts, art and poetry, sky-high temples, priests—and the symbol of the cross and a belief in a Creator of All. Last but not least, there were the legends of white and bearded gods who had left but did promise to return.

The mysteries and enigmas of the Maya, the Aztecs, the Incas, and their predecessors that puzzled the conquistadores still baffle scholar and layman alike five centuries later.

How, when, and why did such great civilizations arise in the New World, and is it mere coincidence that the more that is known about them, the more they appear to have been molded after the civilizations of the ancient Near East?

It is our contention that the answers can be found only by accepting as fact, not as myth, the presence on Earth of the Anunnaki, "Those Who From Heaven to Earth Came."

This book offers the evidence.

1

1

EL DORADO

Nowadays Toledo is a quiet provincial city situated about an hour's drive south of Madrid; yet hardly does a visitor to Spain miss seeing it, for within its walls there have been preserved the monuments of diverse cultures and the lessons of history.

Its beginnings, local legends tell, go back two millennia before the Christian era and its foundation is attributed to the biblical descendants of Noah. Its name, many hold, comes from the Hebrew *Toledoth* ("Generational Histories"); its olden homes and magnificent houses of worship bear witness to the Christianization of Spain—the rise and fall of the Moors and their Moslem dominion and the uprooting of the splendid Jewish heritage.

For Toledo, for Spain, and for all other lands, 1492 was a pivotal year, for a triple history was made therein. All three events took place in Spain, a land geographically known as "Iberia"—a name for which the only explanation can be found in the term *Ibri* ("Hebrew") by which its earliest settlers might have been known. Having lost the greater part of Iberia to the Moslems, the warring splintered kingdoms in the peninsula saw their first major union when Ferdinand of Aragon and Isabella of Castile married in 1469. Within ten years of the union they launched a military campaign to roll back the Moors and bring Spain under the banner of Catholicism; in January 1492 the Moors were decisively defeated with the fall of Granada, and Spain was made a Christian land. In March of that same year, the king and queen signed an edict for the expulsion from Spain, by July 31 of that year, of all Jews who would not convert to Christianity by that time. And on August 3 of that same year, Christopher Columbus—Cristobal Colon to the Spaniards—sailed under the Spanish flag to find a western route to India.

He sighted land on October 12, 1492. He returned to Spain in January 1493. As proof of his success he brought back four

3

"Indians"; as corroboration of his contention that a larger, second expedition under his command was justified, he brought with him a collection of golden trinkets obtained from the natives and tales of a city, a golden city, where the people wore golden bracelets on their arms and legs and adorned their necks and ears and noses with gold, all this gold coming from a fabulous mine near that city.

Of the first gold thus brought to Spain from the new lands, Isabella—so pious that they called her "The Catholic"—ordered that an elaborate Custody be fashioned, and presented it to the Cathedral of Toledo, traditional seat of Spain's Catholic hierarchy. And so it is that nowadays, when a visitor to the cathedral is taken to see its Treasury—a room protected by heavy grillwork and filled with the precious objects donated to the Church over the centuries—one can see, though not touch, the very first gold brought back by Columbus.

It is now recognized that there had been much more to the voyage than a search for a new route to India. Strong evidence suggests that Columbus was a Jew forced into conversion; his financial backers, likewise converted, could have seen in the enterprise an avenue of escape to freer lands. Ferdinand and Isabella had visions of the discovery of the rivers of Paradise and everlasting youth. And Columbus himself had secret ambitions, only some of which he expressed in his personal diaries. He saw himself as the fulfiller of ancient prophesies regarding a new age that shall begin with the discovery of new lands "at the extremity of the Earth."

But he was realistic enough to recognize that of all the information he had brought back from the first voyage, the mention of gold was the attention-getter. Asserting that "the Lord would show him" the enigmatic place "where gold is born," he succeeded in persuading Ferdinand and Isabella to provide him with a much larger fleet for a second voyage, then a third. By then, however, the monarchs sent along various administrators and men known for less vision but more action, who supervised and interfered with the admiral's operations and decisions. The inevitable conflicts culminated in the return of Columbus to Spain in chains, on the pretext that he had mistreated some of his men. Although the king and queen at once released him and offered him monetary compensation, they agreed with the view that Columbus was a good admiral but a bad governor—and clearly one who could not force out of the Indians the true location of the City of Gold.

Columbus countered all that with yet more reliance on ancient prophecies and biblical quotes. He collected all the texts into a book, *The Book of Prophecies,* which he presented to the king and queen. It was meant to convince them that Spain was destined to reign over Jerusalem, and that Columbus was the one chosen to achieve that by being the first to find the place where gold is born.

Themselves believers in the Scriptures, Ferdinand and Isabella agreed to let Columbus sail once more, convinced especially by his argument that the mouth of the river (now called the "Orinoco") that he had discovered was that of one of the four rivers of Paradise; and as the Scriptures had stated, one of those rivers encompassed the land of Havila, "whence the gold came." This last voyage encountered more hardships and heartbreaks than any of the previous three.

Crippled with arthritis, a ghost of his old self, Columbus returned to Spain on November 7, 1504. Before the month was out, Queen Isabella died; and although King Ferdinand still had a soft spot for Columbus, he decided to let others act on the last memorandum prepared by Columbus, in which he compiled the evidence for the presence of a major gold source in the new lands.

"Hispaniola will furnish your invincible majesties with all the needed gold," Columbus assured his royal sponsors regarding the island that is nowadays shared by Haiti and the Dominican Republic. There, Spanish settlers using local Indians as slave labor, indeed succeeded in mining gold in fabulous quantities: in less than two decades the Spanish treasury received from Hispaniola gold equivalent to 500,000 ducats.

As it turned out, the Spanish experience in Hispaniola was to repeat itself over and over again across an immense continent. Within those two short decades, as the natives died out or fled and the gold veins were exhausted, the Spaniards' euphoria turned to disappointment and despair, and they grew ever more audacious in landing on ever more unknown coasts in search of riches. One of the early destinations was the peninsula of Yucatán. The very first Spaniards there, in 1511, were survivors of a shipwreck; but in 1517 a purposeful convoy of three ships under Francisco Hernandez de Córdoba sailed to Yucatán from Cuba for the purpose of procuring slave labor. To their amazement they came upon stone buildings, temples, and idols of goddesses; to the misfortune of the local inhabitants (whom the

Spaniards understood to have called themselves "Maya") the Spaniards also "found certain objects of gold, which they took."

The record of the Spanish arrival at and the conquest of Yucatán is primarily based on the report titled *Relacion de las cosas de Yucatan* written by Friar Diego de Landa in 1566 (the English translation by William Gates is titled *Yucatan, Before and After the Conquest).* Hernandez and his men, Diego de Landa reported, saw on this expedition a large step-pyramid, idols and statues of animals, and a large inland city. However, the Indians they tried to capture put up a fierce fight, undaunted even by the cannon fire from the ships. The heavy casualties—Hernandez himself was badly wounded—forced a retreat. Yet, on his return to Cuba, Hernandez recommended further expeditions, for "that land was good and rich, because of its gold."

A year later another expedition left Cuba for Yucatán. They landed on the island of Cozumel and discovered New Spain, Pánuco and the province of Tabasco (having thus named the new places). Armed with a variety of goods for barter and not only with weapons, the Spaniards this time met both hostile and friendly Indians. They saw more stone edifices and monuments, felt the sting of arrows and spears tipped with sharp obsidian stone, and examined artfully made objects. Many were made of stone, common or semiprecious; others shined as gold, but on close examination proved to be of copper. There were, contrary to expectations, very few gold objects; and there were absolutely no mines or other sources for gold, or any other metals, in the land.

Where then had the gold, as little as there was, come from? They obtain it by trading, the Mayas said. It comes from the northwest: there, in the land of the Aztecs, it is plentiful and abundant.

The discovery and conquest of the realm of the Aztecs, in the highland heartland of Mexico, is linked historically with the name of Hernando Cortés. In 1519 he sailed from Cuba in command of a veritable armada of eleven ships, some six hundred men, and a large number of highly prized, scarce horses. Stopping, landing and re-embarking, he slowly proceeded along Yucatán's gulf coast. In the area where Maya influence waned and Aztec domination began he established a base camp and called it Veracruz (by which name the place is still called).

It was there that to the Spaniards' great astonishment emissaries of the Aztec ruler appeared offering greetings and bearing exquisite gifts. According to an eyewitness, Bernal Díaz del Castillo *(Historia verdadera de la conquista de la Nueva Espana,* English translation by A. P. Maudslay), the gifts included "a wheel like the sun, as big as a cartwheel, with many sorts of pictures on it, the whole of fine gold and a wonderful thing to behold, which those who afterwards weighed it said it was worth more than ten thousand dollars." Then another, even larger wheel, "made of silver of great brilliancy in imitation of the moon." Also a helmet filled to the brim with grains of gold; and a headdress made of the plumes of the rare *quetzal* bird (a relic still kept at Vienna's Museum für Völkerkunde).

These were gifts, the emissaries explained, of their ruler Moctezuma to the divine Quetzal Coatl, the "Plumed Serpent" god of the Aztecs; a great benefactor who was forced long ago by the God of War to leave the land of the Aztecs. With a band of followers he went to Yucatán, and then sailed off eastward, vowing to return on the day of his birth in the year "1 Reed." In the Aztec calendar, the cycle of years completed itself every fifty-two years, and therefore the year of the promised return, "1 Reed," could occur once in fifty-two years. In the Christian calendar these were the years 1363, 1415, 1467—and 1519, precisely the year in which Cortés appeared from the waters on the east at the gateway of the Aztec domain. Bearded and helmeted as Quetzalcoatl was (some also held that the god was fair skinned), Cortés seemed to fulfill the prophecies.

The gifts offered by the Aztec ruler were not casually selected. Rather, they were rich with symbolism. The heap of gold grains was offered because gold was a divine metal belonging to the gods. The silver disk representing the moon was included because some legends held that Quetzalcoatl sailed off to return to the heavens, making the moon his abode. The plumed headdress and the richly adorned garments were for the returning god to wear. And the golden disk was a sacred calendar depicting the cycle of fifty-two years and indicating the Year of Return. We know that it was such a calendar because others like it, made however of stone rather than pure gold, have since been discovered (Fig. 1).

Whether the Spaniards had grasped the symbolism or not is not recorded. If they did, they did not respect it. To them the objects represented one thing: proof of the vast riches that awaited them in the Aztec realm. These irreplaceable objects were among the artful treasures that arrived in Seville from Mexico on December 9, 1519, on board the first treasure ship

Figure 1

sent back to Spain by Cortés. The Spanish king Charles I, grandson of Ferdinand and sovereign of other European lands as Emperor Charles V of the Holy Roman Empire, was then in Flanders, and the ship was sent on to Brussels. The golden hoard included in addition to the symbolic gifts golden figurines of ducks, dogs, tigers, lions, and monkeys; and a golden bow and arrows. But overwhelming them all was the "sun disk," seventy-nine inches in diameter and thick as four *real* coins. The great painter and artist Albrecht Dürer, who saw the treasure that arrived from "the New Golden Land," wrote that "these things were all so precious that they were valued at 100,000 gulden. But I have never seen in all my days what so rejoiced my heart as these things. For I saw among them amazing artistic objects and I marvelled over the subtle ingenuity of the men in these distant lands. Indeed I cannot say enough about the things which were there before me."

But whatever unique artistic, religious, cultural, or historical value "these things" had, to the king they represented first and last gold—gold with which he could finance his struggles against internal insurrections and external wars. Losing no time, Charles ordered that these and all future objects made of precious metals be melted down on arrival and recast as gold or silver bullion.

In Mexico, Cortés and his men adopted the same attitude. Advancing slowly and overcoming whatever resistance was encountered by force of superior arms or by diplomacy and treachery, the Spaniards arrived at the Aztec capital Tenochtitlán—today's Mexico City—in November 1519. The city, situated in the midst of a lake, could be reached only via causeways that could be easily defended. Yet, still awed by the prophecy of the Returning God, Moctezuma and all the nobles came out to greet Cortés and his entourage. Only Moctezuma wore sandals; all the others were barefoot, humbling themselves before the white god. He made the Spaniards welcome in his magnificent palace; there was gold everywhere, even the tableware was made of gold; and they were shown a storage room filled with golden artifacts. Using a ruse, the Spaniards seized Moctezuma and held him in their quarters; for his release they demanded a ransom in gold. The nobles thereupon sent out runners throughout the kingdom to collect the ransom; the golden objects that were handed over were enough to fill a ship that sailed back to Spain. (It was, however, seized by the French, causing war to break out.)

Obtaining gold through cunning and weakening the Aztecs by sowing dissent among them, Cortés was planning to release Moctezuma and leave him on the throne as a puppet ruler. But his second-in-command lost patience and ordered a massacre of the Aztec noblemen and commanders. In the turmoil that followed Moctezuma was killed and the Spaniards had a full-fledged battle on their hands. With heavy losses Cortés retreated from the city; he reentered it, heavily reinforced from Cuba and after prolonged battles, only in August of 1521. By the time Spanish rule was irrevocably imposed on the crushed Aztecs, gold weighing some 600,000 pesos was forced out, plundered, and melted down into ingots.

Mexico, while being conquered, was indeed a New Golden Land; but once the gold artifacts created and accumulated over centuries, if not millennia, were hauled off, it was becoming apparent that Mexico was not the biblical land of Havila, and Tenochtitlán not the legendary City of Gold. And so the search for gold, which neither adventurers nor kings were prepared to give up, turned to other parts of the New World.

The Spaniards had by then established a base, Panama, on the Pacific coast of America, and from there they were sending out expeditions and agents into Central and South America. It was there that they heard the alluring legend of El Dorado— short for *el hombre dorado,* the Gilded Man. He was a king whose kingdom was so rich in gold that he was painted each morning with a gum or oil on which gold dust was sprinkled, covering him from head to toe. In the evening he dipped in the lake and washed off the gold and oil, only to repeat the rite the next day. He reigned in a city that was in the center of a lake, situated on an island of gold.

According to the chronicle titled *Elejias de Varones Ilustres de Indias,* the first concrete report of El Dorado was brought to Francisco Pizarro in Panama by one of his captains in the following version: It was said that an Indian from Colombia heard of "a country rich in emeralds and gold. Among the things in which they engaged was this: their king disrobed, and went aboard a raft to the midst of a lake to make oblations to the gods. His regal form was overspread with fragrant oil, on which was laid a coat of powdered gold, from sole of foot unto his highest brow, making him resplendent as the beaming of the sun." To view the ritual many pilgrims had been coming, making "rich votive offerings of golden trinkets and emeralds rare, and diverse other of their ornaments," by throwing them into the sacred lake.

Another version, suggesting that the sacred lake was somewhere in northern Colombia, had the gilded king carrying the "great quantity of gold and emeralds" into the center of the lake. There, acting as emissary of the multitudes that stood shouting and playing musical instruments all around the lake, he threw the treasure into the lake as an offering to its god. Still another version gave the name of the golden city as Manoa and said it was in the land of *Biru*—Peru to the Spaniards.

Word of El Dorado spread among the Europeans in the New World like wildfire, and in time back in Europe itself. The word of mouth was soon put in writing; pamphlets and books began to circulate in Europe describing the land and the lake and the city and the king whom no one had yet seen, and even the actual ritual of gilding the king each morning (Fig. 2).

While some, like Cortés who went to California or others who went to Venezuela, had searched in directions of their own choosing, Francisco Pizarro and his lieutenants relied entirely on the Indian reports. Some went indeed to Colombia and searched the waters of Lake Guatavita—a search that continued on and off for four centuries, yielded golden votive objects and left ensuing generations of treasure hunters convinced that if only the lake could be completely drained, the golden riches would be raised from its bottom.

Others, like Pizarro himself, accepted Peru as the right location. Two expeditions launched from their base in Panama along the Pacific coast of South America yielded enough gold objects to convince them that a major effort in Peru would pay off. After obtaining a royal charter for the purpose and the titles Captain General and Governor (of the province yet to be conquered), Pizarro sailed to Peru at the head of two hundred men. The year was 1530.

Figure 2

How did he expect to take over with such a small force a large country protected by thousands of warriors fiercely loyal to their lord, the *Inca,* whom they considered to be the personification of a god? Pizarro's plan was to repeat the strategy successfully employed by Cortés: to lure the ruler, seize him, obtain gold as ransom, then release him to be a Spanish puppet.

The fact that the Incas, as the people themselves came to be called, were engaged in a civil war when the Spaniards landed was an unexpected boon. They found out that upon the death of the Lord Inca, his firstborn son by a "secondary wife" challenged the legitimacy of the succession by a son born to the Inca's principal wife. When news of the advancing Spaniards reached the challenger, Atahualpa by name, he decided to let the Spaniards advance inland (and thus away from their ships and reinforcements) while he completed the seizing of the capital, Cuzco. On reaching a major city in the Andes, the Spaniards sent to him emissaries bearing gifts and offering peace talks. They suggested that the two leaders meet in the city square, unarmed and without military escort, as a show of goodwill. Atahualpa agreed. But when he reached the square, the Spaniards attacked his escort and held the Inca captive.

To release him they asked for a ransom: let a large room be

filled with gold as high as a man's outstretched hand can reach up toward the ceiling. Atahualpa understood that to mean filling up the room with golden objects, and agreed. On his orders golden utensils were brought out of temples and palaces—goblets, ewers, salvers, vases of all shapes and sizes—ornaments that included imitations of animals and plants, and plates that lined the walls of public buildings. For weeks the treasures were being brought to fill up the room. But then the Spaniards claimed that the deal was to fill the room with solid gold, not the space-filling artifacts; and for over a month, Inca goldsmiths were engaged in melting down all the artful objects into ingots.

As if history insisted on repeating itself, the fate of Atahualpa was exactly the same as that which befell Moctezuma. Pizarro intended to release him to rule as a puppet king; but zealous lieutenants and Church representatives, at a mock trial, sentenced Atahualpa to death for the crime of idolatry and the murder of his half brother, his rival for the throne.

The ransom obtained for the Inca lord, according to one of the chronicles of that time, was the equivalent of 1,326,539 *pesos de oro* ("weights of gold")—about 200,000 ounces—a wealth that was quickly divided among Pizarro and his men after setting aside the required fifth for the king. But as much as what each man received was beyond his fanciest dreams, it was nothing compared to what was yet to come.

When the conquistadores entered the capital, Cuzco, they saw temples and palaces literally covered and filled with gold. In the royal palace there were three chambers filled with gold furnishings and five with silver, and a hoard of 100,000 gold ingots weighing about five pounds each, a reserve of the precious metal waiting to be fashioned into artful objects. The golden throne, outfitted with a golden stool, designed to convert into a litter on which the king could recline, weighed 25,000 pesos (about 4,000 ounces); even the carrying poles were overlaid with gold. Everywhere there were chapels and burial chambers honoring ancestors, filled with statuettes and images of birds, fish, and small animals, ear spools, breastplates. In the great temple (which the Spaniards named Temple of the Sun) the walls were covered with heavy gold plates. Its garden was an artificial garden where everything—trees, shrubs, flowers, birds, a fountain—was fashioned of gold. In the courtyard there was a field of maize (the local corn) where every stalk was made of silver and the ears of gold; it was a field that covered an area of 300 by 600 feet—180,000 square feet of golden corn!

In Peru, the conquering Spaniards saw within a short space of time their initial easy victories give way to hard-fought Inca rebellions, and the initial wealth give way to the scourge of inflation. To the Incas, as to the Aztecs, gold was a gift or the property of the gods, not a means of exchange. They never used it as a commodity, as money. To the Spaniards, gold was a means to acquire whatever their hearts desired. Flush with gold but short of homegrown luxuries or even daily necessities, the Spaniards were soon paying sixty golden pesos for a bottle of wine, 100 for a cloak, 10,000 for a horse.

But back in Europe, the inflow of gold, silver, and precious stones raised the gold fever and encouraged more speculation about El Dorado. No matter how much treasure was coming in, the conviction persisted that El Dorado had not yet been found, that with persistence and luck and the correct reading of Indian clues and enigmatic maps someone was going to find it. German explorers were certain that the golden city would be found at the headwaters of the Orinoco river in Venezuela, or perhaps in Colombia. Others concluded that the river to be followed was another one, even the Amazon in Brazil. Perhaps the most romantic of all of them, on account of his background and his royal sponsor, was Sir Walter Raleigh, who sailed from Plymouth in 1595 to find the legendary Manoa and add its golden glory to Queen Elizabeth's crown.

In his vision he saw Manoa as

> Imperial El Dorado, roofed with gold!
> Shadows to which—
> Despite of all shocks of change,
> all onset of capricious accident—
> Men clung with yearning hope
> which would not die.

He, like others before and after him, still saw El Dorado—the king, the city, the land—as a dream yet to be fulfilled, "a yearning hope which would not die." In that, all who went in quest of El Dorado were a link in a chain that began before the pharaohs and continues with our wedding rings and national hoards.

Yet it was those dreamers, those adventurers, who in their lust for gold revealed to Western man the unknown peoples and civilizations of the Americas. And thereby, unknowingly, reestablished links that had existed in forgotten times.

Why did the quest for El Dorado continue so intensively for so long even after the discovery of the incredible gold and silver treasures of Mexico and Peru, to say nothing of the lesser plundered lands? The continued and intensified search can be attributed mostly to the conviction that the *source* of all those riches had yet to be found.

The Spaniards extensively questioned the natives about the fountainhead of the amassed treasures and tirelessly followed every clue. It soon became clear to them that the Caribbean and Yucatán were not primary sources at all: the Maya in fact indicated that they had obtained gold mostly by trading with their neighbors to the south and the west, and explained that they had learned the arts of goldsmithing from earlier settlers (whom scholars nowadays identify by the name *Toltecs*). Yes, the Spaniards said, but where do the others obtain the gold from? From the gods, the Maya answered. In the local tongues, gold was called *teocuitlatl*, literally meaning "the gods' excretion," their perspiration and their tears.

In the Aztec capital the Spaniards learned that gold was indeed deemed to be the gods' metal, the stealing of which was a capital offense. The Aztecs too pointed to the Toltecs as their teachers of the art of goldsmithing. And who had taught the Toltecs? The great god Quetzalcoatl, the Aztecs replied. Cortés, in his reports to the Spanish king, wrote that he had questioned the Aztec king Moctezuma extensively about the source of the gold. Moctezuma revealed that the gold came from three provinces of his kingdom, one on the Pacific coast, one on the gulf coast, and one inland in the southwest where the mines were. Cortés sent men to investigate the three indicated sources. In all three they found that the Indians were actually obtaining the gold in riverbeds or collecting nuggets that were lying on the surface where rains had washed the gold down. In the province where mines did exist, they appeared to have been mined only in the past; the Indians encountered by the Spaniards were not working in the mines at all. "There were no active mines," Cortés wrote in his report. "Nuggets were found on the surface; the principal source was the sand of the riverbeds. The gold was kept in the form of dust in small cane tubes or quilts, or was melted in small pots and cast in bars." Once ready, it was sent on to the capital, returned to the gods to whom the gold had always belonged.

While most experts on mining and metallurgy accept the conclusions of Cortés—that the Aztecs engaged in placer mining only (the collection of gold nuggets and dust from surfaces and river beds) and not in actual mining involving the cutting of shafts and tunnels into mountainsides—the issue is far from being resolved. The conquering Spaniards, and mining engineers in following centuries, persistently spoke of prehistoric gold mines found at various Mexican sites. Since it seems inconceivable that earlier settlers of Mexico, such as the Toltecs, whose beginnings are traced to a few centuries before the Christian era, would have possessed a higher mining technology than the later (and thus presumably more advanced) Aztecs, the purported "prehistoric mines" have been dismissed by researchers as old shafts begun and abandoned by the conquering Spaniards. Expressing the current views at the beginning of this century, Alexander Del Mar *(A History of the Precious Metals)* stated that, "With regard to Prehistoric mining it must be premised that the Aztecs had no knowledge of iron, and therefore, that subterranean mining . . . is practically out of the question. It is true that modern prospectors have found in Mexico old shafts and remains of mining works which appeared to them to have been the scene of prehistoric mining." Although such reports had even found their way into official publications, Del Mar believed that the sites were "ancient workings coupled with volcanic upheavals, or else with deposits of lava or tarp, both of which were regarded as evidence of vast antiquity." "This inference," he concluded, "is hardly warranted."

This, however, is not what the Aztecs themselves had reported. They attributed to their predecessors, the Toltecs, not just the craftsmanship but also the knowledge of the hidden place of gold and the ability to mine it out of the rocky mountains. The Aztec manuscript known as *Codice Matritense de la Real Academia* (vol. VIII), in a translation by Miguel León-Portilla *(Aztec Thought and Culture)* describes the Toltecs thus:

"The Toltecs were skillful people; all of their works were good, all were exact, all well made and admirable. . . . Painters, sculptors, carvers of precious stones, feather artists, potters, spinners, weavers, skillful in all they made. They discovered the precious green stones, the turquoise; they knew the turquoise and its mines. They found its mines and they found the mountains hiding silver and gold, copper and tin and the metal of the moon."

The Toltecs, most historians agree, had come to the central highland of Mexico in the centuries preceding the Christian era —at least a thousand years, perhaps fifteen hundred years, before the Aztecs appeared on the scene. How was it possible that they had known mining, real mining of gold and other metals as well as of precious stones such as turquoise, whereas those who had followed them—the Aztecs—could only scrape nuggets off the surface? And who was it who had taught the Toltecs the secrets of mining?

The answer, as we have seen, was Quetzalcoatl, the Feathered Serpent god.

The mystery of the accumulated gold treasures on the one hand and the limited ability of the Aztecs to obtain it, repeated itself in the land of the Incas.

In Peru, as in Mexico, the natives did obtain gold by collecting grains and nuggets washed down from the mountains into the riverbeds. But the annual production through these methods could in no way account for the immense treasures of gold found in Inca hands. The immensity of the hoards is obvious from the Spanish records kept at Seville, the official port of entry into Spain of the New World's riches. The *Archives of the Indies*—still available—recorded the receipt in the five years 1521–1525 of 134,000 *pesos de oro*. In the next five years (the loot from Mexico!) the quantity was 1,038,000 pesos. From 1531 to 1535, when the shipments from Peru began to augment those from Mexico, the quantity increased to 1,650,000 pesos. During 1536–1540, when Peru was the main source, the gold received weighed 3,937,000 pesos; and in the decade of the 1550s the receipts totaled almost 11,000,000 pesos.

One of the leading chroniclers of that time, Pedro de Cieza de León *(Chronicles of Peru),* reported that in the years following the conquest the Spaniards "extracted" from the Inca empire annually 15,000 *arrobas* of gold and 50,000 of silver; this is equivalent to over 6,000,000 ounces of gold and over 20,000,000 ounces of silver *annually!* Though Cieza de León does not mention over how many years such fabulous quantities had been "extracted," his numbers give us an idea of the quantities of precious metals that the Spaniards were able to plunder in the Inca lands.

The chronicles relate that after the initial great ransom obtained from the Inca lord, the plunder of the riches of Cuzco, and the tearing apart of a sacred temple at Pachácamac on the coast, the Spaniards became expert in "extracting" gold from the provinces in equally vast quantities. Throughout the Inca empire, provincial palaces and temples were richly decorated with gold. Another source was burial sites containing golden objects. The Spaniards learned that the Inca custom was to seal the residences of deceased noblemen and rulers, leaving there their mummified bodies surrounded by all the precious objects they had possessed in life. The Spaniards also suspected, correctly, that the Indians had carried off to hiding places various gold treasures; some were stashed away in caves, some were buried, others were thrown into lakes. And there were the *huacas,* venerated places set aside for worship or for divine use, where gold was piled up and kept at the disposal of its true owners, the gods.

Tales of treasure finds, as frequently as not obtained by torturing Indians to reveal the hidden places, permeate the records of the fifty years following the conquest, and even into the seventeenth and eighteenth centuries. In this manner Gonzalo Pizarro found the hidden treasure of an Inca lord who reigned a century earlier. One Garcia Gutiérrez de Toledo found a series of mounds covering sacred treasures from which over a million pesos worth of gold was extracted between 1566 and 1592. As late as 1602, Escobar Corchuelo secured from the *huaca* La Tosca objects valued at 60,000 pesos. And when the waters of the river Moche were diverted, a treasure worth some 600,000 pesos was found; it included, the chroniclers reported, "a large golden idol."

Writing a century and a half ago, and thus much closer to the events than can be done nowadays, two explorers (M. A. Ribero and J. J. von Tschudi, *Peruvian Antiquities)* described the situation thus: "In the second half of the sixteenth century, in the short space of twenty-five years, the Spaniards exported from Peru to the mother country more than four hundred million ducats of gold and silver, and we may well be assured that nine-tenths of this quantity composed the mere booty taken by the conquerors; in this computation we leave out of view the immense masses of precious metals buried by the natives to hide from the avarice of the foreign invaders; as also the celebrated chain of gold which the Inca Huayna Capac commanded to be made in honor of the birth of his firstborn son, Inti Cusi Huallapa Huáscar, and which they say was thrown into the lake of Urcos." (The chain was said to be seven hundred feet long and thick as a man's wrist.) "Also not included are the eleven thousand llamas loaded with gold dust in precious vases of this metal, with which the unfortunate Atahualpa wished to purchase his life and liberty, and which the conductors interred in the Puna as soon as they heard of the new punishment to which their adored monarch had been treacherously condemned."

That these immense quantities were the result of the plunder of accumulated riches and not of ongoing production is known not only from the chronicles but is also confirmed by the numbers. Within decades, after the visible and hidden treasures had been exhausted, the gold receipts in Seville dwindled to a mere 6,000–7,000 pounds of gold a year. It was then that the

Spaniards, using their iron tools, began to conscript the natives for work in the mines. The toil was so harsh, that by the end of the century the land was almost depopulated and the Spanish Court imposed restrictions on the exploitation of native labor. Great silver lodes were discovered and worked, such as at Potosí; but the quantity of gold obtained never matched, nor does it explain, the vast treasures amassed before the Spanish arrival.

Seeking an answer to the puzzle, Ribero and von Tschudi wrote, "The gold, although it was the Peruvians' most esteemed metal, they possessed in a quantity greater than that of any other. Upon comparing its abundance, in the time of the Incas, with the quantity which, in the space of four centuries, the Spaniards have been able to extract from the mines and rivers, it becomes certain that the Indians had a knowledge of veins of this precious material which the conquerors and their descendants never succeeded in discovering." (They also predicted that "the day will come when Peru will withdraw from her bosom the veil which now covers more wonderful riches than those which are offered at the present day in California." And when the gold rushes of the late nineteenth century gripped Europe with a new gold fever, many mining experts came to believe that the so-called "mother lode," the ultimate source of all gold on Earth, would be found in Peru.)

As in Mexico, the generally accepted notion regarding the Lands of the Andes has been (in the words of Del Mar) that "the precious metals obtained by the Peruvians previous to the Spanish conquest consisted nearly altogether of gold secured by washing the river gravels. No native shafts were found. A few excavations had been made into the sides of hills with outcrops of native gold or silver." That is true insofar as the Incas of the Andes (and the Aztecs of Mexico) were concerned; but in the Andean lands, as in Mexico, the question of *prehistoric* mining —the hewing of the metal out of vein-rich rocks—has not been settled.

The possibility that at a time long before the Incas someone had access to gold at its vein sources (at places the Incas did not disclose or even did not know about), remains a plausible explanation for the accumulated treasures. Indeed, according to one of the best contemporary studies on the subject (S. K. Lothrop, *Inca Treasure As Depicted by Spanish Historians*), "modern mines are located at sites of aboriginal operations. Ancient shafts have been frequently reported and also finds of primitive tools, even the bodies of entombed miners."

The amassing of gold by the American natives, no matter

how obtained, poses still another, yet very basic, question: What for?

The chroniclers, and contemporary scholars after centuries of studies, agree that those peoples had no practical use for gold, except to adorn with it the temples of the gods and those who ruled over the people in the name of the gods. The Aztecs literally poured their gold at the Spaniards' feet, believing that they represented the returning deity. The Incas, who at first also saw in the arriving Spaniards the fulfillment of their deity's promise to return from across the seas, later on could not understand why the Spaniards had come so far and behaved so ill for a metal for which Man had no practical use. All scholars are agreed that the Incas and the Aztecs did not use gold for monetary purposes, nor did they attach to it a commercial value. Yet they extracted from their subject nations a tribute of gold. Why?

In the ruins of a pre-Inca culture at Chimu, on the Peruvian coast, the great nineteenth-century explorer Alexander von Humboldt (a mining engineer by profession) discovered a mass of gold buried alongside the dead in tombs. The discovery of the metal made him wonder why would gold, being deemed of no practical use, be buried with the dead? Was it that somehow it was believed that they would need it in an afterlife—or that in joining their ancestors, they could use the gold the way their ancestors had once done?

Who was it who had brought about such customs and beliefs, and when?

Who had caused gold to be so valued, and perhaps gone after it at its sources?

The only answer the Spaniards were given was "the gods."

It was of the gods' tears that gold was formed, the Incas said.

And in so pointing to the gods, they unknowingly echoed the statement of the biblical Lord through the prophet Haggai:

> The silver is mine
> and the gold is mine,
> So sayeth the Lord of Hosts.

It is this statement, we believe, that holds the key to unraveling the mysteries, enigmas, and secrets of gods, men, and ancient civilizations in the Americas.

2

THE LOST REALM
OF CAIN?

The Aztec capital, Tenochtitlán, was an impressive metropolis when the Spaniards arrived. Their reports describe it as large, if not larger, than most European cities of the time, well laid out and administered. Situated on an island in Lake Texcoco, in the highlands' central valley, it was surrounded by water and intersected by canals—a Venice of the New World. The long and wide causeways that connected the city to the mainland made a great impression upon the Spaniards; so did the numerous canoes sailing the canals, the streets teeming with people, the marketplaces filled with merchants and merchandise from all over the realm. The royal palace was many-roomed, filled with riches and surrounded by gardens that included an aviary and a zoo. A great plaza, humming with activity, was the setting for festivities and military parades.

But the heart of the city and the empire was the vast religious center—an immense rectangle of more than a million square feet, surrounded by a wall fashioned to resemble writhing serpents. There were scores of edifices within this sacred precinct; the most outstanding of them were the Great Temple with its two towers, and the partly circular temple of Quetzalcoatl. Nowadays Mexico City's great plaza and the cathedral occupy parts of the ancient sacred precinct, as do many adjoining streets and buildings. Following a chance excavation in 1978, important portions of the Great Temple can be now seen and visited, and enough has become known in the past decade to make possible a scale-model reconstruction of the precinct as it was in its times of glory.

The Great Temple had the shape of a step-pyramid, rising in stages to a height of some 160 feet; its base measured about 150 by 150 feet. It represented the culmination of several phases of construction: Like a Russian doll, the outer structure was built over a previous smaller one, and that one enclosed an even earlier structure. In all, seven structures were encasing each other. Archaeologists were able to peel the layers back to Tem-

ple II, which was built sometime around A.D. 1400; that one, like the last one, already had the distinctive twin towers upon its top.

Representing a curious dual worship, the tower on the northern side was a shrine dedicated to Tlaloc, god of storms and earthquakes (Fig. 3a). The southern tower was dedicated to the Aztec tribal deity Huitzilopochtli, their war god. He was usually depicted holding the magical weapon called Fire Serpent (Fig. 3b) with which he had defeated four hundred lesser gods.

Two monumental stairways led up to the pyramid's top on its western side, one for each tower-shrine. Each was decorated at its base with two ferocious serpent heads carved of stone, one being the Fire Serpent of Huitzilopochtli and the other the Water Serpent symbolizing Tlaloc. At the base of the pyramid excavators found a large, thick stone disk whose top was carved with a representation of the dismembered body of the goddess Coyolxauhqui (Fig. 3c). According to Aztec lore, she was a sister of Huitzilopochtli and came to grief by his own hand,

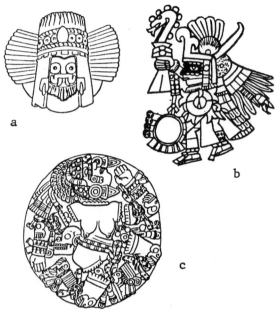

a

b

c

Figure 3

during the rebellion of the four hundred gods in which she was involved. It seems that her fate was one of the reasons for the Aztec belief that Huitzilopochtli had to be appeased by offering him the torn out hearts of human victims.

The motif of twin towers was further enhanced in the sacred precinct by the erection of two pyramids topped by towers, one on each side of the Great Temple, and two more somewhat back, westward. The latter two flanked the temple of Quetzalcoatl. It had the unusual shape of a regular step-pyramid in front but a circular stepped structure in the back, where it spiraled up to become a circular tower with a conical dome (Fig. 4). Many believe that this temple served as a solar observatory. A. F. Aveni *(Astronomy in Ancient Mesoamerica)* determined in 1974 that on the dates of the equinox (March 21 and September 21), when the Sun rises in the east precisely on the equator, sunrise could be seen from the Quetzalcoatl tower right between the two towers atop the Great Temple. This was possible only because the planners of the sacred precinct erected the temples along an architectural axis aligned not precisely with the cardinal points, but one that shifted to the southeast by 7½ degrees; this compensated exactly for the geographical position of Tenochtitlán (north of the equator), enabling the viewing of

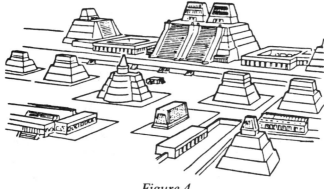

Figure 4

the Sun on the crucial dates rising between the two towers.

Although the Spaniards may have been unaware of this sophisticated feature of the sacred precinct, the records they left bespeak their amazement at encountering not merely a cultured people, but also a civilization so similar to the Spaniards' own. Here, across what had been a forbidding ocean, for all intents and purposes isolated from the civilized world, was a state headed by a king—just as in Europe. Noblemen, functionaries, courtesans filled the royal court. Emissaries came and went. Tribute was extracted from vassal tribes, taxes were paid by loyal citizens. Royal archives kept written records of tribal histories, dynasties, wealth. There was an army with an hierarchical command and perfected weapons. There were arts and crafts, music and dancing. There were festivals connected with the seasons and holy days prescribed by religion—a state religion, just as in Europe. And there was the sacred precinct with its temples and chapels and residences, surrounded by a wall— just as the Vatican in Rome—run by a hierarchy of priests who, just as in Europe of the time, were not only keepers of the faith and interpreters of divine will, but also guardians of the secrets of scientific knowledge. Of that, astrology, astronomy, and the mysteries of the calendar were paramount.

Some Spanish chroniclers of the time, aiming to counteract the embarrassingly positive impressions of what should have been Indian savages, attributed to Cortés a reprimand to Moctezuma for worshiping "idols that are not gods, but evilly named demons," an evil influence Cortés supposedly offered to counteract by constructing atop the pyramid a shrine with a cross "and the image of our Lady" (Bernal Díaz del Castillo, *Historia verdadera*). But to the Spaniards' astonishment, even the symbol of the cross was known to the Aztecs and, deemed by them

Figure 5

a symbol with celestial significance, was depicted as the emblem of Quetzalcoatl's shield (Fig. 5).

Moreover, through the maze of a pantheon of numerous deities, there could be seen an underlying belief in a Supreme God, a Creator of All. Some of the prayers to him even sounded familiar; here are a few verses from an Aztec prayer, recorded in Spanish from the original Nahuatl language:

> You inhabit the heavens,
> You uphold the mountains...
> You are everywhere, everlasting.
> You are beseeched, you are entreated.
> Your glory is eminent.

Yet with all the baffling similarities, there was a troubling difference about Aztec civilization. It was not just the "idolatry," of which the flocking friars and *padres* made a *casus belli;* not even the barbaric customs of cutting out the hearts of prisoners and offering the pulsating hearts in sacrifice to Huitzilopochtli (a practice, incidentally, apparently introduced only in 1486 by the king preceding Moctezuma). It was, rather, the whole gamut of this civilization, as though it was the result of a progress that had been arrested in its course, or an imported higher culture covering, as a thin veneer, a coarser understructure.

The edifices were impressive and ingeniously laid out, but they were not built of dressed stones; rather, they were of adobe construction—field stones crudely held together with simple mortar. Trade was extensive, but it was all a barter trade. Tribute was in kind; taxes were paid in personal services—there was no knowledge of money of any kind. Textiles were woven on a most rudimentary loom; cotton was spun on clay spindles the likes of which have been found in the Old World, in the ruins of Troy (second millennium B.C.) and sites in Palestine (third millennium B.C.). In their tools and weapons the Aztecs were in a stone age, unaccountably devoid of metal tools and weapons although they possessed the craft of goldsmithing. For cutting they used chips of the glasslike obsidian stone (and one of the prevalent objects from Aztec times was the obsidian knife used to cut out prisoners' hearts . . .).

Because other peoples in the Americas have been held to have had no writing, the Aztecs seemed more advanced at least on this score because they did have a system of writing. But the writing was neither alphabetical nor phonetic; it was a series of pictures, like cartoons in a comic strip (Fig. 6a). By comparison, in the ancient Near East where writing began circa 3800 B.C. (in Sumer) in the form of pictographs, it quickly changed through stylization to a cuneiform script, advanced to a phonetic script where signs stood for syllables, and, by the end of the second millennium B.C., to a complete alphabet. Pictorial writing appeared in Egypt at the beginning of kingship there, circa 3100 B.C., and quickly evolved into a system of hieroglyphic writing.

Expert studies, as that by Amelia Hertz *(Revue de Synthèse Historique,* vol. 35), have concluded that Aztec picture-writing in A.D. 1500 was similar to the earliest Egyptian writing, as that on the stone tablet of king Narmer (Fig. 6b) whom some consider to have been the first dynastic king in Egypt—four and a half millennia earlier. A. Hertz found another curious analogy between Aztec Mexico and early dynastic Egypt: In both, while copper metallurgy was yet to develop, goldsmithing was so advanced that the craftsmen could inlay golden objects with turquoise (a semiprecious stone cherished in both lands).

The National Museum of Anthropology in Mexico City—certainly one of the world's best in its field—displays the country's archaeological heritage in a U-shaped building. Consisting of connected sections or halls, it takes the visitor through time and place, from prehistoric origins to Aztec times and from south and north to east and west. The central section is devoted to the Aztecs; it is the heart and pride of national Mexican archaeology, for "Aztecs" was a name given these people only lately. They called themselves *Mexica,* thus giving their preferred name not only to the capital (built where the Aztec Tenochtitlán had been) but also to the whole country.

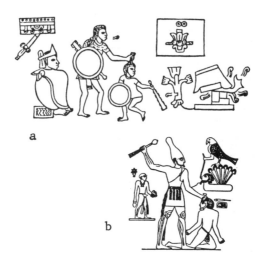

Figure 6

The Mexica Hall, as it is designated, is portrayed by the Museum as "the most important hall. . . . Its grandiose dimensions were designed to amply frame the culture of the Mexican people." Its monumental stone sculptures include the immense Calendar Stone (see Fig. 1) that weighs some twenty-five tons, huge statues of various gods and goddesses, and a great thick stone disk carved in the round. Smaller stone and clay effigies, earthenware utensils, weapons, golden ornaments and other Aztec remains, plus the scale model of the sacred precinct, fill up this impressive hall.

The contrast between primitive clay and wood objects and grotesque effigies on the one hand, and the powerful stone carvings and monumental sacred precinct on the other hand, is astounding. It is inexplicable in terms of the less than four centuries of Aztec presence in Mexico. How could two such layers of civilization be accounted for? When the answer is sought in known history, the Aztecs appear as a nomadic, uncouth immigrant tribe that forced its way into a valley peopled by tribes with a more advanced culture. At first they made a living by serving the settled tribes, mostly as hired mercenaries. In time they managed to overpower their neighbors and borrowed not only their culture but also their artisans. Themselves followers of Huitzilopochtli, the Aztecs adopted their neighbors' pantheon, including the rain god Tlaloc and the benevolent Quetzalcoatl, god of crafts, writing, mathematics, astronomy, and time reckoning.

But the legends, what scholars call "migration myths," put events in a different light—mainly by beginning the tale at a much earlier time. The sources for this information are not only verbal traditions, but the various books called codices. These, such as the Codex Boturini, relate that the ancestral home of the Aztec tribe was called *Azt-lan* ("White Place"). It was the abode of the first patriarchal couple, *Itzac-mixcoatl* ("White Cloud Serpent") and his spouse *Ilan-cue* ("Old Woman"); they gave birth to sons from whom the Nahuatl-speaking tribes, among them the Aztecs, had come forth. The Toltecs too were descended of Itzac-mixcoatl, but their mother was another woman; they were thus only half brothers of the Aztecs.

Where Aztlan was located, no one can say for certain. Of the numerous studies dealing with the matter (which include theories that it was the legendary Atlantis), one of the best is Eduard Seler's *Wo lag Aztlan, die Heimat der Azteken?* It was a place apparently associated with the number seven, having been sometimes called Aztlan of the Seven Caves. It was also depicted in the codices as a place recognizable by its seven temples: a central large step-pyramid surrounded by six lesser shrines.

In his elaborate *Historia de las cosas de la Nuéva Espana,* the Friar Bernardino de Sahagún, using the original texts in the native Nahuatl language written after the Conquest, deals with the multitribal migration from Aztlan. There were seven tribes in all. They left Aztlan by boats. The pictorial books show them passing by a landmark whose pictograph remains an enigma. Sahagún provides various names for the way stations, calling the place of landfall "Panotlan"; it simply means "Place of Arrival by Sea," but from various clues scholars conclude that it was what is nowadays Guatemala.

The arriving tribes had with them four Wise Men to guide and lead them, because they had carried with them ritual manuscripts and also knew the secrets of the calendar. From there the tribes went in the direction of the Place of the Cloud-Serpent, apparently dispersing as they did so. At long last some, including the Aztecs and the Toltecs, reached a place called Teotihuacan, where two pyramids were built, one to the Sun and the other to the Moon.

Kings reigned at Teotihuacan and were buried there, for to be buried in Teotihuacan was to join the gods in an afterlife. How long it was before the next migratory trek is not clear; but at some point the tribes began to abandon the holy city. First to leave were the Toltecs, who left to build their own city, Tollan. Last to leave were the Aztecs. Their wanderings took them to various places, but they found no respite. At the time of their final migration their leader's name was *Mexitli,* meaning "The Anointed." That, according to some scholars (e.g., Manuel Orozoco y Berra, *Ojeada sobre cronologia Mexicana),* was the origin of the tribal name *Mexica* ("The Anointed People").

The signal for the last migration was given to the Aztecs/ Mexica by their god Huitzilopochtli, who promised them a land where there are "houses with gold and silver, multicolored cotton and cacao of many hues." They were to keep on going in the indicated direction until they would see an eagle perched on a cactus growing from a rock surrounded by water. They were to settle there and call themselves "Mexica," for they were a chosen people destined to rule over the other tribes.

Thus it was that the Aztecs arrived—according to these legends, for the second time—in the Valley of Mexico. They reached Tollan, also known as "The Middle Place." Although the inhabitants were their own ancestral kinfolk, they did not make the Aztecs welcome. For nearly two centuries the Aztecs lived on the central lake's marshy edges. Gaining strength and knowledge, they finally established their own city, Tenochtitlán.

The name meant "City of Tenoch." Some think it was so called because the Aztec leader at the time, the actual builder of the city, was named Tenoch. But since it is known that the Aztecs considered themselves at the time to have been *Tenochas*—descendants of Tenoch—others believed that Tenoch was the name of a tribal ancestor, a legendary paternal figure from way, way back.

Scholars now generally hold that the Mexica or Tenochas arrived in the valley circa A.D. 1140 and established Tenochtitlán in A.D. 1325. They then gained influence through a series of alliances with some tribes and warfare with others. Some researchers doubt whether the Aztecs dominated a true empire. The fact is that when the Spaniards arrived, they were the dominant power in central Mexico, lording over allies and subjugating enemies. The latter served as a source of captives for sacrifices; the Spanish conquest was facilitated by their insurrections against the Aztec oppressors.

Like the biblical Hebrews, who traced back their genealogies not only to patriarchal couples but also to the beginning of Mankind, so did the Aztecs and Toltecs and other Nahuatl tribes possess Legends of Creation that followed the same themes. But whereas the Old Testament compressed its detailed Sumerian sources by devising one plural entity *(Elohim)* out of the various deities active in the creative processes, the Nahuatl tales retained the Sumerian and Egyptian concepts of several divine beings acting either alone or in concert.

Tribal beliefs, prevalent from the southwestern United States in the north to today's Nicaragua in the south—Mesoamerica— held that at the very beginning there was an Olden God, Creator of All Things, of the Heaven and of the Earth, whose abode was in the highest heaven, the twelfth heaven. Sahagún's sources attributed the origin of this knowledge to the Toltecs:

> And the Toltecs knew
> that many are the heavens.
> They said there are twelve superimposed divisions;
> There dwells the true god and his consort.
> He is the Celestial God, Lord of Duality;
> His consort is Lady of Duality, Celestial Lady.
> This is what it means:
> He is king, he is Lord, above the twelve heavens.

This amazingly sounds like a rendering of Mesopotamian celestial-religious beliefs, according to which the head of the pantheon was called Anu ("Lord of Heaven") and who, with his consort Antu ("Lady of Heaven") resided on the outermost planet, the twelfth member of our Solar System. The Sumerians depicted it as a radiating planet whose symbol was the cross (Fig. 7a). The symbol was thereafter adopted by all the peoples of the ancient world and evolved to the ubiquitous emblem of the Winged Disk (Fig. 7b,c). Quetzalcoatl's shield (Fig. 7d) and symbols depicted on early Mexican monuments (Fig. 7e) are uncannily similar.

The Olden Gods of whom the Nahuatl texts related legendary tales were depicted as bearded men (Fig. 8), as befits ancestors of the bearded Quetzalcoatl. As in Mesopotamian and Egyptian theogonies, there were tales of divine couples and of brothers who espoused their own sisters. Of prime and direct concern to the Aztecs were the four divine brothers Tlatlauhqui, Tezcatlipoca-Yaotl, Quetzalcoatl, and Huitzilopochtli, in the order of their birth. They represented the four cardinal points and the four primary elements: Earth, Wind, Fire, Water—a concept of the "root of all things" well known in the Old World from end to end. These four gods also represented the colors red, black, white, and blue, and the four races of Mankind, who were often depicted (as on the front page of the *Codex Ferjervary-Mayer*) in appropriate colors together with their symbols, trees and animals.

This recognition of four separate branches of Mankind is in-

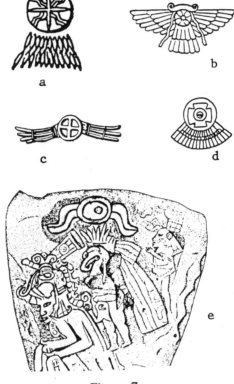

Figure 7

teresting, perhaps even significant in its difference from the three-branched Mesopotamian-biblical concept of an Asian-African-European division stemming from the Shem-Ham-Japhet line of Noah. A fourth people, the people of the color red, had been added by the Nahuatl tribes—the peoples of the Americas.

The Nahuatl tales spoke of conflict and even warfare among the gods. These included an incident when Huitzilopochtli defeated four hundred lesser gods and a fight between Tezcatlipoca-Yaotl and Quetzalcoatl. Such wars for dominion over Earth or its resources have been described in the lore ("myths") of all the ancient peoples. Hittite and Indo-European tales of the wars between Teshub or Indra with their brothers arrived in Greece via Asia Minor. The Semitic Canaanites and Phoenicians wrote down the tales of Ba'al's wars with his brothers, in the course of which Ba'al slaughtered hundreds of lesser "sons

Figure 8

of the gods" when they had been lured to his victory banquet. And in the lands of Ham, Africa, Egyptian texts related the dismemberment of Osiris by his brother Seth and the ensuing bitter and long warfare between Seth and Horus, the son and avenger of Osiris.

Were the gods of the Mexicans original conceptions, or were they memories of beliefs and tales that had their roots in the ancient Near East? The answer will emerge as we examine additional aspects of Nahuatl tales of creation and prehistory.

We find the Creator of All Things, to continue the comparisons, to have been a god who "gives life and death, good and evil fortune." The chronicler Antonio de Herrera y Tordesillas *(Historia general)* wrote that the Indians "call to him in their tribulations, gazing toward the sky where they believe him to be." This god first created the Heaven and the Earth; then he fashioned a man and a woman out of clay, but they did not last. After additional endeavors, a human pair was created of cinders and metals and from them the world was peopled. But all these men and women were destroyed in a flood, save for a certain priest and his wife who, with seeds and animals, floated in a hollowed-out log. The priest discovered land by sending out birds. According to another chronicler, the Friar Gregorio Garcia, the flood lasted a year and a day during which the whole Earth was covered with water and the world was in chaos.

The early or prehistoric events affecting Mankind and the progenitors of the Nahuatl tribes were divided by legends, pictorial depictions, and stone carvings such as the Calendar Stone, into four ages or "Suns." The Aztec considered their times to have been the most recent of five eras, the Age of the Fifth Sun. Each of the previous four Suns had come to an end through some catastrophe, sometimes a natural one (such as a deluge) and sometimes a calamity triggered by wars between the gods.

The great Aztec Calendar Stone (it was discovered within the area of the sacred precinct) is believed to be a record in stone of the five ages. The symbols encircling the central panel and the central depiction itself have been the subject of numerous studies. The first inner ring clearly depicts the twenty signs for the twenty days of the Aztec month. The four rectangular panels surrounding the central face are recognized as the glyphs representing the past four eras and the calamity that ended each of them—Water, Wind, Quakes & Storms, and Jaguar.

The tales of the four ages are valuable for their information regarding the lengths of the eras and their principal events. Though versions vary, suggesting a long verbal tradition preceding the written records, they all agree that the first age came to an end by a deluge, a great flood that engulfed the Earth. Mankind survived because one couple, Nene and his wife Tata, managed to save themselves in a hollowed-out log.

Either this first age or the second one was the age of the White Haired Giants. The Second Sun was recalled as "Tzoncuztique," "Golden Age"; it was brought to an end by the Wind Serpent. The Third Sun was presided over by the Fire Serpent; it was the age of the Red Haired People. According to the chronicler Ixtlilxochitl, they were survivors of the second age who had come by ship from the east to the New World, settling in the area he called Botonchan; they encountered there giants who also survived the second age, and became enslaved by them.

The Fourth Sun was the era of the Black Headed People. It was during that era that Quetzalcoatl appeared in Mexico—tall of stature, bright of countenance, bearded, and wearing a long tunic. His staff, shaped like a serpent, was painted black, white, and red; it was inlaid with precious stones and adorned with six stars. (Not by coincidence, perhaps, the staff of Bishop Zumárraga, the first bishop of Mexico, was fashioned to look like the staff of Quetzalcoatl). It was during this era that Tollan, the Toltec capital, was built. Quetzalcoatl, master of wisdom and knowledge, introduced learning, crafts, laws, and time reckoning according to the fifty-two-year cycle.

Toward the end of the Fourth Sun wars between the gods were taking place. Quetzalcoatl left, going east back to the place whence he had come. The gods' wars brought havoc to the land; wild animals overran mankind, and Tollan was abandoned. Five years later the Chichimec tribes, alias the Aztecs, arrived; and the Fifth Sun, the Aztec era, began.

Why were the eras called "Suns" and how long did they last? The reason is unclear and the length of the various eras is either unstated or differs according to the version. One that appears orderly and, as we shall show, astoundingly plausible, is the *Codex Vaticano-Latino 3738*. It relates that the first Sun lasted 4,008 years, the second 4,010, the third 4,081. The fourth Sun "began 5,042 years ago," leaving unstated the time of its ending. Be it as it may, we have here a tale of events going back 17,141 years from the time the tales have been recorded.

This is quite a time span for supposedly backward people to recall, and scholars, while agreeing that the events of the Fourth Sun contain historical elements, tend to dismiss the earlier eras as sheer myth. How then explain the tales of Adam and Eve, a global deluge, the survival of one couple—episodes (in the words of H. B. Alexander, *Latin-American Mythology)* "strikingly reminiscent of the creation-narrative in Genesis 2 and of the similar Babylonian cosmogony"? Some scholars suggest that Nahuatl texts reflect in some way what the Indians had already heard from the Bible-spouting Spaniards. But since not all codices are post-Conquest, the biblical-Mesopotamian similarities can only be explained by admitting that the Mexican tribes had some ancestral ties to Mesopotamia.

Moreover, the Mexica-Nahuatl timetable correlates events and times with a scientific and historical accuracy that ought to make everyone stop and wonder. It dates the deluge, at the end of the First Sun, to 13,133 years before the time of writing the codex; i.e., to about 11,600 B.C. Now, in our book *The 12th Planet* we have concluded that a global deluge had indeed engulfed the Earth circa 11,000 B.C.; such a correspondence not only of the tale itself but also of its approximate time suggests that there is more than myth to Aztec tales.

We are equally intrigued by the tales' statement that the fourth era was the time of the "black-headed people" (the earlier ones having been deemed eras of white-haired giants, then red-haired people). This is precisely the term by which the Sumerians were called in their texts. Do the Aztec tales then deem the Fourth Sun to have been the time when the Sumerians appeared on the human scene? Sumerian civilization began circa 3800 B.C.; we should not, it would seem by now, be surprised to find that by dating the beginning of the Fourth Age to 5,026 years before their own time, the Aztecs in effect date it to circa 3500 B.C.—amazingly correct for the start of the age of the "black-headed people."

The feedback explanation (that the Aztecs told the Spaniards what they had heard from the Spaniards to begin with) certainly does not hold water where the Sumerians are concerned; the Western world uncovered the remains and legacy of the great Sumerian civilization only four centuries after the Conquest.

The Genesis-like tales, one must conclude, had to be known to the Nahuatl tribes from their own ancestral sources. But how?

The question had already baffled the Spaniards themselves. Astounded to discover not just a civilization in the New World, and one so akin to Europe's, but also "the great number of people there," they were doubly puzzled by the biblical threads in the Aztec yarns. Trying to find an explanation, the answer seemed to be a simple one: these were descendants of the Ten Lost Tribes of Israel who were exiled by the Assyrians in 722 B.C. and then vanished without a trace (the remaining kingdom of Judea was retained by the two tribes Judah and Benjamin).

If not the originator, then the one who expounded it first in a detailed manuscript, was the Dominican Friar Diego Duran, who was brought to New Spain in 1542 at the age of five. His two books, one known by the English title *Book of the Gods and Rites and the Ancient Calendar* and *Historia de las Indias de Nueva España,* have been translated into English by D. Heyden and F. Horcasitas. It is in the second book that Duran, citing the many similarities, stated emphatically his conclusion regarding the natives "of the Indies and the mainland of this new world": that "they are Jews and Hebrew people." His theory was confirmed, he wrote, "by their nature: These natives are part of the ten tribes of Israel which Shalmaneser, King of the Assyrians, captured and took to Assyria."

His reports of conversations with old Indians elicited tribal traditions of a time when there had been "men of monstrous stature who appeared and took possession of the country. . . . And these giants, not having found a way to reach the Sun, decided to build a tower so high that its summit would reach unto Heaven." Such an episode paralleling the biblical tale of the Tower of Babel matched in significance another tale, of an Exodus-like migration.

No wonder then that as such reports increased, the theory of the Ten Lost Tribes became the favorite one of the sixteenth and seventeenth centuries, the assumption being that, somehow, wandering eastward through the Assyrian domains and beyond, the Israelites reached America.

The notion of the Ten Lost Tribes, at its height sponsored by Europe's royal courts, came to be ridiculed by later scholars. Current theories hold that Man initially arrived in the New World from Asia across an icy land bridge to Alaska some 20,000–30,000 years ago, spreading gradually southward. Considerable evidence consisting of artifacts, language and ethnological and anthropological evaluations indicates influences from across the Pacific—Hindu, Southeast Asian, Chinese, Japanese, Polynesian. Scholars explain them by periodic arrival of such people in the Americas; but they are emphatic in stating that these occurred during the Christian era, just centuries before the conquest and not at any time B.C.

While established scholars continue to downplay all evidence for transatlantic contacts between the Old and New World, they employ the concession to relatively recent transpacific contacts as the explanation for the currency of Genesis-like tales in the Americas. Indeed, legends of a global deluge and of the creation of Man out of clay or similar materials have been themes of mythologies all over the world, and one possible route to the Americas from the Near East (where the tales had originated) could have been Southeast Asia and the Pacific islands.

But there are elements in the Nahuatl versions that point to a very early source, rather than to relatively recent pre-Conquest centuries. One is the fact that the Nahuatl tales of the creation of Man follow a very ancient Mesopotamian version that did not even find its way into the Book of Genesis!

The Bible, in fact, has not one but two versions of the creation of Man; both draw on earlier Mesopotamian versions. But both ignore a third version, and probably the oldest one, in which Mankind was fashioned not of clay but out of the blood of a god. In the Sumerian text on which this version is based, the god Ea, collaborating with the goddess Ninti, "prepared a purifying bath." "Let one god be bled into it," he ordered; "from his flesh and blood, let Ninti mix the clay." From this mixture, men and women were created.

We find it highly significant that it is this version—which is not in the Bible—that is repeated in an Aztec myth. The text is known as *Manuscript of 1558;* it relates that after the calamitous end of the Fourth Sun the gods assembled in Teotihuacan.

As soon as the gods came together, they said:
"Who shall inhabit the Earth?

The sky has already been established
and the Earth has been established;
but who, oh gods, shall live on Earth?"

The gathered gods "were grieved." But Quetzalcoatl, a god of wisdom and science, had an idea. He went to Mictlan, the Land of the Dead, and announced to the divine couple in charge of it: "I have come for the precious bones which you keep here." Overcoming objections and trickery, Quetzalcoatl managed to get hold of the "precious bones":

He gathered the precious bones;
The bones of man were put together on one side,
the bones of woman were put together on the other side.
Quetzalcoatl took them and made a bundle.

He carried the dry bones to Tamoanchan, "Place of Our Origin" or "Place From Which We Are Descended." There he gave the bones to the goddess Cihuacoatl ("Serpent Woman"), a goddess of magic.

She ground up the bones
and put them in a fine earthen tub.
Quetzalcoatl bled his male organ on them.

As the other gods looked on, she mixed the ground bones with the god's blood; from the claylike mixture, the *Macehuales* were fashioned. Mankind was re-created!

In the Sumerian tales, the fashioners of Man were the god Ea ("Whose Home Is Water"), also known as Enki ("Lord Earth") whose epithets and symbols often implied his being crafty, a metallurgist—all words that found their linguistic equivalent in the term "Serpent." His companion in the feat, Ninti ("She Who Gives Life") was the goddess of medicine—a craft whose symbol from antiquity has been the entwined serpent. Sumerian depictions on cylinder seals showed the two deities in a laboratorylike setting, flasks and all (Fig. 9a).

It is truly amazing to find all these elements in the Nahuatl tales—a god of knowledge known as the Plumed Serpent, a goddess of magical powers called Serpent Woman; a bathtub of loam in which earthly elements are mixed with a god's essence (blood); and the fashioning of Man, male and female, out of the mixture. Even more astounding is the fact that the myth has been pictorially depicted in a Nahuatl codex found in the area of the Mixtec tribe. It shows a god and a goddess mixing an ele-

a

b

Figure 9

ment that flows into a huge flask or vat with the blood of a god that drips into the flask; out of the mixture, a man emerges (Fig. 9b).

Coupled with the other Sumerian-related data and terminology, contacts at a very early time are indicated. The evidence, it appears, also challenges the current theories about Man's first migrations to the Americas. By that we do not mean simply the suggestions (made earlier this century at the International Congresses of Americanists) that the migration was not from Asia via the Bering Strait in the north but from Australia/New Zealand via Antarctica to South America—an idea revived recently after the discovery in northern Chile, near the border with Peru, of buried human mummies 9,000 years old.

The trouble we have with both arrival theories is that they require the trekking by men, women, and children over thousands of miles of frozen terrain. We wonder *how* this could have been done 20,000 or 30,000 years ago; moreover, we wonder *why* such a journey would have been undertaken. Why would men, women, and children journey for thousands of miles over frozen terrain, seemingly achieving nothing except the experience of more ice—unless they were aware that there was a Promised Land beyond the ice?

But how could they know what was beyond the endless ice if

they had not been there yet, nor anyone else before them—for, by definition, they were the first men to cross over to the Americas?

In the biblical tale of the Exodus from Egypt, the Lord describes the Promised Land as "a land of wheat and barley and of the vine and of the fig-tree and of the pomegranate, a land of the olive-tree and of honey . . . A land whose stones are iron and of whose mountains thou canst hew copper." The Aztec god described their Promised Land to them as one of "houses with gold and silver, multicolored cotton and cacao of many hues." Would the early migrants to America have undertaken their impossible trek had not someone—their god—told them to go and described to them what to expect? And if that deity was not a mere theological entity, but a being physically present on Earth, could he have helped the migrants overcome the hardships of the journey, just as the biblical Lord had done for the Israelites?

It is with such thoughts, of why and how an impossible journey would have been undertaken, that we have read and reread the Nahuatl tales of migrations and the Four Ages. Since the First Sun had ended with the Deluge, that era had to be the final phase of the last Ice Age, for we have concluded in *The 12th Planet* that the Deluge was caused by the slippage of the Antarctic ice sheet into the oceans, thereby bringing the last Ice Age to an abrupt end circa 11,000 B.C.

Was the legendary original home of the Nahuatl tribes called Aztlan, "The White Place," for the simple reason that that is what it was—a snow-covered land? Is this why the First Sun was deemed the time of the "white-haired giants?" Do Aztec historical recollections, by harking back to the beginning of the First Sun 17,141 years earlier, in fact speak of a migration into America circa 15,000 B.C., when the ice formed a land-bridge with the Old World? Moreover, could it be that the crossing was not at all across the ice sheet, but by boats across the Pacific Ocean, as the Nahuatl legends relate?

Legends of prehistoric arrival by sea and landings on the Pacific coast are not confined to the Mexican peoples. Farther south the Andean peoples retained memories of a similar nature, told as legends. One, the Legend of Naymlap, may relate to the very first settlement on those coasts by people from elsewhere. It tells of the arrival of a great fleet of balsa-reed boats (of the kind used by Thor Heyerdahl to simulate Sumerian seafaring in reed boats). A green stone that could utter the words of the people's god, placed in the lead boat, directed the migrants' leader, Naymlap, to the chosen beach. The deity, speaking through the green idol, then instructed the people in the arts of farming, building, and handicrafts.

Some versions of the legend of the green idol pinpointed Cape Santa Helena in Ecuador as the landing site; there the South American continent projects westward into the Pacific. Several of the chroniclers, among them Juan de Velasco, related native traditions that the first settlers in the equatorial regions were giants. The human settlers who followed there worshiped a pantheon of twelve gods, headed by the Sun and the Moon. Where Ecuador's capital is situated, Velasco wrote, the settlers built two temples facing each other. The temple dedicated to the Sun had in front of its gateway two stone columns, and in its forecourt a circle of twelve stone pillars.

The time then came when the leader, Naymlap, his mission accomplished, had to depart. Unlike his successors, he did not die: he was given wings and flew away, never to be seen again —taken heavenward by the god of the speaking stone.

In believing that divine instructions could be received through a Speaking Stone, the American Indians were in good company: all the ancient peoples of the Old World described and believed in oracle stones, and the Ark that the Israelites had carried during the Exodus was topped by the *Dvir*—literally, "Speaker"—a portable device through which Moses could hear the Lord's instructions. The detail concerning the departure of Naymlap by being taken heavenward also has a biblical parallel. We read in Chapter 5 of Genesis that in the seventh generation of Adam's line through Sheth, the patriarch was Enoch; after he had reached the age of 365 years "he was gone" from the Earth, for the Lord had taken him heavenward.

Scholars have a problem with a crossing of the oceans by boats 15,000 or 20,000 years ago: Man, they hold, was too primitive then to have oceangoing vessels and navigate the high seas. Not until the Sumerian civilization, at the beginning of the fourth millennium B.C., did Mankind begin to attain the land (wheeled craft) and water (boats) means of long-range transportation.

But that, according to the Sumerians themselves, was the course of events after the Deluge. There had been, they stated and restated, a high civilization upon Earth *before* the Deluge —a civilization begun on Earth by those who had come from the planet of Anu and continued through a line of long-living "demigods," the offspring of intermarriage between the Extraterrestrials (the biblical *Nefilim)* and the "daughters of Man." Egyptian chronicles, such as the writings of the priest Manetho, followed the same concept. So of course did the Bible, which describes both rural life (farming, sheepherding) and urban civilization (cities, metallurgy) before the Deluge. All that, however—according to all those ancient sources—was wiped off the face of the Earth by the Deluge, and everything had to be restarted from scratch.

The Book of Genesis begins with creation tales that are concise versions of much more detailed Sumerian texts. In these it consistently speaks of "*the* Adam," literally "the Earthling." But then it switches to the genealogy of a specific ancestor named Adam: "This is the book of the generations of Adam" (Genesis 5:1). He had two sons at first, Cain and Abel. After Cain killed his brother, he was banished by Yahweh. "And Adam knew his wife again and she bore a son and called his name Sheth." It is this line, the line of Sheth, that the Bible follows through a genealogy of patriarchs to Noah, the hero of the Deluge story. The tale then focuses on the Asian-African-European peoples.

But whatever happened to Cain and his line? All we have in the Bible are a dozen verses. Yahweh punished Cain to become a nomad, "a fugitive and a vagabond on the Earth."

And Cain went away from the presence of Yahweh
and dwelt in the land of Nod, east of Eden.
And Cain knew his wife and she conceived and bore Enoch;
And he built a city
and called the name of the city by his son's name, Enoch.

Several generations later, Lamech was born. He had two wives. Of one Jabal was born; "he was the father of such as dwell in tents and have cattle." Of the other, two sons were born. One, Jubal, "was the father of all such as play the lyre and pipe." The other son, Tubal-Kain, was "an artificer of gold and copper and iron."

This meagre biblical information is somewhat augmented by the pseudepigraphical Book of Jubilees, believed to have been composed in the second century B.C. from earlier sources. Relating events to the passage of Jubilees, it states that "Cain took Awan his sister to be his wife and she bare him Enoch at the close of the fourth jubilee. And in the first year of the first week of the fifth jubilee, houses were built on Earth, and Cain built a city and called its name after the name of his son, Enoch."

Biblical scholars have long been puzzled by the naming of both a descendant of Adam through Sheth and through Cain "Enoch" (meaning "Founding," "Foundation"), as well as other similarities in descendants' names. Whatever the reason, it is evident that the sources on which the Bible's editors had relied attributed to both Enochs—who were perhaps one prehistoric person—extraordinary deeds. The Book of Jubilees states that Enoch "was the first among men that were born on Earth who learnt writing and knowledge and wisdom and who wrote down the signs of heaven according to their months in a book." According to the Book of Enoch, this patriarch was taught mathematics and knowledge of the planets and the calendar during his heavenly journey, and was shown the location of the "Seven Metal Mountains" on Earth, "in the west."

The pre-biblical Sumerian texts known as King Lists also relate the story of a pre-Deluvial ruler who was taught by the gods all manner of knowledge. His epithet-name was EN.ME.DUR.AN.KI—"Lord of the Knowledge of the Foundations of Heaven and Earth"—and a very probable prototype of the biblical Enochs.

The Nahuatl tales of wandering, arrival at a final destination, settling marked by the building of a city; of a patriarch with two wives and sons of whom tribal nations have evolved; of one that became renowned for being a craftsman in metals—do they not read almost as the biblical tales? Even the Nahuatl stressing of the number seven is reflected in the biblical tales, for the seventh descendant through the line of Cain, Lamech, enigmatically proclaimed that "Seven-fold shall Cain be avenged, and Lamech seventy and seven."

Are we, then, encountering in the traditions of the seven Nahuatl tribes echoes—olden memories—of the banished line of Cain and his son Enoch?

✗ The Aztecs called their capital *Tenochtitlán*, the City of Tenoch, so naming it after their ancestor. Considering that in their dialect the Aztecs had prefixed many words with the sound *T*, *Tenoch* could have originally been *Enoch* if the prefixed T is dropped.

✗ A Babylonian text based in the opinion of scholars on an earlier Sumerian text from the third millennium B.C. enigmatically relates a conflict, ending in murder, between an earth-tilling and a shepherding brother, just as the biblical Cain and Abel were. Doomed to "roam in sorrow," the offending leader, called *Ka'in*, migrated to the land of Dunnu and there "he built a city with twin towers."

Twin towers atop the temple-pyramids were a hallmark of Aztec architecture. Did this commemorate the building of a "city with twin towers" by Ka'in? And was Tenochtitlán, the

"City of Tenoch," so named and built because Cain, millennia earlier, "built a city and called the city by his son's name, Enoch"?

Have we found in Mesoamerica the lost realm of Cain, the city named after Enoch? The possibility certainly offers plausible answers to the enigma of Man's beginnings in these domains.

It may also shed light on two other enigmas—that of the "Mark of Cain" and the hereditary trait common to all the Amerindians: the absence of facial hair.

According to the biblical tale, after the Lord had banished Cain from the settled lands and decreed that he become a wanderer in the East, Cain was concerned about being slain by vengeance seekers. So the Lord, to indicate that Cain was wandering under the Lord's protection, "set a sign unto Cain, that any one finding him should not smite him." Although no one knows what this distinguishing "sign" had been, it has been generally assumed that it was some kind of a tattoo on Cain's forehead. But from the ensuing biblical narrative it appears that the matter of vengeance and the protection against it continued into the seventh generation and beyond. A tattoo on the forehead could not last that long nor be transmittable from generation to generation. Only a genetic trait, transmitted hereditarily, can fit the biblical data.

And, in view of the particular genetic trait of the Amerindians—the absence of facial hair—one wonders whether it was this genetic change that was the "mark of Cain" and his descendants. If our guess is right, then Mesoamerica, as a focal point from which Amerindians spread north and south in the New World, was indeed the Lost Realm of Cain.

3

REALM OF THE
SERPENT GODS

When Tenochtitlán attained its greatness, the Toltec capital of Tula had already been recalled as the legendary Tollan. And when the Toltecs had built their city, Teotihuacan was already enshrined in myth. Its name has meant "Place of the Gods"; and that, according to recorded tales, was exactly what it had been.

It is told that there was a time when calamities befell the Earth and the Earth fell into darkness, for the sun failed to appear. Only at Teotihuacan there was light, for a divine flame remained burning there. The concerned gods gathered at Teotihuacan, wondering what should be done. "Who shall govern and direct the world," they asked each other, unless they could make the sun reappear?

They asked for a volunteer among the gods to jump into the divine flame and, by his sacrifice, bring back the sun. The god Tecuciztecatl volunteered. Putting on his glittering attire he stepped forward toward the flame; but each time he neared the fire he stepped back, losing courage. Then the god Nanauatzin volunteered and unhesitatingly jumped into the fire. Thus shamed, Tecuciztecatl followed suit; but he landed only at the flame's edge. As the gods were consumed, the Sun and Moon reappeared in the skies.

But though they could now be seen, the two luminaries remained motionless in the sky. According to one version, the Sun began to move after one god shot an arrow at it; another version says that it resumed its coursing after the Wind God blew at it. After the Sun had resumed its motion, the Moon too began to move; and so was the cycle of day and night resumed and the Earth was saved.

The tale is intimately connected with Teotihuacan's most renowned monuments, the Pyramid of the Sun and the Pyramid of the Moon. One version has it that the gods built the two pyramids to commemorate the two gods who had sacrificed themselves; another version states that the pyramids had already existed when the event was taking place, that the gods jumped into the divine fire from atop preexisting pyramids.

Whatever the legend, the fact is that the Pyramid of the Sun and the Pyramid of the Moon still rise majestically to this very day. What only a few decades ago were mounds covered by vegetation have now become a major tourist attraction, just thirty miles north of Mexico City. Rising in a valley whose surrounding mountains act as a backdrop to an eternal stage (Fig. 10), the pyramids force the visitor's eyes to follow their upward slope, to the mountains beyond and the vista of the skies above. The monuments exude power, knowledge, intent; the setting bespeaks a conscious linking of Earth with Heaven. No one can miss the sense of history, the presence of an awesome past.

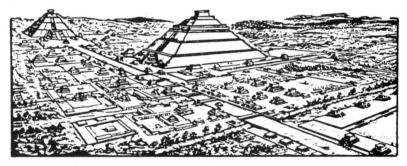

Figure 10

How far back in the past? Archaeologists had assumed at first that Teotihuacan was established in the first centuries of the Christian era; but the date keeps slipping back. On-site work indicates that the city's ceremonial center had already occupied 4.5 square miles by 200 B.C. In the 1950s a leading archaeologist, M. Covarrubias, incredulously admitted that radiocarbon dating gave the place "the almost impossible date of 900 B.C." (*Indian Art of Mexico and Central America*). In fact, further radiocarbon tests gave a date of 1474 B.C. (with a possible small error either way). A date of circa 1400 B.C. is now widely accepted; that is when the Olmecs, who may have been the people to actually toil in the building of Teotihuacan's monumental structures, were establishing great "ceremonial centers" elsewhere in Mexico.

Teotihuacan had clearly undergone several phases of development and its pyramids reveal evidence of earlier inner structures. Some scholars read in the ruins a tale that may have begun 6,000 years ago—in the fourth millennium B.C. This would certainly conform to the Aztec legends that spoke of this Place of the Gods as existing in the Fourth Sun. Then, when the Day of Darkness happened circa 1400 B.C., the two great pyramids were raised to their monumental sizes.

The Pyramid of the Moon rises at the northern end of this ceremonial center, flanked by smaller auxiliary structures and fronted by a great plaza. From there a wide avenue runs southward as far as the eye can see; it is flanked by low-profile shrines, temples, and other structures that were believed to have been tombs; consequently the avenue was given the name Avenue of the Dead. Some 2,000 feet to the south the Avenue of the Dead reaches the Pyramid of the Sun that rises on the eastern side of the avenue (Fig. 11) beyond a plaza and a series of shrines and other structures.

Past the Pyramid of the Sun, and another 3,000 feet southward, one reaches the *Ciudadela,* a quadrangle that contains at its eastern side the third pyramid of Teotihuacan, called the Quetzalcoatl Pyramid. It is now known that facing the Ciudadela, across the Avenue of the Dead, there existed a similar quadrangle that served mostly as a lay administrative-commercial center. The avenue then continues further south; the Teotihuacan Mapping Project led by René Millon in the 1960s established that this north–south avenue extended for nearly five miles—longer than the longest runways at modern airports. In spite of this remarkable length, the wide avenue runs straight as an arrow—quite a technological feat at any time.

An east–west axis, perpendicular to the north–south avenue, extended eastward from the Ciudadela and westward from the administrative quadrangle. Members of the Teotihuacan Mapping Project found south of the Pyramid of the Sun a marker chiseled into the rocks in the shape of a cross within two concentric circles; a similar marker was found about two miles to the west, on a mountainside. A sight line connecting the two markers precisely indicates the direction of the east–west axis, and the other arms of the crosses match the orientation of the north–south axis. The researchers concluded that they had found markers used by the city's original planners; they did not offer a theory to explain what means were used in antiquity to draw a beadline between two such distant spots.

That the ceremonial center had been oriented and laid out deliberately is evident from several other facts. The first one is that the San Juan river that flows in the Teotihuacan valley has

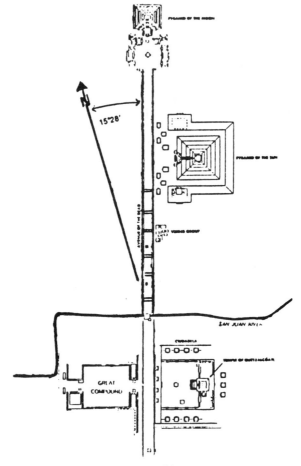

Figure 11

been deliberately diverted where it crosses the ceremonial center: artificial channels divert the river to flow at the Ciudadela and along the quadrangle facing it exactly parallel to the east–west axis, then after two precise right-angle turns along the west-leading avenue.

The second fact indicating a deliberate orientation is that the two axes are not pointing to the cardinal points, but are tilted to the southeast by 15½ degrees (Fig. 11). Studies show that this was not an accident or a miscalculation by the ancient planners. A. F. Aveni *(Astronomy in Ancient Mesoamerica)*, calling this a "sacred orientation," points out that later ceremonial centers (such as Tula and ones even farther away) adhered to this orientation although it made no sense at their locations and when they were built. The conclusion of his researches was that, at Teotihuacan and at the time of its construction, the orientation was devised to enable celestial observations on certain key dates of the calendar.

Zelia Nuttal, in a paper delivered to the twenty-second International Congress of Americanists (Rome, 1926) suggested that the orientation was keyed to the passage of the Sun at the observer's zenith, which occurs twice a year as the Sun appears to move from north to south and back. If such celestial observations were the purpose of the pyramids, their ultimate shape— step pyramids equipped with staircases, leading to presumed viewing-temples on the topmost platform—would make sense. However, because strong evidence suggests that what we now see are the latest outer layers of the two major pyramids (and as arbitrarily resurfaced by archaeologists, to boot), one cannot state for certain that these pyramids' original purpose was not a different one. The possibility, even probability, that the stairways were a late addition is suggested to us by the fact that the first stage of the grand stairway of the Sun Pyramid is tilted and improperly aligned with the pyramid's orientation (Fig. 12).

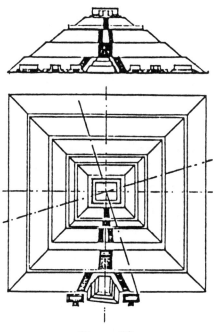

Figure 12

Of the three pyramids at Teotihuacan the smallest is the Quetzalcoatl pyramid in the "Citadel." A later addition was partly excavated to reveal the original step-pyramid. The partly exposed facade reveals sculpted decorations in which the serpent symbol of Quetzalcoatl alternates with a stylized face of Tlaloc against a background of wavy waters (Fig. 13). This pyramid is ascribed to Toltec times and is akin to many other Mexican pyramids.

Figure 13

The two larger pyramids, by contrast, are totally undecorated. They are of a different size and shape and stand out in their massiveness and antiquity. In all these aspects they resemble the two great pyramids of Giza, which likewise differ on all these counts from all the other, subsequent Egyptian pyramids; the latter were built by Pharaohs, whereas the unique ones at Giza were built by the "gods." Perhaps that is also what had happened at Teotihuacan; in which case the archaeological evidence would support the legends of how the Pyramid of the Sun and the Pyramid of the Moon had come to be.

Although, in order to enable their use as observatories, the two great pyramids of Teotihuacan were built as step-pyramids topped by platforms and equipped with stairways (as the Mesopotamian ziggurats had been), there can be no doubt that their architect was acquainted with the Giza pyramids in Egypt and, except for adjusting the outer shape, emulated the unique Giza pyramids. One amazing similarity: although the Second Pyramid at Giza is shorter than the Great Pyramid, their peaks are at the same height above sea level because the Second Pyramid is built on correspondingly higher ground; the same holds true at Teotihuacan, where the smaller Pyramid of the Moon is built on ground some thirty feet higher than that of the Pyramid of the Sun, giving their peaks equal height above sea level.

The similarities are especially obvious between the two greater pyramids. Both are built on artificial platforms. Their sides measure almost the same: about 754 feet in Giza, about 745 feet at Teotihuacan, and the latter would fit neatly into the former (Fig. 14).

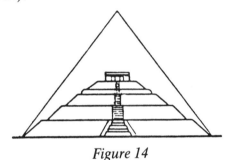

Figure 14

While such similarities and correspondences bespeak a hidden link between the two sets of pyramids, one need not ignore the existence of certain and considerable differences. The Great Pyramid of Giza is built of large stone blocks, carefully shaped and matched and held together without mortar, weighing an aggregate 7,000,000 tons with a mass of 93,000,000 cubic feet. The Sun Pyramid was built of mud bricks, adobe, pebbles, and gravel, held together by a sheath of crude stones and stucco, with an aggregate mass of only 10,000,000 cubic feet. The Giza pyramid contains an inner complex of corridors, galleries, and chambers of intricate and precise construction; the Teotihuacan pyramid does not appear to have such inner structures. The one at Giza rises to a height of 480 feet, the Sun Pyramid (including the erstwhile uppermost temple) to a mere 250. The Great Pyramid has four triangular sides that rise at the tricky angle of 52 degrees; the two at Teotihuacan consist of stages that rest one atop the other, with sides that slope inward for stability, beginning with a slope of 43½ degrees.

These are significant differences that reflect the different times and purposes of each set of pyramids. But in the very last difference lies, hitherto unnoticed to all previous researchers, a key to the solution of some puzzles.

The rather steep angle of 52 degrees has been attained in Egypt only in the Giza pyramids, which were built neither by Cheops or any other Pharaoh (as proven in previous books of *The Earth Chronicles)* but by the gods of the ancient Near East, as beacons for landing at their spaceport in the Sinai peninsula. All the other Egyptian pyramids—lesser, smaller, decayed, or collapsed—were indeed built by Pharaohs, millennia later, in emulation of the gods' "stairways to heaven." But none succeeded in attaining the perfect angle of 52 degrees and whenever this was attempted, the attempt ended in collapse.

The lesson was learned when the Pharaoh Sneferu (circa 2650 B.C.) embarked on his grasp for monumental glory. In a brilliant analysis of the ancient events, K. Mendelssohn *(The Riddle of the Pyramids)* suggested that Sneferu's architects were building his second one at Dahshur when his first one, built at Maidum at the 52 degree angle, collapsed. The architects then hurriedly changed the angle of the Dahshur pyramid to the safer 43½ degrees in midconstruction, giving that pyramid the shape and thus the name The Bent Pyramid (Fig. 15a). Still determined to leave behind a true pyramid, Sneferu then proceeded to build a third one nearby; it is called the Red Pyramid for the color of its stones, and it rises at the safe angle of 43½ degrees (Fig. 15b).

But in this retreat to the safety of 43½ degrees, Sneferu's architects in fact fell back to a choice made more than a century earlier, circa 2700 B.C. by the Pharaoh Zoser. His pyramid, the earliest pharaonic one that still stands (at Sakkara), was a step pyramid that rose in six stages (Fig. 15c) conforming to the shallower angle of 43½ degrees.

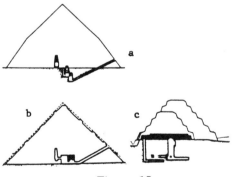

Figure 15

Is it only a coincidence that the Pyramid of the Sun and the Great Pyramid of Giza have the same base measurements? Perhaps. Is it by mere chance that the precise 43½ degree angle adopted by the Pharaoh Zoser and perfected in his step-pyramid was followed at Teotihuacan? We doubt it. Whereas a shallower angle, say 45 degrees, could have been attained by an unsophisticated architect simply by dividing in two a right angle (90 degrees), the 43½ degree angle resulted in Egypt from a sophisticated adaptation of the factor *Pi* (about 3.14), which is the ratio of a circle's circumference to its diameter.

The 52 degree angle of the Giza pyramids required familiarity with this factor; it was attained by giving the pyramid a height (H) equal to half the side (S) divided by *Pi* and multiplied by four ($754 \div 2 = 377 \div 3.14 = 120 \times 4 = 480$ feet in height). The angle of 43½ degrees was attained by reducing the height from a final multiple of four to a multiple of three. In both instances, knowledge of *pi* was required; and there is absolutely nothing to indicate such knowledge among the peoples of Mesoamerica. How then did the 43½ degree angle appear in the structures of the two unique (to Mesoamerica) pyramids of Teotihuacan, if not through someone familiar with the constructions of the Egyptian pyramids?

Except for the unique Great Pyramid of Giza, Egyptian pyramids were equipped only with a lower passageway (see Figs. 15) that usually began at or near the edge of the pyramid's base and continued under it. Should one ascribe to mere coincidence the existence of such a passageway under the Pyramid of the Sun?

The accidental discovery was made in 1971, after heavy rainfalls. Just in front of the pyramid's central stairway, a subterranean cavity was unearthed. It contained ancient steps that led some twenty feet down to an entrance into a horizontal passageway. The excavators concluded it was a natural cave that had been artificially enlarged and improved, running under the bedrock on which the pyramid was built. That the original cave was converted to some purpose intentionally is evidenced by the fact that the ceiling is made of heavy stone blocks and that the tunnel's walls are smoothed with plaster. At various points along this subterranean passageway adobe walls divert its course at sharp angles.

About 150 feet from the ancient stairway, the tunnel sprouts two elongated side chambers, like spread wings; it is a spot exactly under the first stage of the step-pyramid. From there the subterranean passageway, generally about seven feet high, continues for almost another 200 feet; in this inner portion the construction becomes more complex, using a variety of materials; the floors, laid in segments, were man-made; drainage pipes were provided for now unknown purposes (perhaps connected to an underground watercourse now extinct). Finally, the tunnel ends below the fourth stage of the pyramid in a hollowed-out area that resembles a cloverleaf, supported by adobe columns and basalt slabs.

What was the purpose of the complex subterranean structure? Since the segmenting walls had been breached before the discovery in modern times, it is not possible to say whether the remains of clay vessels, obsidian blades and charcoal ashes belong to the earliest phase of the tunnel's use. But the question of what, besides celestial observation, was going on at Teotihuacan, has been compounded by other discoveries.

The Avenue of the Dead seems to stretch as a wide, smooth runway from the plaza of the Pyramid of the Moon to the southern horizon; but in fact its smooth flow is interrupted in a section situated between the Pyramid of the Sun and the San Juan river. The overall slope from the Pyramid of the Moon to the Pyramid of the Sun is even more accentuated in this section of the Avenue, and the on-site examination clearly indicates that the slope was achieved by deliberate cutting into the native rock; overall, the drop from the Pyramid of the Moon to a point past the Ciudadela is some ninety feet. Here six segments have been created by the erection of a series of double walls perpendicularly to the course of the Avenue. The Avenue's cavity is further lined with walls and low structures, resulting in six semi-misubterranean compartments open to the sky. The perpendicular walls are fitted with sluices at their floor level. The impression is that the whole complex served to channel water that flowed down the Avenue. The flow may have begun at the Pyramid of the Moon (where a subterranean tunnel was found encircling it), and been linked in some manner to the subterranean tunnel of the Pyramid of the Sun. The series of compartments then retained and eventually let out the water from one to the other, until ultimately the water reached the diverting channel of the San Juan river.

Could these artificially flowing and cascading waters have been the reason for decorating the facade of the Quetzalcoatl Pyramid with wavy waters—at an inland site, hundreds of miles away from any sea?

The association of this inland site with water is further suggested by the discovery of a huge stone statue of Chalchiuhtlicue, the goddess of water and the spouse of Tlaloc, the rain god. The statue (Fig. 16), now on exhibit at the National Museum of

Figure 16

Anthropology in Mexico City, was found standing in the center of the plaza in front of the Pyramid of the Moon. In her pictorial depictions, the goddess, whose name means "Lady of Waters," was usually shown wearing a jade skirt decorated with conch shells. Her adornments were turquoise earrings and a necklace of jade or other blue-green stones from which there hung a gold medallion. The statue repeats these dress and decorative elements, and it appears that it was also adorned with an actual golden pendant, embedded in an appropriate cavity, which has been removed by robbers. Her pictorial depictions often showed her wearing a crown of serpents or otherwise adorned with them, indicating her being one of the serpent gods of the Mexicans.

Was Teotihuacan laid out and constructed as some kind of a waterworks, employing water for some technological processes? Before we answer the question, let us mention another puzzling discovery there.

Alongside the third segment down from the Pyramid of the Sun, excavations of a series of interconnected subterranean chambers revealed that some of the floors were covered with layers of thick sheets of mica. This is a silicone whose special properties make it resistant to water, heat, and electrical currents. It has therefore been used as an insulator in various chemical processes and electrical and electronic applications, and in recent times in nuclear and space technologies.

The particular properties of mica depend to some extent on its content of other trace minerals, and thus on its geographic source. According to expert opinions, the mica found at Teotihuacan is of a type that is found only in faraway Brazil. Traces of this mica were also found on remains removed from the Pyramid of the Sun's stages when it was being uncovered early in this century. What was the use to which this insulating material was put at Teotihuacan?

Our own impression is that the presence of the Lord and Lady of Water alongside the principal deity, Quetzatcoatl; the sloping avenue; the series of structures, subterranean chambers, tunnels; the diverted river; the semisubterranean sections with their sluices; and the underground compartments lined with mica—were all components of a scientifically conceived plant for the separation, refining or purification of mineral substances.

Whether in the middle of the first millennium B.C., or more probably in the middle of the second millennium B.C., someone familiar with the secrets of pyramid building had come to this valley; and equally knowledgeable in the physical sciences, created from locally available materials a sophisticated processing plant. Was this someone in search of gold, as the pendant of the Lady of Water would suggest, or of some other, even rarer mineral?

And if it was not Man—was it his gods, just as the legends concerning Teotihuacan and its very name have suggested all along?

Who, besides the gods, were the original dwellers of Teotihuacan? Who had carried the stones and mortar to raise its first pyramids? Who had channeled the waters and operated the sluices?

Those who assume that Teotihuacan is no older than a few centuries B.C. have a simple answer: the Toltecs. Those who now lean toward a much earlier beginning have started to point to the Olmecs, an enigmatic people who emerged on the Mesoamerican scene in the middle of the second millennium B.C. But the Olmecs themselves pose many puzzles, for they appear to have been black Africans; and that too is anathema to those who simply cannot accept transatlantic crossings millennia ago.

Even if the origin of Teotihuacan and its builders is shrouded in mystery, it is almost certain that in the centuries preceding the Christian era Toltec tribesmen began to drift in. At first performing manual chores, they gradually learned the city's crafts and adopted the culture of its masters, including picture-writing, the secrets of goldsmithing, knowledge of astronomy and the calendar, and the worship of the gods. Circa 200 B.C. whoever had lorded over Teotihuacan picked up and left, and the place became a Toltec city. For centuries it was renowned for its tools, weapons, and artifacts made of obsidian stone, and its cultural and religious influence extended widely. Then, a thousand years after they had drifted in, the Toltecs too packed up and left. No one knows why; but the departure was total and Teotihuacan became a desolate place, living only in memories of a golden past.

Some believe that the event coincided with the establishment of Tollan as the Toltecs' new capital, circa A.D. 700. A place of human settlement for millennia on the banks of the Tula river, it was built up by the Toltecs as a mini-Teotihuacan. Codices and lore described Tollan as a legendary city, a center of arts and crafts, resplendent in its palaces and temples, glittering with gold and precious stones. But for a long time scholars questioned its very existence . . . Now it is known beyond doubt that Tollan did indeed exist, at a site nowadays called Tula, some fifty miles northwest of Mexico City.

The rediscovery of Tollan began toward the end of the nineteenth century and the beginning of the process is mainly associated with the French traveller Désiré Charnay (*Les anciennes villes du nouveau monde*). Serious excavation work began only in the 1940s under the leadership of the Mexican archaeologist Jorge R. Acosta. This work of excavation and restoration focused on the principal ceremonial compound referred to as Tula Grande; later work, as that by teams from the University of Mississippi, expanded the area of unearthing the past.

The discoveries confirmed not only the city's existence but also its history as told in various codices, especially the one known as *Anales de Cuauhtitlan*. It is now known that Tollan was ruled by a dynasty of priest-kings who claimed to have been descendants of the god Quetzalcoatl and therefore, in addition to their given name, also bore the god's name as a patronym—a custom that was prevalent among the Egyptian pharaohs. Some of these priest-kings were warriors, bent on expanding Toltec rule; others were more concerned with the faith. In the second half of the tenth century A.D. the ruler was Ce Acatl Topiltzin-Quetzalcoatl; his name and time are certain because a portrait of his, accompanied by a date equivalent to A.D. 968, can still be seen carved on a rock overlooking the site of the city.

It was in his time that a religious conflict broke out among the Toltecs; it seems that it concerned the demand by part of the priesthood to introduce human sacrifices in order to pacify the War God. In A.D. 987 Topiltzin-Quetzalcoatl and his followers left Tollan and migrated eastward, emulating the earlier legendary departure of the divine Quetzalcoatl. They settled in Yucatán.

Two centuries later natural calamities and onslaughts by

other tribesmen brought the Toltecs to their knees. The calamities were deemed signs of divine wrath, foretelling the city's doom. The chronicler Sahagún recorded that in the end the ruler, who many think was called Huemac but who also bore the patronym Quetzalcoatl, convinced the Toltecs that Tollan must be abandoned. "And so they left by his command, although they had lived there many years and had built beautiful and large houses and their temples and their palaces...At last they had to depart, leaving their houses, their lands, their city and their riches, and since they could not take all their wealth with them, they buried many things, and even today some of them are brought up from under the ground and not without admiration for their beauty and workmanship."

Thus it was that in A.D. 1168 or thereabouts Tollan became a desolate city, left to decay and disintegrate. It is told that when the first Aztec chieftain laid eyes on the city's remains, he cried bitterly. The destructive forces of nature were aided by invaders, marauders, and robbers who desecrated the temples, toppled monuments, and wrecked whatever was left standing. And so Tollan, flattened and forgotten, became only a legend.

What is known about Tollan eight centuries later attests to the appropriateness of its name, which means "Place of many neighborhoods"; for it appears to have consisted of many neighborhoods and precincts that occupied as much as seven square miles. As at Teotihuacan (which its planners tried to emulate), Tollan's heart was a sacred precinct that extended along a mile-long north–south axis; it was flanked by ceremonial groups built with an east–west orientation perpendicular to the north–south axis. As we have already noted, the orientations were given the "sacred tilt" of Teotihuacan, although at the period and geographic location of Tollan it no longer made astronomical sense.

At what might have been the northern limit of the sacred precinct there were found the remains of an unusual structure. In front it was built like a regular step-pyramid with its staircase; but in the back the structure is circular and was probably surmounted by a tower. The building might have served as an observatory; it certainly could have been a model for the later Aztec temple of Quetzalcoatl in Tenochtitlán and for other circular observatory pyramids elsewhere in Mexico.

The principal ceremonial compound, about a mile away to the south, was laid out around a large central square in the midst of which stood the Great Altar. The main temple stood atop a large five-stage pyramid on the square's eastern side. A smaller five-stage pyramid on the northern side served as the

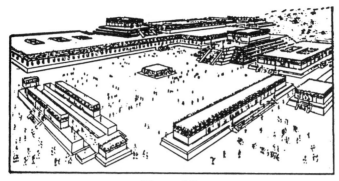

Figure 17

raised platform for another temple; it was flanked by multi-chambered buildings that show evidence of fires and that may have served for some industrial purpose. Elongated buildings or vestibules whose roofs rested on rows of pillars connected the two pyramids and also lined the square's southern side. A ball-court for the sacred *tlachtli* rubber-ball game completed the square on the west (Fig. 17, an artist's reconstruction suggested by the archaeologist P. Salazar Ortegon).

Between this principal compound of Tula Grande and the northern edge of the sacred precinct, various structures and groups of buildings evidently existed; another ballcourt was excavated. In the particular compounds and throughout the precinct, relatively many stone statues have been found. These include not only those of animals, such as a familiar coyote and an unfamiliar tiger, but also of a reclining demigod called Chac-mool (Fig. 18). The Toltecs also sculpted statues of their chieftains, depicting them mostly as men of short stature. Others, attired as warriors and holding (in their left hand) the *atl-atl* weapon (a curved spear or arrow thrower), were depicted in

Figure 18

a   b

Figure 19

relief on square columns (Fig. 19a), both in profile and in back views (Fig. 19b).

When methodical and sustained archaeological work began in the 1940s under Jorge R. Acosta, attention was directed at the Great Pyramid, which, facing the Great Altar, provided an obvious astronomical purpose. At the time the archaeologists wondered why the local Indians referred to the desolate mound as *El Tesoro,* The Treasure; but when several artifacts of gold were found after excavations began, the workmen insisted that the pyramid rose atop a "field of gold" and refused to continue work. "Be it reality or superstition," Acosta wrote, "the result was that work stopped and was never resumed."

Work then focused on the smaller pyramid that has variably been referred to (at first) as Pyramid of the Moon, then as Pyramid "B," and lately as the Quetzalcoatl Pyramid. The designation stems primarily from the long native name for the mound that means "Lord of the Morning Star," presumably one of the epithets of Quetzalcoatl, and from the remains of colored plasterwork and low reliefs that adorned the pyramid's stages, evidencing that its rich decorations were dominated by the Feathered Serpent motif. Archaeologists also believe that two round stone columns, several of whose sections have been found, were carved with the Feathered Serpent image and stood as gateway pillars at the entrance to the temple atop this pyramid.

The greatest archaeological treasure trove was found when the Acosta teams realized that the northern side of this pyramid was disturbed in pre-Hispanic times. A ramplike aggregate seemed to run down the middle of this side, replacing the stepped incline. Excavating there, the archaeologists found that a trench had been cut through this side of the pyramid, reaching well into its interior; and the trench, which was as high as the pyramid, was used to bury in it a great number of stone sculptures. When these were taken out, stood up and fitted together, it became clear that these were sections of the two round gateway columns, four square columns that are believed to have held up the roof of the pyramid's temple, and four colossal humanlike statues, more than fifteen feet high, that came to be known as the *Atlantes* (Fig. 20). Believed to have also served as caryatids (sculptures used as pilasters to uphold a roof or its beams), they were re-erected by the archaeologists atop the pyramid when the restoration work was completed.

Each one of the *Atlantes* (as illustrated in Fig. 21) consists of four sections that were carved to fit together. The topmost section forms the statue's head, showing the giants wearing a headdress of feathers held together by a band decorated with star symbols; two elongated objects cover the ears. The facial features are not readily identifiable and so far have defied comparison with any known racial group; but although the four faces hold the same remote expression, a close examination shows them to be slightly different and individual.

The torso is made up of two sections. The upper or breast section's main feature is a thick breastplate whose shape has been compared to a butterfly. The lower part of the torso has its main feature on the back; it is a disk with a human face in its center, surrounded by undeciphered symbols and, in the opinion of some, a "wreath" of two entwined serpents. The bottom section provides the giant's thighs, legs, and sandaled feet. Ribbons hold these accoutrements in place; armbands, anklets, and a loincloth are included in the elaborate attire (see Fig. 21).

Whom do these giant statues represent? Their first discoverers called them "idols," certain that they represented deities. Popular writers nicknamed them *Atlantes*, which implied both that they might have been offspring of the Goddess Atlatona, "She Who Shines in the Water," and also that they might have come from the legendary Atlantis. Less imaginative scholars see

Figure 20

them simply as Toltec warriors, who hold in their left hand a bunch of arrows and an atl-atl in the right hand. But this interpretation cannot possibly be correct, for the "arrows" in the left hand are not straight but curved; and we have seen that the left-handed weapon was the atl-atl. At the same time, the weapon held in the right hand (Fig. 22a) is not curved as the atl-atl must be; what is it, then?

The instrument looks rather like a pistol in its holster, held by two fingers. An interesting theory suggesting that it was not a weapon but a tool, a "plasma pistol," was advanced by Gerardo Levet *(Mision Fatal)*. He discovered that one of the square pilasters depicting Toltec chieftains has, engraved in an upper-left-hand corner (Fig. 22b), the image of a person wearing a backpack and holding the tool in question; he uses it as a flamethrower to shape a stone (Fig. 22c). The tool is unques-

Figure 21

tionably the same instrument held by the giants' right hands. Levet suggests that it was a high-energy "pistol" that was used to cut and carve stones, and he points out that such Thermo-Jet torches were used in modern time to carve the giant monument of Georgia's Stone Mountain.

The significance of Levet's discovery may go beyond his own theory. Since stone stellas and carvings have been found throughout Mesoamerica, the product of its native artists, one need not search for high-tech tools to explain the stone carvings. On the other hand, the depicted tool may serve to explain another enigmatic aspect of Tollan.

As they examined the depths of the pyramid after they had removed the ramp's soil, the archaeologists discovered that the external and visible pyramid was built over and hid an earlier pyramid whose stepped stages lay some eight feet away on each side. They also discovered remains of vertical walls that suggested the existence of inner chambers and passages within the earlier pyramid (but have not pursued these leads). They did come upon an extraordinary feature—a stone pipe made of perfectly fitting tubular sections (Fig. 23) with an inner diameter of about eighteen inches. The long pipe was installed inside the pyramid at the same angle as its original incline and ran through its whole height.

Acosta and his team presumed that the pipe had served to drain rainwater; but this could have been achieved without such an elaborate internal installation, and with simple clay pipes rather than by precision-sculpted stone sections. The position and incline of the unusual, if not unique, tubular contraption was obviously part of the original plan of the pyramid and inte-

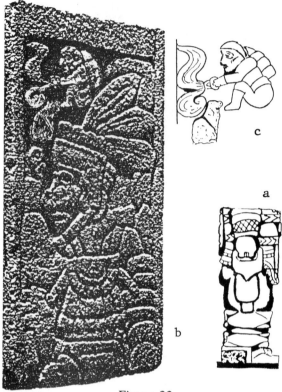

c

a

b

Figure 22

gral to the structure's purpose. The fact that the remains of the
adjoining multichambered and multistoried buildings suggest
some industrial processing, and also the fact that in antiquity
water from the Tula river was channeled to flow by these buildings, raise the possibility that at this site, as at Teotihuacan,
some kind of a purification and refining process had taken place
at a very early period.

What comes to our mind is this: Was the enigmatic tool a
tool not to engrave stones, but to break up stones for their ores?
Was it, in other words, a sophisticated mining tool?

And was the mineral sought after, gold?

The possession by "Atlanteans" of high-technology tools
more than a thousand years ago in Central Mexico raises the
question of who they were. Certainly, to judge by their facial
features, not Mesoamericans; and probably "gods" and not
mortal men, if the statues' size is an indication of veneration,

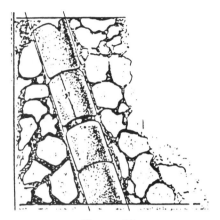

Figure 23

for alongside these giant figures there were erected the square columns on which images of Toltec rulers were carved in normal size. The fact that at some pre-Hispanic time the colossal images were disassembled and carefully lowered into the depths of the pyramid and buried there, implies a measure of sanctity. Indeed, it all confirms the statement by Sahagún, earlier quoted, that when the Toltecs abandoned Tollan "they buried many things" some of which, even in Sahagún's time, "were brought up from under the ground and not without admiration for their beauty and workmanship."

The archaeologists believe that the four Atlanteans stood atop the Pyramid of Quetzalcoatl, supporting the ceiling of the temple atop the pyramid as though they were holding up the Celestial Canopy. This is the role played in Egyptian beliefs by the four sons of Horus, who were holding up the sky at the four cardinal points. According to the Egyptian *Book of the Dead,* it was these four gods, who linked Heaven and Earth, who accompanied the deceased pharaoh to a sacred stairway whereby he would ascend heavenward for an eternal afterlife. This "Stairway to Heaven" was depicted hieroglyphically as either a single or a double stairway, the latter representing a step pyramid (Fig. 24a). Was it just a coincidence that the stairway symbol decorated the walls around the Tollan pyramid and became a major Aztec iconographic symbol (Fig. 24b)?

At the center of all this symbolism and religious beliefs of the Nahuatl peoples was their hero-god, giver of all their knowledge, Quetzalcoatl—"The Feathered Serpent." But what, one may ask, was a "feathered" serpent if not a serpent that, birdlike, had wings and could fly?

And if so, the concept of Quetzalcoatl as the "Feathered

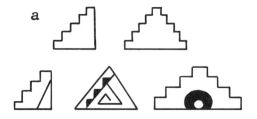

Figure 24

Serpent" was none other than the Egyptian concept of the Winged Serpent (Fig. 25) that facilitated the transfiguration of the deceased pharaoh to the realm of the ever-living gods.

In addition to Quetzalcoatl, the Nahuatl pantheon was replete with deities associated with serpents. Cihuacoatl was the "Serpent Female." Coatlicue was "the one with the skirt of serpents." Chicomecoatl was "Seven Snake." Ehecacoamixtli was the "Cloud of wind snakes," and so on. The great god Tlaloc was frequently depicted with the mask of a double-serpent.

And so, unacceptable as this might be to pragmatic scholars, mythology, archaeology, and symbolism lead to the unavoidable conclusion that Central Mexico, if not all of Mesoamerica, was the realm of the Serpent Gods—the gods of ancient Egypt.

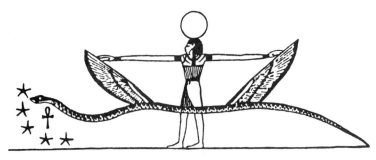

Figure 25

4

SKYWATCHERS
IN THE JUNGLES

Maya.

The name evokes mystery, enigma, adventure. A civilization that was, and is gone, vanished though its people have remained. Incredible cities abandoned intact, swallowed by the green jungle canopy; pyramids that reach sky high, aiming to touch the gods; and monuments, elaborately carved and decorated, that speak out in artful hieroglyphs whose meaning is still mostly lost in the mists of time.

The Maya mystique seized the imagination and curiosity of Europeans from the moment the Spaniards first set foot in the Yucatán peninsula and saw the vestiges of cities lost in the jungle. It was all so unbelievable, yet there it was: stepped pyramids, platformed temples, decorated palaces, engraved stone pillars; and as they stared at the astounding remains they listened to the natives' tales of monarchies, city-states and glories that once had been. One of the most notorious of the Spanish priests who wrote of Yucatán and the Maya during and following the Conquest, Friar (later Bishop) Diego de Landa *(Relacion de las cosas de Yucatan),* reported that "there are in Yucatán many edifices of great beauty, this being the most outstanding of all things discovered in the Indies; they are all built of stone and finely ornamented, though there is no metal found in the country for this cutting."

With other interests on their minds, such as the search for riches and the conversion of the natives to Christianity, it took nearly two centuries for the Spaniards to turn their attention to the ruins. It was only in 1785 that a royal commission inspected the then-discovered ruins of Palenque. Fortunately, a copy of the commission's illustrated report found its way to London; its eventual publication attracted to the Mayan enigma a wealthy nobleman, Lord Kingsborough. Fervently believing that the inhabitants of Mesoamerica were descended from the Ten Lost

Tribes of Israel, he spent the rest of his life and all of his fortune in the exploration and description of the ancient monuments and writings of Mexico. His *Antiquities of Mexico* (1830–1848), together with Landa's *Relacion,* has been an invaluable source of data on the Maya past.

But in the popular mind, the honor of launching the archaeological discovery of the Maya civilization belongs to a native of New Jersey, John L. Stephens. Appointed U.S. envoy to the Central American Federation, he went to the Maya lands with his friend Frederick Catherwood, an accomplished artist. The two books that Stephens wrote and Catherwood illustrated, *Incidents of Travel in Central America, Chiapas, and Yucatán* and *Incidents of Travel in Yucatán,* are still recommended reading a century and a half after their original publication (1841 and 1843). Catherwood's own volume, *Views of Ancient Monuments of Central America, Chiapas, and Yucatán,* further fueled interest in the subject. When Catherwood's drawings are put side by side with current photographs, one is amazed to see the accuracy of his work (and saddened to realize the erosion that has taken place since).

The team's reports were especially detailed regarding the great sites of Palenque, Uxmal, Chichén Itzá, and Copan; the latter is above all associated with Stephens for, in order to investigate it without hindrance, he bought the site from its local landlord for fifty American dollars. All in all the two explored nearly fifty Maya cities; the profusion not only staggered the imagination but also left no doubt that the emerald canopy of the rain forests hid not just a few lost outposts but a whole lost civilization. Of particular importance was the realization that some of the symbols and glyphs carved upon the monuments in fact stated the date thereof, so that the Maya civilization could be placed in a time frame. Although the complete hieroglyphic writing of the Maya is still a long way from being deciphered, scholars have been successful in reading the date inscriptions and establishing the parallel dates in the Christian calendar.

We could have known much more about the Maya from their own extensive literature—books that were written on paper made from tree barks and laminated with white lime to create a base for the inked glyphs. But these books, by the hundreds, were systematically destroyed by the Spanish priests—most notably by the very same Bishop Landa who ended up being the one who preserved much of the "pagan" information in his own writings.

Only three (or, if authentic, a fourth) codices ("picture-books") have remained. The parts scholars find most interesting in them are the sections dealing with astronomy. Two other major literary works are also available because they had been rewritten, either from original picture-books or from oral traditions, into the native tongues but using Latin script.

One of these is the books of *Chilam Balam,* meaning the Oracles or Utterings of Balam the priest. Many villages in Yucatán possessed copies of this book; the one best preserved and translated is the *Book of Chilam Balam of Chumayel.* Balam, it appears, was a kind of a Maya "Edgar Cayce": the books record information regarding the mythical past and the prophetic future, on rites and rituals, astrology, and medical advice.

The word *balam* means "jaguar" in the native tongue, and has caused much consternation among scholars, for it has no apparent connection with oracles. We find it intriguing, however, that in ancient Egypt a class of priests called *Shem*-priests, who pronounced oracles during certain royal ceremonies as well as secret formulas intended to "Open the Mouth" so that a deceased pharaoh could join the gods in the Afterlife, wore leopard skins (Fig. 26a). Maya depictions of similarly clad priests have been found (Fig. 26b); since in the Americas this would have to be a jaguar skin rather than that of an African leopard, this could explain the "jaguar" meaning of the name Balam. It would also indicate, once more, an Egyptian ritual influence.

We are even more intrigued by the similarity of this name of the Maya oracle-priest to that of the seer Balaam, who, according to the Bible, was retained by the king of Moab during the Exodus to put a curse on the Israelites, but who ended up being pronounced their favorable oracle. Was this just a coincidence?

The other book is the *Popol Vuh,* the "Council Book" of the highland Maya. It gives an account of divine and human origins and of royal genealogies; its cosmogony and creation traditions

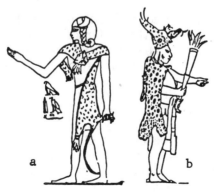

Figure 26

are basically similar to those of the Nahuatl peoples, indicating a common original source. Regarding Maya origins the *Popol Vuh* states that their forefathers had come "from the other side of the sea." Landa wrote that the Indians "have heard from their ancestors that this land was occupied by a race of people who came from the East and whom God had delivered by opening twelve paths through the sea."

These statements are in accord with a Maya tale known as the Legend of Votan. It was reported by several Spanish chroniclers, particularly Friar Ramon Ordóñez y Aguiar and Bishop Nuñez de la Vega. It was later collected from its various sources by the Abbé E. C. Brasseur de Bourbourg *(Histoire de nations civilisées du mexique)*. The legend relates the arrival in Yucatán, circa 1000 B.C. by the chroniclers' calculations, of "the first man whom God had sent to this region to people and parcel out the land that is now called America." His name was Votan (meaning unknown); his emblem was the Serpent. "He was a descendant of the Guardians, of the race of *Can*. His place of origin was a land called *Chivim*." He made a total of four voyages. The first time he landed he established a settlement near the coast. After some time he advanced inland and "at the tributary of a great river built a city which was the cradle of this civilization." He called the city *Nachan*, "which means Place of Serpents." On his second visit he surveyed the newfound land, examining its subterranean zones and underground passages; one such passage was said to have gone right through a mountain near Nachan. When he returned to America the fourth time he found discord and rivalry among the people. So he divided the realm into four domains, establishing a city to serve as the capital of each. Palenque is mentioned as one of them; another appears to have been near the Pacific coast. The others are unknown.

Nuñez de la Vega was convinced that the land whence Votan had come bordered on Babylonia. Ordóñez concluded that Chivim was the land of the Hivites whom the Bible (Genesis 10) listed as sons of Canaan, cousins of the Egyptians. More recently Zelia Nuttal, writing in the *Papers of the Peabody Museum*, Harvard University, pointed out that the Maya word for serpent, *Can*, paralleled the Hebrew *Canaan*. If so, the Maya legend, telling that Votan was of the race of Can and his symbol was the serpent, could be using a play of words to state that Votan came from Canaan. This certainly justifies our wondering why *Nachan*, "Place of Serpents," is virtually identical to the Hebrew *Nachash* that means "serpent."

Such legends strengthen the scholarly school that considers

the Gulf Coast as the place where Yucatec civilization began—not only of the Maya, but also of the earlier Olmecs. In this view much more consideration has to be given to a site that is little known to visitors, which belongs to the very beginnings of Maya culture "between 2000 and 1000 B.C. if not earlier," according to its excavators from Tulane University–National Geographic Society. Called Dzibilchaltun, it is situated near the port city Progreso on Yucatán's northwestern coast. The remains, extending over an area of twenty square miles, reveal that the city was occupied from the earliest times through Spanish times, its edifices having been built and rebuilt and overbuilt, and its cut and ornamented stones having been hauled away to be used in Spanish and modern constructions near and far. Besides immense temples and pyramids, the city's outstanding feature is a Great White Way, a causeway paved with limestones that ran straight for a mile and a half as an east–west axis of the city.

A string of major Maya cities stretches across the northern tip of Yucatán, bearing names well known not just to archaeologists but to millions of visitors: Uxmal, Izamal, Mayapan, Chichén Itzá, Tulum—to mention the most outstanding sites. Each played a role in Maya history; Mayapan was the center of an alliance of city-states, Chichén Itzá was made great by Toltec migrants. Either one of them could have been the capital from which, according to the Spanish chronicler Diego Garcia de Palacio, a great Maya lord from Yucatán had conquered the southern highlands and built the southernmost Maya center of Copan. It was all, Garcia wrote, written in a book that the Indians of Copan had shown him when he visited that place.

Notwithstanding all this legendary and archaeological evidence, another school of archaeologists believes that Maya culture—or at least the Mayas themselves—originated in the southern highlands (today's Guatemala), spreading from there northward. Studies of the Maya language trace its origins to "a proto-Maya community that, perhaps around 2600 B.C., existed in what is now the department of Huehuetenango in northwest Guatemala" (D. S. Morales, *The Maya World)*. But wherever and however Maya civilization developed, scholars consider the second millennium B.C. as its "Pre-Classic" phase and the beginning of the "Classic" phase of maximal achievement circa A.D. 200; by A.D. 900 the realm of the Maya extended from the Pacific coast to the Gulf of Mexico and the Caribbean. During those many centuries the Maya built scores of cities whose pyramids, temples, palaces, plazas, stelae, sculptures, inscriptions, and decorations overwhelm both scholar and visitor in their profusion, variety and beauty, to say nothing of their monumental size and imaginative architecture. Except for a few cities that were walled, Maya cities were in reality open-ended ceremonial centers surrounded by a population of administrators, artisans, and merchants, and supported by an extensive rural population. In these centers each successive ruler added new structures or enlarged older ones by building bigger edifices over the previous ones, like adding a new layer of skin over an onion.

And then, five centuries before the Spanish arrival, for reasons unknown, the Maya abandoned their sacred cities and let the jungle take them over.

Palenque, one of the earliest Maya cities, is situated near the Mexican–Guatemalan border and is reachable from the modern city Villahermosa. In the seventh century A.D. it marked the western reaches of Maya expansion. Its existence was known to Europeans since 1773; the remains of its temples and palaces have been uncovered and its rich stucco decorations and hieroglyphic inscriptions have been studied by archaeologists since the 1920s. Yet, its fame and allure took off only after the discovery in 1949 (by Alberto Ruiz Lhuillier) that the stepped pyramid called the Temple of Inscriptions contained a secret internal stairway that led all the way down. Several years of excavation and removal of the soil and debris that filled and hid the inner structure yielded in the end a most exciting discovery: a burial chamber (Fig. 27). At the bottom of the twisting stairway a triangular stone block masked an entranceway through the

Figure 27

Figure 28

blank wall that was still guarded by the skeletons of Maya warriors. Behind it there was a vaulted crypt, its walls painted with murals. Within, a stone sarcophagus was covered by a large rectangular stone slab that weighs about five tons and is 12½ feet long. When this stone lid was moved, there came into view the skeletal remains of a tall man, still bedecked with pearls and jade jewelry. His face was covered with a mosaic jade mask; a small jade pendant bearing the image of a deity lay among the beads that once were a jade collar.

The discovery was astounding, for until then no other pyramid or temple in Mexico had been found to have served as a tomb. The enigma of the tomb and its occupant was deepened by the depiction carved upon the stone lid: it was the image of a barefoot Maya sitting upon a plumed or flaming throne and seemingly operating mechanical devices inside an elaborate chamber (Fig. 28). The Ancient Astronaut Society and its sponsor, Erich von Däniken, have seen in this a depiction of an astronaut inside a spacecraft driven by flaming jets. They suggest that an Extraterrestrial is buried here.

Archaeologists and other scholars ridicule the idea. Inscriptions on the walls of this funerary edifice and in adjoining structures convince them that the person buried here is the ruler

Pacal ("Shield") who reigned in Palenque in A.D. 615–683. Some see in the scene a depiction of the deceased Pacal being taken by the Dragon of the Underworld to the realm of the dead; they consider the fact that at the winter solstice the Sun sets exactly behind the Temple of Inscriptions as added symbolism of the king's departure with the setting Sun God. Others, prompted to revised interpretations by the fact that the depiction is framed by a Sky Band, a chain of glyphs that represent celestial bodies and the zodiac constellations, regard the scene as showing the king being carried by the Celestial Serpent to the celestial realm of the gods. The crosslike object that the deceased is facing is now recognized as a stylized Tree of Life, suggesting that the king is being transported to an eternal afterlife.

In fact a similar tomb, known as Burial 116, was discovered in the Great Plaza of Tikal, at the foot of one of its major pyramids. Buried some twenty feet below the ground was found the skeleton of an unusually tall man. His body was placed on a platform of stone masonry, he was bedecked with jade jewelry, and was surrounded (as at Palenque) by pearls, jade objects, and pottery. Also, depictions of persons carried in the jaws of fiery serpents (whom scholars call Sky Gods) are known from various Maya sites, such as this one (Fig. 29) from Chichén Itzá.

All considered, scholars have admitted that "one cannot avoid an implicit comparison to the crypts of the Egyptian pharaohs. The similarities between the tomb of Pacal and those who ruled earlier beside the Nile are striking" (H. La Fay, "The Maya, Children of Time" in the *National Geographic Magazine*). Indeed, the scene on Pacal's sarcophagus conveys the very same image as that of a pharaoh transported, by the Winged Serpent, to an eternal afterlife among the gods who came from the heavens. The pharaoh, who was not an astro-

Figure 29

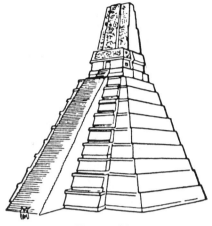

Figure 30

naut, had become one upon his death; and that, we suggest, is what the carved scene has implied for Pacal.

Not only tombs have been discovered in the jungles of Mesoamerica, Central America, and the equatorial zones of South America. Repeatedly, a hill overgrown with tropical vegetation turned out to be a pyramid; groups of pyramids were peaks of a lost city. Until excavations began at El Mirador, a jungle site astride the Guatemalan–Mexican border, in 1978, revealing a major Maya city dating back to 400 B.C. and occupying six square miles, those of the southern-beginnings school (viz. S. G. Morley, *The Ancient Maya)* believed that Tikal was not only the largest Maya city but also the earliest. Situated in the northeastern part of Guatamela's province of Petén, Tikal still raises its tall pyramids high above the jungle's sea of green. It is so large that its boundaries seem to be constantly expanding as more remains are found. Its main ceremonial center alone covers more than a square mile; the space for it was not only hacked out of the rain forest; it was physically created atop a mountain ridge that was laboriously flattened out. The flanking ravines were converted into water reservoirs linked by a series of causeways.

Tikal's pyramids, tightly grouped together in several sections, are a marvel of construction. Tall and narrow, they are true skyscrapers, rising steeply to heights nearing and even exceeding 200 feet. Rising in sheer stages, the pyramids served as raised platforms for the temples that stood atop them. The rectangular temples, containing but a couple of narrow rooms, were in turn topped by massive ornamental superstructures that further increased the height of the pyramids (Fig. 30). The ar-

Figure 31

chitectural result was to make the sanctuary appear suspended
between the Earth and the Sky, reachable by steep steps that
were truly symbolic Stairways to Heaven. Within each temple a
series of doorways led from the outside in, each doorway a step
higher than the one before it. The lintels were made of rare
woods and exquisitely carved. There were as a rule five exterior
and seven interior doorways, a total of twelve—a symbolism
whose meaning has not attracted, so far, particular attention.

The construction of an airstrip near Tikal's ruins speeded up
its exploration after 1950 and extensive archaeological work has
been conducted there especially by teams from The University
Museum, University of Pennsylvania. They discovered that the
great plazas of Tikal served as a necropolis, where rulers and
noblemen were buried; also, that many of the lesser structures
were in fact funerary temples, built not over the tombs but next
to them and serving as cenotaphs. They also uncovered about
one hundred and fifty stelas, carved stone slabs erected mostly
so as to face either east or west. They depict, it was ascertained,
portraits of actual rulers and commemorate major events in
their lives and reigns. The hieroglyphic inscriptions carved upon
them (Fig. 31) recorded accurate dates associated with these
events, named the ruler by his hieroglyph (here "Jaguar Paw
Skull," A.D. 488) and identified the event; the textual hiero-

glyphs, scholars are by now certain, were not merely pictorial or ideographic "but also written phonetically in syllables similar to those of Sumerian, Babylonian, and Egyptian" (A. G. Miller, *Maya Rulers of Time*).

It was with the aid of such stelas that the archaeologists were able to identify a sequence of fourteen rulers at Tikal who had reigned from A.D. 317 to A.D. 869. But it is certain that Tikal was a royal Maya center long before: carbon-dating of remains in some of the royal tombs result in dates going back to 600 B.C..

Lying about a hundred and fifty miles to the southeast of Tikal is Copán, the city that Stephens had purchased. It was located at the southeastern periphery of the Maya realm, in today's Honduras. Though lacking Tikal's steep skyscrapers, it was perhaps more typical of Maya cities in its scope and layout. Its vast ceremonial center occupied seventy-five acres and consisted of pyramid-temples grouped about several great plazas (Fig. 32). The pyramids, wide-based and just seventy feet or so high, were distinguished by wide monumental stairways decorated with elaborate sculptures and hieroglyphic inscriptions. The plazas were dotted with shrines, altars, and—most important to the historians—carved stone stelas that portrayed rulers and gave their dates. They reveal that the main pyramid was completed in A.D. 756 and that Copán reached its glorious peak in the ninth century A.D.—just before the sudden collapse of Mayan civilization.

But, as ongoing discoveries and excavations have shown, site after new site in Guatemala, Honduras, and Belize indicates the existence of monuments and dated stelas as early as 600 B.C., revealing a developed system of writing that, all scholars agree, must have had a prior developmental phase or source.

Copán, as we shall soon see, played a special role in Maya life and culture.

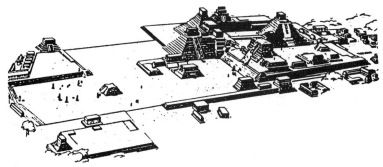

Figure 32

Students of the Maya civilization have been especially impressed by the accuracy, ingenuity and diversity of Maya time reckoning, attributing them to an advanced Maya astronomy.

The Maya had, indeed, not one but three calendars; but one —the most significant one in our opinion—had nothing to do with astronomy. It is the so-called Long Count. It stated a date by counting the number of days that had passed from a certain starting day to the day of the event recorded by the Maya on the stela or monument. That enigmatic Day One, most scholars now agree, was August 13, 3113 B.C. according to the current Christian calendar—a time and an event that clearly preceded the emergence of the Maya civilization.

The Long Count, like the two other time-reckoning systems, was based on the vigesimal ("times twenty") mathematical system of the Maya, and—as in ancient Sumer—employed the "place" concept, whereby 1 in the first column would be one, in the next column twenty, then four hundred, and so on. The Maya Long Count dating system, using vertical columns where values were lowest at the bottom, named these various multiples and identified them with glyphs (Fig. 33). Starting with *kin* for ones, *uinal* for twenties and so on, the multiples reached the glyph *alau-tun,* which stood for the fantastic number of 23,040,000,000 days—a period of 63,080,082 years!

But, as stated, in their actual calendrical dating on their monuments, the Maya went back not to the age of the dinosaurs but to a specific day, an event as crucial to them as the date of Christ's birth is to the followers of the Christian calendar. Thus, Stela 29 at Tikal (Fig. 34), which bears the earliest date so far

KIN　　　UINAL　　　TUN

KATUN　　　BAKTUN　　　PICTUN

CALABTUN　　　KINCHILTUN　　　ALAUTUN

Figure 33

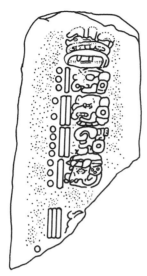

Figure 34

found on a royal monument there (A.D. 292), gives the Long Count date 8.12.14.8.15 by using dots for the numeral one and bars for five:

8 bak-tun	(8 × 400 × 360)	=	1,152,000 days
12 ka-tun	(12 × 20 × 360)	=	86,400 days
14 tun	(14 × 360)	=	5,040 days
8 uinal	(8 × 20)	=	160 days
15 kin	(15 × 1)	=	15 days
		Total =	1,243,615 days

Dividing the 1,243,615 days by the number of days in a solar year, 365¼, the date on the stela states that it, or the event depicted on it, occurred 3,404 years and 304 days after the mysterious Day One; i.e., since August 13, 3113 B.C. Therefore, according to the now accepted correlation, the date on the stela is A.D. 292 (3,405 − 3,113 = 292). Some scholars see evidence that the Maya began to use the Long Count in the era of Baktun 7, which equaled the fourth century B.C.; others do not dismiss an even earlier use.

Alongside this continuous calendar there were two cyclical calendars. One was the *Haab* or Solar Year of 365 days that was divided into 18 months of 20 days, plus an additional 5 days at year's end. The other was the *Tzolkin* or Sacred Year calendar in which the basic 20 days were rotated 13 times, resulting in a

Sacred Year of 260 days. The two cyclical calendars were then meshed together, as though they were gear wheels driven by each other to create the grand Sacred Round of 52 solar years; for the combination of 13, 20, and 365 could not repeat itself except once in 18,980 days, which equals 52 years. This Calendar Round of 52 years was sacred to all the peoples of ancient Mesoamerica and they related to it events both past and future —such as the messianic expectation of the return of Quetzal-coatl.

The earliest Sacred Round date was found in Mexico's Oaxaca valley and goes back to 500 B.C. Both time reckoning systems, the continuing one and the Sacred Round one, are quite old. One is historical, counting the passage of time (days) from an event in the long-ago whose significance and nature are still a puzzle. The other is cyclical, geared to a peculiar period of 260 days; scholars are still trying to guess what, if anything, happened or still happens once every 260 days.

Some believe that this cycle is purely mathematical: since five cycles of 52 years is 260 years, somehow a shorter count of 260 days was adopted. But such an explanation of 260 only shifts the problem to a need to explain 52: where, then, is the origin and reason for 52?

Others suggest that the period of 260 days had to do with agriculture, such as the length of the rainy season or the dry intervals. In view of the Mayan propensity for astronomy, others attempt to somehow calculate a relationship between 260 days and the motions of Venus or Mars. One must wonder why a solution offered by Zelia Nuttal at the twenty-second International Congress of Americanists (Rome, 1926) did not gain the full recognition it deserves. She pointed out that the easiest way for the people of the New World to apply seasonal movements of the Sun to their own locality was to determine Zenith Days, when the Sun passed precisely overhead at midday. This happens twice a year as the Sun appears to travel northward, then southward, passing overhead twice. The Indians, she suggested, measured the interval between the two Zenith Days and the resulting number of days became the basis for the Calendar Round.

This interval is half a solar year at the equator; it lengthens as one moves away, northward or southward. At 15 degrees north, for example, it is 263 days (from August 12 to the following May 1). This is the rainy season and to this day the descendants of the Maya begin planting on May 3 (conveniently also the Mexican Day of the Holy Cross). The interval was precisely 260 days at latitude 14° 42' north—*the latitude of Copán.*

That Nuttal has come up with the correct explanation for the manner in which the 260-day ritual year was fixed is borne out by the fact that Copán was considered the astronomical capital of the Maya. Besides the usual celestial orientation of edifices, some of its stelas have been found to be aligned for determining key calendar dates. In another instance a stela ("Stela A") that bears a Long Count date equivalent to a day in A.D. 733 also bears two other Long Count dates, one greater by 200 days and one smaller by 60 days (splitting up a cycle of 260 days). A. Aveni *(Skywatchers of Ancient Mexico)* assumes that this was an attempt to realign the Long Count (which counted an actual 365¼ days per year) with the cyclical *Haab* of 365 days. The need to readjust or reform the calendars may have been the reason for a conclave of astronomers that was held in Copán in A.D. 763. It was commemorated by a square monument known as Altar Q on which the sixteen astronomers that took part in the conclave were portrayed, four to a side (Fig. 35). It will be noted that the "teardrop" glyph in front of their noses—as was done on the Pacal depiction—identifies them as Skywatchers. The date carved on this monument appears on monuments at other Maya sites, suggesting that the decisions reached at Copán were applied throughout the realm.

Figure 35

The reputation of the Maya as accomplished astronomers has been enhanced by the fact that their various codices contain astronomical sections dealing with solar and lunar eclipses and the planet Venus. Closer study of the data revealed, however, that these were not records of observations by the Maya astronomers. Rather, they were almanacs copied from some earlier sources that provided the Maya with ready-made data against which they were to look for phenomena applicable to the 260-day cycle. As stated by E. Hadingham *(Early Man and the*

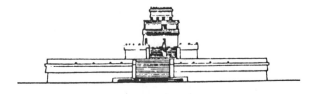

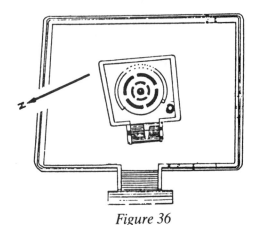

Figure 36

Cosmos), these almanacs displayed "a curious blend of long-term exactness and short-term inaccuracy."

The main task of the local astronomers, it appears, was to keep verifying or adjusting the 260-day sacred year against data from earlier times that dealt with the movements of celestial bodies. Indeed, the most renowned and still standing observatory in Yucatán, the *Caracol* in Chichén Itzá (Fig. 36), has frustrated successive researchers who had tried, in vain, to find in its orientation and aperture viewlines to the solstices or equinoxes. Some viewlines, however, do seem to be related to the Tzolkin (260-day) cycle.

But why the number 260? Just because it happened to equal the number of days between Zeniths at Copán? Why not, say, the easier number 300 if a site near latitude 20° north would have been chosen, such as Teotihuacan?

The number 260 appears to have been an arbitrary, deliberate choice; the explanation that it results from multiplying a natural number, 20 (the number of fingers and toes), by 13 only shifts the problem to the question, Why and Wherefrom 13? The Long Count too contains an arbitrary number, 360: inexplicably it abandons the pure vigesimal progression and, after the kin (1) and uinal (20), introduces the tun (360) into the system. The Haab calendar also considers 360 as its basic length, dividing this number into 18 "months" of 20 days; it rounds off the year by the addition of 5 "bad days" to complete the solar cycle of 365.

All three calendars thus are based on numbers that are not natural, numbers deliberately selected. We will show that both 260 and 360 reached Mesoamerica from Mesopotamia—via Egypt.

We are all familiar with the number 360: it is the number of degrees in a circle. But few know that we owe the number to the Sumerians, and that it stems from their sexagesimal ("Base 60") mathematical system. The first known calendar was the Nippur Calendar of the Sumerians; it was devised by dividing the circle of 360 into 12 parts, twelve being the sacred celestial number from which followed the twelve months of the year, the twelve houses of the zodiac, the twelve Olympian gods, and so on. The problem of the shortfall of 5¼ days was solved by intercalation —the addition of a thirteenth month after the passage of a number of years.

Although the Egyptian arithmetical system was not sexagesimal, they adopted the Sumerian system of $12 \times 30 = 360$. But unable to pursue the very complex calculations involved in intercalation, they simplified matters by rounding off each year by having a short "month" of five days at year's end. It was this very system that was adopted in Mesoamerica. The Haab calendar was not just similar to the Egyptian one, it was identical to it. Moreover, just as the Mesoamericans had a ritual year alongside the solar one, so did the Egyptians have a ritual year relating to the rising of the star Sirius and the rising at the same time of the waters of the Nile.

The Sumerian imprint on the Egyptian and hence Mesoamerican calendars was not limited to the sexagesimal number 360. Various studies, principally by B. P. Reko, in the early issues of *El Mexico Antiguo,* leave little doubt that the thirteen months of the Tzolkin calendar were in fact a reflection of the 12-month system of the Sumerians plus the thirteenth intercalary month, except that in Egypt (and hence in Mesoamerica) the thirteenth month had shrunk to an annual 5 days. The term *tun* for 360 meant in the Maya language "celestial," a star or planet within the zodiacal band. Interestingly, a "heap of stars" —a constellation—was called *Mool,* virtually the same term MUL that the Sumerians had used to mean "celestial body."

The association of the Mesoamerican calendar with the Old World will become additionally evident as we look at the most sacred number, 52, to which all the great Mesoamerican events were geared. The many attempts to explain it (like the statement that it is 13 times 4) ignore its most obvious source: the 52 weeks of the Near Eastern calendar (and thereafter the European one). This number of weeks, however, is arrived at only if a week of 7 days is adopted. This was not always the case. The origin of the 7-day week has been a subject of study for almost two centuries and the best theory is that it derived from the four phases of the Moon. What is certain is that it emerged as a divinely decreed time period in biblical times, when God commanded the Israelites during the Exodus from Egypt to observe the seventh day as the Sabbath.

Was then 52 the most sacred cycle because it happened to be the common denominator of the Mesoamerican calendars—or was the sacred cycle of 260 adopted because it (rather than, say, 300) was a multiple of 52 ($52 \times 5 = 260$)?

Although a deity whose epithet was "Seven" was a principal Sumerian god, he was honored with theophonic place (e.g., *Beer-Sheba,* The Well of Seven) or personal names *(Elisheva,* My God is Seven) principally in the land of Canaan. The number 7 as a revered number appears in the tales of the Hebrew patriarchs only after Abraham went to Egypt and stayed at the pharaoh's court. The number 7 permeates the biblical tale of Joseph, the pharaoh's dream and the ensuing events in Egypt. And, to the extent that 52 stemmed from the consideration of 7 as a basic calendrical unit, we will show that this most sacred cycle of Mesoamerica was of Egyptian origin.

More specifically: 52 was a magical number that was associated with the Egyptian god Thoth, the god of science, writing, mathematics, and the calendar.

An ancient Egyptian tale known as "The Adventures of Satni-Khamois with the Mummies"—a tale of magic, mystery, and adventure that can match any modern thriller—employs the association of the magical number 52 with Thoth and with the secrets of the calendar for the key scene in the plot. It was written on a papyrus (Cairo 30646) that was discovered in a tomb in Thebes dating to the third century B.C. Fragments of other papyri with the same tale have also been found, indicating that it was an established book in ancient Egyptian literature, belonging to the cycle of tales of gods and men.

The tale's hero, son of a pharaoh, "was well instructed in all things." He was wont to wander in the necropolis of Memphis (then the capital), studying the sacred writings upon temple walls and stelas and researching ancient books of magic. In time he became "a magician who had no equal in the land of Egypt." One day a mysterious old man told him of a tomb "where there is deposited the book that the god Thoth had written with his own hand," in which are revealed the mysteries of the Earth and the secrets of the Heavens, including the divine knowledge concerning "the risings of the Sun and the appearances of the Moon and the motions of the gods [planets] that are in the cycle of the Sun"—the secrets of astronomy and the calendar.

The tomb was that of Nenoferkheptah, son of a former pharaoh (who, scholars believe, had reigned circa 1250 B.C.). When Satni, as expected, became very interested and asked for the location of the tomb, the old man warned him that although mummified, Nenoferkheptah was not dead and could strike down anyone who dared take away the book that was lodged at his feet. Undaunted, Satni went in search of the tomb. It could not be found for it was below the ground. But having reached the right spot Satni "recited a formula over it and a gap opened in the ground and Satni went down to the place where the book was."

Inside the tomb Satni saw the mummies of Nenoferkheptah, of his sister-wife, and of their son. The book that was indeed at Nenoferkheptah's feet "gave off a light as if the sun shone there." As Satni stepped toward it, the wife's mummy spoke up, warning him to advance no farther. She told Satni of the adventures of Nenoferkheptah when he had attempted to obtain the book, for Thoth had hidden it in a secret place, inside a golden box that was inside a silver box that was inside a series of other boxes, the last and outer ones being of bronze and iron. Ignoring all warnings and overcoming all obstacles, Nenoferkheptah found and obtained the book; whereupon they were condemned by Thoth to suspended animation: though alive, they were buried, and though mummified they could see, hear, and speak. She warned Satni that Thoth's curse would be upon him if he touched the book.

But having gone so far Satni was determined to get the book. As he took another step toward it, the mummy of Nenoferkheptah spoke up. There was a way to possess the book without incurring Thoth's wrath, he said: it was to play and win the Game of Fifty-Two, the magical number of Thoth.

Satni readily agreed. He lost the first game and found himself partly sunk into the ground. He lost the next game, and the next, sinking down more and more. How he managed to escape with the book, the calamities that befell him as a result, and how he in the end returned it to its hiding place, make up the rest of this ancient version of "Raiders of the Lost Ark."

The tale's moral was that no man, as knowledgeable as he might be, could learn the mysteries of the Earth, the Sun, the Moon, and the planets without divine permission; unauthorized by Thoth, Man will lose the game of Fifty-Two. And he would lose it even if he tried to find out the secrets by opening up the protective layers of Earth's minerals and metals.

It is our belief that it was the same Thoth, alias Quetzalcoatl, who had bestowed the Calendar of Fifty-Two, and all other knowledge, upon the peoples of Mesoamerica. In Yucatán the Maya called him Kukulcan; in the Pacific regions of Guatemala and El Salvador he was called Xiuhtecuhtli; the names all meant the same: Feathered or Winged Serpent.

The architecture, inscriptions, iconography, and monuments of the lost cities of the Maya have enabled scholars to trace and reconstruct not only their and their rulers' histories, but also their changing religious concepts. At first temples were lofted atop step pyramids to worship the Serpent God, and the skies were observed to watch for the key celestial cycles. But there came a time when the god—or all the celestial gods—had left. Seen no more, they were presumed to have been swallowed by the ruler of the night, the jaguar; and the image of the great god was henceforth covered by the jaguar's mask (Fig. 37) through which the serpents, his erstwhile symbol, still emerge.

Figure 37

But had not Quetzalcoatl promised to return?

Fervently the skywatchers of the jungles consulted ancient almanacs. Priests advanced the notion that the vanished deities would return if offered the throbbing hearts of human victims.

But at some crucial calendrical date in the ninth century A.D., a prophesied event failed to occur. All the cycles came together, and added up to naught. And so were the ceremonial centers and the cities dedicated to the gods abandoned, and the jungle cast its green mantle over the domain of the Serpent Gods.

5

STRANGERS FROM ACROSS THE SEAS

When the Toltecs under their leader Topiltzin-Quetzalcoatl left Tollan in A.D. 987, disgusted by the religious abominations and seeking a place where they could worship as in the olden days, they went to Yucatán. Surely they could have found a new home closer by, a less arduous journey, a passage through less hostile tribes. Yet they chose to trek almost a thousand miles, to a land different in all respects—flat, riverless, tropical—from their own. They did not stop until they had reached Chichén Itzá. Why? What was the imperative in reaching the sacred city that the Maya had already abandoned? We can only search the ruins for an answer.

Easily reached from Mérida, Yucatán's administrative capital, Chichén Itzá has been compared to Pompeii in Italy, where after removal of the volcanic ash under which it had been buried, a Roman city with its streets and houses and murals, graffiti and all, has been brought to light. Here it was the jungle canopy that had to be removed, rewarding the visitor with a double treat: a visit to an "Old Empire" Maya city, and to a mirror-image of Tollan as its emigrants had last seen it; for when the Toltecs arrived, they rebuilt and built over Chichén Itźa in the image of their erstwhile capital.

Archaeologists believe that the site was an important settlement even in the first millennium B.C. The Chronicles of *Chilam Balam* attest that by A.D. 450 it was the principal sacred city of Yucatán. It was then called *Chichén*, "The Well's Mouth," for its most sacred features was a *cenote* or sacred well to which pilgrims came from near and far. Most of the visible remains from that era of Maya dominion are located in the southern or "Old Chichén" part of the site. It is there that the edifices described and drawn by Stephens and Catherwood are mostly located, bearing such romantic names as *Akab-Dzib* ("Place of

Figure 38

Occult Writing"), the Nunnery, Temple of the Thresholds, and so on.

Last to occupy (or rather, reoccupy) Chichén Itzá before the arrival of the Toltecs were the Itzas, a tribe that some believe were kinsmen of the Toltecs and others see as migrants from the south. It is they who gave the place its current name, meaning "The Well Mouth of the Itzas." They built their own ceremonial center north of the Maya ruins; the site's most renowned edifices, the great central pyramid ("El Castillo") and the observatory (the Caracol) were built by them—only to be taken over and built over by the Toltecs when they re-created Tollan at Chichén Itzá.

A chance discovery of an entranceway enables today's visitor to enter the space between the Itzá pyramid and the Toltec pyramid that envelops it, and to climb up the earlier stairway to the Itzá sanctum, where the Toltecs had installed an image of Chacmool and of a jaguar. From the outside one can only see the Toltec structure—a pyramid that rises in nine stages (Fig. 38) to a height of some 185 feet. Dedicated to the God of the Plumed Serpent, Quetzalcoatl-Kukulcan, it honors him not only with plumed-serpent decorations but also by incorporating in the structure various calendrical aspects, such as the construction on

Figure 39

each of the four faces of the pyramid of a stairway with 91 steps, which with the topmost "step" or platform add up to the days of the solar year (91 × 4 + 1 = 365). A structure called the Temple of Warriors literally duplicates the pyramid of the *Atlantes* in Tula by its location, orientation, stairway, flanking plumed serpents of stone, decorations, and sculptures.

As at Tula (Tollan), facing this pyramid-temple across the great plaza is the main ball court. It is an immense rectangular arena, 545 feet long—the largest in Mesoamerica. High walls rise along the two long sides; at the center of each, thirty-five feet above the ground, there protrudes a stone ring decorated with carvings of entwined serpents. To win the game the ball players had to throw a ball of solid rubber through the rings. There were seven players in each team; the team that lost paid a heavy price: its leader was decapitated. Stone panels decorated in bas-relief were installed along the long walls, depicting scenes from the game. The central panel on the eastern wall (Fig. 39)

still shows the leader of the winning tèam (on the left) holding
the decapitated head of the leader of the losing team.

The severe end suggests that there was more than play and
entertainment to this ball game. At Chichén Itzá, as at Tula,
there were several ball courts, perhaps for training or lesser
matches. The main ball court was unique in its size and splen-
dor, and the importance of what took place in it was under-
scored by the fact that it was provided with three temples that
were richly decorated with scenes of warriors, mythological encounters, the Tree of Life, and a winged and bearded deity with
two horns (Fig. 40).

Figure 40

All this, and the diversity and regalia of the ball players,
suggest to us an intertribal, if not international, aspect of an
event of great political–religious significance. The number of
players (seven), the decapitation of the losers' leader, and the
use of a rubber ball seem to mimic a mythological tale in the
Popol Vuh of a combat between the gods conducted as a contest
with a rubber ball. It pitched the gods Seven-Macaw and his two
sons against various Sky Gods, including the Sun, Moon, and
Venus. The defeated son Seven-Huanaphu was executed: "His
head was cut off from his body and rolled away, his heart was
cut out from his chest." But being a god, he was resurrected and
became a planet.

Such a reenactment of godly events would have made the
Toltec custom akin to religious plays in the ancient Near East.
In Egypt, the dismemberment and resurrection of Osiris was
reenacted annually in a mystery play in which actors, including
the pharaoh, played the roles of various gods; and in Assyria, a
complex play, also performed annually, reenacted a battle between two gods in which the loser was executed, only to be
pardoned and resurrected by the God of Heaven. In Babylon,
Enuma elish, the epic describing the creation of the solar system, was read annually as part of the New Year celebrations; it
depicted the celestial collision that led to the creation of Earth
(the Seventh Planet) as the cleaving and decapitating of the
monstrous Tiamat by the supreme Babylonian god Marduk.

Figure 41

The Maya myth and its reenactment, in echoing Near Eastern "myths" and their reenactments, appear to have retained the celestial elements of the tale and the symbolism of the number seven as it relates to the planet Earth. It is significant that in the Mayan–Toltec depictions along the walls of the ball court, some players carry as their emblem the Sun Disk, while others carry that of a seven-pointed star (Fig. 41). That this was a celestial symbol and not just a chance emblem is confirmed, in our opinion, by the fact that elsewhere in Chichén Itzá a four-pointed star was repeatedly depicted in combination with the "eight" symbol for the planet Venus (Fig. 42a) and that at other sites in northwestern Yucatán temple walls were decorated with symbols of six-pointed stars (Fig. 42b).

The depiction of planets as pointed stars is so common that we tend to forget how this custom had arisen: As so much else, it began in Sumer. Based on what they had learned from the Nefilim, the Sumerians counted the planets not as we do, from the Sun outward, but from the outside in. Thus, Pluto was the first planet, Neptune the second, Uranus the third, Saturn the fourth, Jupiter the fifth. Mars accordingly was the sixth, Earth the seventh, and Venus the eighth. The usual explanation by scholars why the Maya/Toltecs considered Venus the eighth is that it takes eight Earth years ($8 \times 365 = 2,920$ days) to repeat a synodic alignment with Venus after five orbits of Venus ($5 \times 584 = 2,920$ days). But if so, Venus should have been "Five" and Earth "Eight."

We find the Sumerian method much more elegant and accurate, and suggest that the Maya/Toltec depictions followed the Near Eastern iconography; for, as one can see, the symbols found at Chichén Itzá and elsewhere in Yucatán are almost identical to those by which the various planets had been depicted in Mesopotamia (Fig. 42c).

Indeed, the employment of pointed-star symbols in the Near Eastern manner becomes more prevalent the more one moves toward the northwestern corner of Yucatán and its coast. A most remarkable sculpture has been found there, at a site called Tzekelna; it is now on exhibit at the Mérida museum. Carved out of a large stone block to which the statue's back is still attached, it depicts a man of strong facial features, possibly wearing a helmet. His body is covered by a tight-fitting suit made of scales or ribs. Under his bent arm he holds an object the museum identifies as "the geometric form of a five-pointed star" (Fig. 43). An enigmatic circular device is held by belts to his belly; scholars believe that it somehow identified its bearers as Water Gods.

Large sculptures of deities forming part of massive stone blocks were discovered at a nearby site called Oxkintok; they are presumed by archaeologists to have served as structural supporting columns in temples. One of them (Fig. 44) looks like a female counterpart of the above-described male one. Her ribbed and scalelike garb appears on several statues and statuettes from Jaina, an island that lies offshore from this northwestern part of Yucatán on which there had stood a most

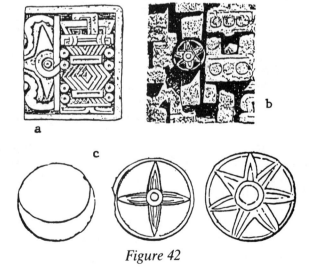

Figure 42

Figure 43   *Figure 44*

unusual temple. The island had served as a hallowed necropolis because according to legends it was the final resting place of Itzamna, the god of the Itzas—a great olden god who had waded there ashore from the sea, and whose name meant "He Whose Home Is Water."

Texts, legends, and religious beliefs have thus combined to point to the gulf shore of Yucatán as the place where a divine or deified being had come ashore, to begin settlement and civilization in these lands. This powerful combination, these collective recollections, must have been the reason for the Toltec trek to this corner of Yucatán, and specifically to Chichén Itzá, when they migrated in search of the revival and purity of their original beliefs; a return to the spot where it all began, and where the Returning God would land again, coming from across the sea.

The focal point of the worship of Itzamna and Quetzalcoatl, and perhaps also of the memories of Votan, was the Sacred Cenote of Chichén Itzá—a huge well that gave Chichén Itzá its name.

Situated directly north of the main pyramid and connected to the ceremonial plaza by a long paved processional avenue, the well is nowadays about seventy feet deep from the surface to the water level, with another one hundred feet or so of water and silt farther down. The well mouth, oval in shape, measures about 250 feet in length and about 170 feet in width. There is evidence that the well had been artificially enlarged and that a stairway had once led down. There can still be seen the remains of a platform and a shrine at the well mouth; there, Bishop Landa wrote, rites were held for the god of water and rains, maidens were thrown down in sacrifice, and worshipers who had gathered from all over threw in precious offerings, preferably made of gold.

In 1885 Edward H. Thompson, who had made a reputation for himself as the author of a treatise titled *Atlantis Not a Myth,* obtained an assignment as an American consul in **Mexico**. Before long he purchased for seventy-five dollars one **hundred** square miles of jungle, which included the ruins of **Chichén Itzá**. Making the ruins his home, he organized for the Peabody **Museum** of Harvard University systematic dives into the well to retrieve its sacred offerings.

Only some forty human skeletons were found; but the divers brought up a rich array of artful objects by the thousands. More than 3,400 were made of jade, a semiprecious stone that was the highest prized by the Maya and the Aztecs. The objects included beads, nose bars, ear plugs, buttons, rings, pendants, globes, disks, effigies, figurines. More than 500 objects bore carvings depicting animals and people. Among the latter, some were clearly bearded (Fig. 45a, b), resembling depictions on the temple walls of the ball court (Fig. 45c).

Even more significant were the metal objects that the divers brought up. Hundreds were made of gold, some of silver or copper—significant finds in a peninsula devoid of metals. Some

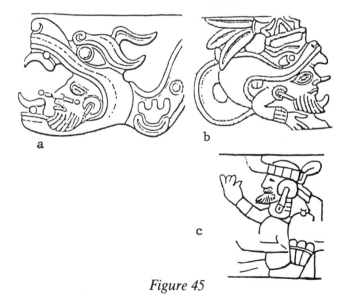

Figure 45

Figure 46

of the objects were made of gilded copper or copper alloys, including bronze, revealing a metallurgical sophistication unknown in the Maya lands and attesting that the objects had been brought from distant lands. Most puzzling of all was the discovery of disks of pure tin, a metal that is not found in its native state and that can be obtained only by a complex refining of ores—ores that are altogether absent in Mesoamerica.

The metal objects, exquisitely crafted, included numerous bells as well as ritual objects (cups, basins), rings, tiaras, masks; ornaments and jewelry; scepters; objects of unknown purpose; and, most important, disks engraved or embossed with encounter scenes. In these, persons in different garbs and of diverse features confront each other, perhaps in combat, in the presence of terrestrial or celestial serpents or Sky Gods. The dominant or victorious hero is always depicted bearded (Fig. 46a, b).

These were clearly not gods, for the serpent or Sky gods were shown separately. The likes of them, distinct from the bearded and winged Sky God (Fig. 40), appear in reliefs carved on walls and columns in Chicheń Itzá together with other heroes and warriors, like this one with his long and narrow beard (Fig. 47) who has been nicknamed by some "Uncle Sam."

Figure 47

The identity of these bearded people is a puzzle; what is certain is that they were not native Indians, who grow no facial hair and have no beards. Who, then, were these foreigners? Their "Semitic" or rather Eastern Mediterranean features (even more prominent in clay objects bearing facial images) have led various researchers to identify them as Phoenicians or "seafaring Jews," perhaps blown off course and carried by the Atlantic's currents to the shores of Yucatán when King Solomon and the Phoenician King Hiram joined forces to send maritime expeditions around Africa in search of gold (circa 1000 B.C.); or a few centuries later, when the Phoenicians were driven away from their port cities in the eastern Mediterranean, established Carthage, and sailed to western Africa.

No matter who the seafarers might have been and the proposed crossing time, established academic researchers dismiss out of hand any notion of deliberate crossings. They either explain the obvious beards as false beards, artificially attached by the Indians to their chins, or as belonging to the chance survivors of shipwrecks. Clearly, the first argument (seriously made

Figure 48

by renowned scholars) only begs the question: if the Indians emulated some other bearded people, who were those other people?

Nor does the explanation of a few shipwrecked survivors seem valid. The native traditions, as in the legend of Votan, speak of repeated voyages, of exploration followed by settlement (the establishment of cities). The archaeological evidence belies the notion of a few chance survivors cast on a single shore. The Bearded Ones, in poses of a variety of activities and circumstances, have been depicted at sites all along the Mexican gulf coast, at inland locations, and as far south as the Pacific coast. Not stylized, not mythified, but as portraits of actual individuals.

Some of the most striking examples of such depictions have been found in Veracruz (Fig. 48a, b). The people they immortalize are clearly identical to West Semitic dignitaries taken prisoner by Egyptian pharaohs during their Asiatic campaigns, as depicted by the victors in their commemorative inscriptions upon temple walls (Fig. 49).

Why, and when, did such Mediterranean seafarers come to Mesoamerica? The archaeological clues are baffling, for they lead to an even greater enigma: the Olmecs, and their apparent black African origins; for, as many depictions—as this one, from Alvarado, Veracruz (Fig. 50)—show, the Bearded Ones

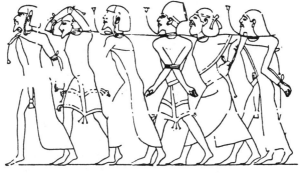

Figure 49

and the Olmecs had met, face to face, in the same domains and at the same time.

Of all the lost civilizations of Mesoamarica, that of the Olmecs is the oldest and the most mystifying. It was by all counts the Mother Civilization, copied and adapted by all the others. It dawned along the Mexican gulf coast at the beginning of the second millennium B.C. It was in full bloom, at some forty sites, by 1200 B.C. (or, some hold, by 1500 B.C.). Spreading in all directions, but mainly southward, it made its mark across Mesoamerica by 800 B.C.

The first Mesoamerican glyphic writing appears in the Olmec realm; so does the Mesoamerican system of numeration, of dots and bars. The first Long Count calendar inscriptions, with the enigmatic starting date in 3113 B.C.; the first works of magnificent and monumental sculpted art; the first use of jade; the first depictions of hand-held weapons or tools; the first ceremonial centers; the first celestial orientations—all were achievements of the Olmecs. No wonder that with so many "firsts," some (as J. Soustelle, *The Olmecs*) have compared the Olmec civilization of Mesoamerica to that of the Sumerians in Mesopotamia, which accounted for all the "firsts" in the ancient Near East. And, like the Sumerian civilization, the Olmecs too appeared suddenly, without a precedent or a prior period of gradual advancement. In their texts, the Sumerians described their civilization as a gift from the gods, the visitors to Earth who could roam the skies and were therefore often depicted as winged beings (Fig. 51a). The Olmecs expressed their "myths" in sculptured art, as on this stela from Izapa (Fig. 51b) of one winged god beheading another. The tale-in-stone is remarkably similar to a Sumerian depiction (Fig. 51c).

Figure 50

Who were the people who had achieved these feats? Nick-named *Olmeca* ("Rubber People") because their gulf-coast area was known for its rubber trees, they were in reality an enigma —strangers in a strange land, strangers from across the seas, people who belonged not just to another land but to another continent. In an area of marshy coasts where stone is rare, they created and left behind stone monuments that amaze to this very day; of these, the most baffling are the ones that portray the Olmecs themselves.

Unique in all respects are giant stone heads sculpted with incredible skill and unknown tools to portray Olmec leaders. The first to see such a gigantic head was J. M. Melgar y Serrano at Tres Zapotes in the state of Veracruz. He described it in the *Bulletin of the Mexican Geographical and Statistical Society* (in 1869) as "a work of art . . . a magnificent sculpture that most amazingly represents an Ethiopian." Accompanying drawings faithfully reproduced the head's negroid features (Fig. 52).

Figure 51

It was not until 1925 that the existence of such colossal stone heads was confirmed by Western scholars, when an archaeological team from Tulane University headed by Frans Blom found "the upper part of a colossal head which has sunk deep into the ground" at La Venta, a site near the gulf coast in the state of Tabasco. When the head was fully unearthed (Fig. 53) it measured about eight feet in height, twenty-one in circumference, and weighed about twenty-four tons. It depicts without question a negroid African wearing a distinct helmet. In time, additional such heads, each portraying a distinctly different individual with

Figure 52

Figure 53

his own different helmet but with the same racial features, were found at La Venta.

Five similar colossal heads were found in the 1940s at San Lorenzo, an Olmec site some sixty miles southwest of La Venta, by archaeological expeditions headed by Matthew Stirling and Philip Drucker. Yale University teams that followed, led by Michael D. Coe, discovered more heads. They took radiocarbon readings that gave dates circa 1200 B.C. This means that organic matter (mostly charcoal) found at the site is that old; but the site itself and its monuments could well be older. Indeed, the Mexican archaeologist Ignacio Bernal, who found another head at Tres Zapotes, dates these colossal sculptures to 1500 B.C.

By now sixteen such colossal heads have been found. They range in height from about five to ten feet and weigh as much as twenty-five tons. Whoever sculpted them was about to sculpt more, for a great deal of "raw material"—large stones that had been quarried and rounded to a ball-like shape—has been found in addition to the finished heads. The basalt stones, finished and unfinished, had been hauled from their source to the stoneless sites over distances of sixty miles or more, through jungle and swamps. How such colossal stone blocks were quarried, transported, and finally sculpted and erected at their destination remains a mystery. Clearly, however, the Olmecs deemed it very important to commemorate their leaders in this manner. That these were individuals, all of the same African negroid stock but with their own personalities and diverse headgear, can be readily seen from a portrait gallery of some of these heads (Fig. 54).

Figure 54

Encounter scenes carved on stone stelae (Fig. 55a) and other monuments (Fig. 55b) clearly depict the Olmecs as tall, heavily built with muscular bodies—"giants" in stature, no doubt, in the eyes of the indigenous Indian population. But lest it be assumed that we are dealing here with just a few leaders and not an actual population of negroid African stock—men, women, and children—the Olmecs left behind, scattered throughout a vast area of Mesoamerica that connected the gulf and Pacific coasts, hundreds if not thousands of depictions of themselves. In sculptures, stone carvings, bas-reliefs, statuettes—we always see the same black African faces, as on jades from the sacred cenote of Chichén Itzá or in golden effigies found there; on

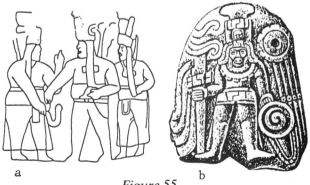

a   b

Figure 55

Figure 56

numerous terra-cottas found all the way from Jaina (as a loving couple) to the central and northern parts of Mexico, or even as ball players (El Tajin reliefs); Fig. 56 shows a few. Some terra-cottas (Fig. 57a) and even more so stone sculptures of the Olmecs (Fig. 57b) portray them as holding babies—an act that must have held special significance for them.

The sites at which the colossal heads and other Olmec depictions have been found are no less intriguing; their size, magnitude, and structures reveal the work of organized settlers, not just of a few shipwrecked visitors. La Venta was actually a small island in the swampy coastal area that has been artificially shaped, landfilled and built up according to a preconceived plan. Major edifices, including an unusual conical "pyramid," elongated and circular mounds, structures, paved courts, altars, stelae, and other man-made features have been laid out with great geometric precision along a north–south axis extending for about three miles. In a place devoid of stones, an amazing variety of stones—each chosen for it special quality—was used in the structures, monuments, and stelae, although all of them required hauling over great distances. The conical pyramid

Figure 57

alone necessitated the bringing and piling up of a million cubic feet of soil. It all called for a tremendous physical effort. It also required a high level of architectural and stoneworking expertise for which there had been no precedent in Mesoamerica; the art was obviously acquired elsewhere.

The extraordinary finds at La Venta included a rectangular enclosure that was surrounded or fenced off by columns of basalt stone (the same material of which the colossal heads were sculpted). The enclosure protected a stone sarcophagus and a rectangular burial chamber that was also roofed and walled with basalt columns. Inside, several skeletons lay on a low platform. All in all, this unique find, with its stone sarcophagus, appears to have been the model for the equally unusual crypt of Pacal in Palenque. At any rate, the insistence on the employment of great blocks of stone, even if it had to be brought from afar, for monuments, commemorative sculptures, and burials must serve as a clue to the enigmatic origin of the Olmecs.

No less puzzling was the discovery at La Venta of hundreds of artistically carved objects of the rare jade, including unusual axes made of this semiprecious stone that is not locally available. Then, to add to the mystery, they were all deliberately buried in long, deep trenches. The trenches, in turn, were filled with layers of clay, each layer of a different kind and color of clay—thousands of tons of soil brought over from diverse distant places. Incredibly, the trenches were paved at the very bottom with thousands of tiles of serpentine, another green-blue semiprecious stone. It has been generally assumed that the trenches were dug to bury in them the precious jade objects; but the floors of serpentine could also suggest that the trenches were constructed earlier, for another purpose altogether; but were used to bury highly valued objects, such as rare axes, once the need for them (and for the trenches) ceased. There is indeed no doubt that the Olmec sites were abandoned by them around the beginning of the Christian era and that the Olmecs even attempted to bury some of the colossal heads. Whoever gained access to their sites afterward, did so with a vengeance: some of the heads were clearly toppled off their bases and rolled downhill into the swamps; others bear marks of attempted mutilation.

As another enigma from La Venta, let us note the discovery in the trenches of concave mirrors of crystallized iron ores (magnetite and hematite), shaped and polished to perfection. After study and experiments scholars at the Smithsonian Institution in Washington, D.C., have concluded that the mirrors could be used to focus the sun's rays, to light fires or for "ritual purposes" (the scholars' way of saying they do not know what an object was for).

The final enigma at La Venta is the site itself, for it is precisely oriented on a north–south axis that is tilted 8 degrees west of true north. Various studies have shown that this was an intentional orientation, intended to permit astonomical sightings, perhaps from atop the conical "pyramid" whose prominent ridges may have served as directional indicators. A special study by M. Popenoe-Hatch. (*Papers on Olmec and Maya Archaeology No. 13, University of California*) concluded that "the pattern of observation being made at La Venta at 1000 B.C. indicates that it must date back to a body of knowledge learned a millennium earlier. . . . The La Venta site and its art of 1000 B.C. seem to reflect a tradition based in large part on the meridian transits of stars occuring on the solstices and equinoxes around 2000 B.C."

A beginning at 2000 B.C. would make La Venta the earliest "sacred center" in Mesoamerica, preceding Teotihuacan except for the legendary time when gods alone were there. It still may not be the true time of the Olmecs' arrival from across the seas, for their Long Count begins at 3113 B.C.; but it does clearly indicate how far ahead of the renowned civilizations of the Maya and the Aztecs the Olmecs had been.

At Tres Zapotes, whose early phase is attributed by archaeologists to the three centuries 1500–1200 B.C., stone constructions (although stone is rare there), terraces, stairways, and mounds that might have been pyramids are scattered about the site. At least another eight sites have been located within a radius of fifteen miles of Tres Zapotes, indicating it was a great center surrounded by satellites. Besides the heads and other sculpted monuments, a number of stelae were unearthed there; one ("Stela C") bears the Long Count date 7.16.6.16.18, which is equivalent to 31 B.C., attesting to the Olmec presence at the site at such time.

At San Lorenzo the Olmec remains consisted of structures, mounds, and embankments, interspersed with artificial ponds. The central part of the site was built upon a man-made platform of about one square mile that was raised some 185 feet above the surrounding terrain—an earthworks project that dwarfs many modern enterprises. The archaeologists discovered that the ponds were interconnected by a system of subterranean conduits "whose meanings or function is not yet understood."

The description of Olmec sites can go on and on—by now, some forty have been uncovered. Everywhere, besides monu-

Figure 58

mental art and edifices of stone, there are mounds by the dozens and other evidence of deliberate, planned earthworks.

The stoneworks, earthworks, trenches, ponds, conduits, mirrors must, however, have some meaningful purpose even if modern scholars cannot fathom it. So, clearly, must the very presence of the Olmecs in Mesoamerica—unless one subscribes to the shipwrecked-survivors theory, which we do not. Aztec historians described the people they nicknamed Olmeca as remnants of an ancient non-Nahuatl-speaking *people*—not a few individuals—who had created the oldest civilization in Mexico. The archaeological evidence supports that and shows that from a base or "metropolitan area" abutting the Gulf of Mexico, where La Venta, Tres Zapotes, and San Lorenzo formed the pivotal triangle, the area of Olmec settlement and influence cut southward toward the Pacific coast of Mexico and Guatemala.

Experts in earthworks, masters of stoneworking, diggers of trenches, channelers of water, users of mirrors—what, thus endowed, were the Olmecs doing in Mesoamerica? Stelae show them emerging from "altars" that represent entrances into the depths of the earth (Fig. 58), or inside caves holding a puzzling array of tools, as on this stela from La Venta (Fig. 59) in which it is possible to discern the enigmatic mirrors being attached to the toolholder's helmets.

All in all, the capabilities, the scenes, the tools appear to us to lead to one conclusion: the Olmecs were miners, come to the New World to extract some precious metals—probably gold, perhaps other rare minerals too.

The legends of Votan, which speak of tunneling through mountains, support this conclusion. So does the fact that among the Olden Gods whose worship was adopted from the Olmecs by the Nahautl people were the god *Tepeyolloti*, meaning "Heart of the Mountain." He was a bearded God of Caves; his temple had to be of stone, preferably built inside a mountain. His glyph-symbol was a pierced mountain; he was depicted (Fig. 60a) holding as his tool a flamethrower—just as we had seen at Tula!

Figure 59

a

b

Figure 60

Figure 61

Our suggestion that the flamethrower seen there (both held by the Atlantes and depicted on a column) was probably used to cut through stone, not just for carving on stone, is manifestly supported by a stone relief known as Daizu No. 40, after the site in Mexico's Oaxaca Valley where it was discovered. It clearly depicts a person inside a confined area, using the flamethrower against the wall in front of him (Fig. 60b). The "diamond" symbol on the wall probably signifies a mineral, but its meaning has not yet been deciphered.

As so many depictions attest, the puzzle of the African "Olmecs" is entwined with the enigma of the Bearded Ones from the eastern Mediteranean. They were depicted on monuments throughout the Olmec sites, in individual portraits or in encounter scenes. Significantly, some encounters are shown to have taken place inside caverns; one, from Tres Zapotes (Fig. 61), even includes an attendant carrying a lighting device (at a time when, supposedly, only torches were used). A no less amazing stela from Chalcatzingo (Fig. 62) depicts a "Caucasian" female operating what looks like technically sophisticated equipment; the base of the stela bears the telltale "diamond" sign. It all spells a connection with minerals.

Did the Mediterranean Bearded Ones come to Mesoamerica at the same time as the African Olmecs? Were they allies, helping each other—or competitors for the same precious minerals or metals? No one can say with any certainty; but it is our own belief that the African Olmecs were there first, and that the

Figure 62

roots of their arrival must be sought in that mysterious beginning date of the Long Count—3113 B.C.

No matter when and why the relationship began, it seems to have ended in a convulsion.

Scholars have wondered why there is, at many Olmec sites, evidence of deliberate destruction—the defacing of monuments (including colossal heads), the smashing of artifacts, the toppling of monuments—all with a vehemence and a vengeance. The destruction does not appear to have taken place all at once; Olmec sites seem to have been abandoned gradually, first in the older "metropolitan center" near the Gulf, circa 300 B.C., then later on at more southern sites. We have seen the evidence of the date equivalent to 31 B.C. at Tres Zapotes; it suggests that the process of the abandonment of Olmec centers, followed by revengeful destruction, may have lasted several centuries, as the Olmecs gave up sites and retreated southward.

The depictions from that turbulent period and from that southern zone of Olmec domains show them more and more as warriors, wearing frightening masks of eagles or jaguars. One such rock carving from the southern areas shows three Olmecs warriors (two with eagle masks) holding spears. The scene includes a naked captive who is bearded. What is not clear is whether the warriors are threatening the captive, or are depicted in the act of saving him. This leaves unclear the intriguing question, were the negroid Olmecs and the Bearded Ones from the eastern Mediterranean on the same side when the troubled times shattered Mesoamerica's first civilization?

They do seem to have shared, though, the same fate.

Figure 63

At a most interesting site near the Pacific coast called Monte Alban—erected on a vast array of man-made platforms and with unusual structures built for astronomical purposes—dozens of stone slabs, erected in a commemorative wall, bear the carved images of the African-negroid men in contorted positions (Fig. 63). For a long time they were nicknamed *Danzantes,* "Dancers"; but scholars now agree that they show the naked bodies of mutilated Olmecs—presumably killed in a violent uprising by the local Indians. Among the depicted negroid bodies there is one of a bearded man with a Semitic nose (Fig. 64) who obviously shared the fate of the Olmecs.

Monte Alban is believed to have been a settlement since 1500 B.C. and a major center since 500 B.C. Thus, within a few

Figure 64

centuries of its grandeur, its builders ended up as mutilated bodies commemorated on stone—victims of those whom they had tutored.

And thus did the millennia, the golden age of the Strangers From Across the Seas, become just a legend.

6

REALM OF THE
GOLDEN WAND

The story of civilization in the lands of the Andes is shrouded in mystery, deepened by the absence of written records or stelae bearing glyphic tales; but myth and legend fill the canvas with tales of gods and giants, and kings who had descended of them.

The coastal peoples could recall traditions of gods who had guided their forebears to the promised lands and of giants who despoiled their crops and raped their women. The highland peoples, of whom the Incas were the dominant at the time of the Spanish conquest, acknowledged divine guidance in all manner of activity and craft, the raising of crops, the building of cities. They recounted Tales of Beginning—tales of creation, of days of upheaval, of an engulfing deluge. And they attributed the beginning of their kingship and the establishment of their capital to the magic of a golden wand.

Spanish chroniclers, as well as native ones who had learned Spanish, had established that the father of the two Inca kings at the time of the conquest, Huayna Capac, was the twelfth *Inca* (a title meaning *lord, sovereign*) of a dynasty that began in Cuzco, the capital, circa A.D. 1020. It was just a couple of centuries before the conquest that the Incas had swooped down from their highland strongholds to the coastal zones, where other kingdoms had existed from much earlier times. In extending their dominions northward to today's Ecuador and southward to today's Chile with the aid of the renowned Highway of the Sun, the Incas essentially superimposed their rule and administration over cultures and organized societies that had thrived in those domains for millennia. The last one to fall under Inca domination was a veritable empire of the Chimu people; their capital, Chan-Chan, was a metropolis whose sacred precincts, step-pyramids and dwelling compounds spread over eight square miles.

Located near the present-day city of Trujillo, where the river

PERU AND ITS NEIGHBORS

Moche flows into the Pacific Ocean, the ancient capital reminded explorers of Egypt and Mesopotamia. The nineteenth-
century explorer E. G. Squier (*Peru Illustrated: Incidents of
Travel and Explorations in the Land of the Incas*) saw vast remains that astounded him even in their ruined and unexcavated
condition. He saw "long lines of massive walls, gigantic cham-
bered pyramids or *huacas,* remains of palaces, dwellings, aqueducts, reservoirs, granaries ... and tombs, extending for many
miles in every direction." Indeed, aerial views of the immense

site, spread out for miles on the flat coastland, bring to mind an aerial view of twentieth-century Los Angeles.

The coastal areas that lie between the western range of the Andes and the Pacific Ocean are climatically rainless areas. Habitation and civilization was able to flourish there because the waters flowing off the high mountains into the ocean do so in the form of rivers large and small that transect the coastal plains every fifty to one hundred miles or so. These rivers create fertile and verdant areas that separate one desertlike stretch from the other. Settlements therefore arose on the banks and at the mouths of these rivers; and the archaeological evidence shows that the Chimus augmented these water sources with supplies brought from the mountains via aqueducts. They also connected the successive fertile and settled areas by a road that on the average was fifteen feet wide—the precursor of the famed Highway of the Sun of the Incas.

At the edge of the built-up area, where the verdant valley ends and the arid desert begins, great pyramids rise from the desert floor, facing each other across the Moche river. They were built of sun-dried mud bricks, reminding explorers such as V. W. von Hagen (*Highway of the Sun* and other books) of the high-rise temple towers (ziggurats) of Mesopotamia, which were also built of mud bricks and, like the ones on the banks of the Moche river, of a slightly convex shape.

The four centuries of Chimu flourishing, from about A.D. 1000 to A.D. 1400, was also a time when goldsmithing was mastered to an extent never attained by the subsequent Incas. Spanish conquistadores described the golden riches of what were in fact Chimu centers (even under Inca rule) in superlatives; the golden enclosure of a town called Tumbes, where plants and animals were mimicked in gold, appears to have been the model after which the Incas fashioned the golden enclosure of the principal shrine in Cuzco. The environs of another city, Tucume, have yielded the greater part of the gold objects that have been found in Peru in the centuries following the conquest (objects buried in tombs with the dead). Indeed, the amount of gold the Chimus possessed astounded the Incas when they overran the coastlands. Those legendary quantities, and the actual finds thereafter, still puzzle scholars; for the gold sources of Peru are not in the arid coastlands, but in the highlands.

The Chimu culture-state was in turn the successor to previous cultures or organized societies. As in the case of Chimu, no one knows what those peoples called themselves; the names that are nowadays applied to them are actually the names of archaeological sites or rivers at which these societies and their recognizable cultures were centered. On the north-central coastal area, the one called Mochica rolls back the fog of history to about 400 B.C. They are known for their artful pottery and graceful textiles; but how and when these arts were acquired remains a mystery. The decorations on their ceramic vessels are replete with illustrations of winged gods and menacing giants, and suggest a religion with a pantheon headed by the Moon God whose symbol was the Crescent and name was *Si* or *Si-An*.

The Mochica artifacts clearly show that, centuries before the Chimu, they had mastered the art of casting gold, of building with mud bricks, and of laying out temple compounds replete with ziggurats. At a site called Pacatnamu, a buried sacred city with no less than thirty-one pyramids was excavated in the 1930s by a German archaeological team (H. Ubbelohde-Doering, *Auf den Koenigsstrassen der Inka*). They determined that the many smaller pyramids were about a thousand years older than the several much larger pyramids that had sides of two hundred feet and were some forty feet high.

The southern border of the Chimu empire was the river Rímac, from which name the Spaniards corrupted *Lima* as the name of their capital. Beyond this boundary the coastal zones were inhabited, in pre-Inca times, by Chincha tribesmen; the highlands were occupied by Aymara-speaking peoples. It is now known that the Incas had obtained their notions of a pantheon from the former, and the tales of Creation and Beginning from the latter.

The Rímac region was a focal point in antiquity as it is nowadays. It was there, just south of Lima, that the largest temple to a Peruvian deity had stood. Its ruins from the time it was rebuilt and enlarged by the Incas can still be seen. It was dedicated to *Pacha-Camac*, meaning "Creator of the World," a god who headed a pantheon that included the divine couples Vis and Mama-Pacha ("Lord Earth" and "Lady Earth") and *Ni* and *Mama-Cocha* ("Lord Water" and "Lady Water"), the Moon God *Si*, the Sun God *Illa-Ra*, and the Hero God *Kon* or *Con* who was also known as *Ira-Ya*—names that evoke a host of Near Eastern divine epithets.

The temple of Pachacamac was a "Mecca" for the ancient people of the southern coasts. Pilgrims came to it from far and near. The act of pilgrimage was so esteemed that even when tribes were at war, enemy pilgrims were granted safe passage. The pilgrims came bearing offerings of gold, for that was the metal deemed belonging to the gods. Only select priests could enter the Holy of Holies where, on certain holidays, the god's image pronounced oracles that the priests then related to the people. But the whole temple precinct was so revered that pilgrims had to take off their sandals to enter it—just as Moses was commanded to do in the Sinai and as Moslems still do as they enter a mosque.

The gold that had accumulated at the temple was too fabulous to escape the attention of the conquering Spaniards. Francisco Pizarro sent his brother Hernandez to loot it. He found some gold, silver, and precious stones, but not the main riches, for the priests had hidden the treasures. No amount of threat or torture could make the priests reveal the hiding place (which is still rumored to be somewhere between Lima and Lurin). Hernandez then smashed the god's golden statue for its metal and pulled out of the walls the silver nails that had held the gold and silver plates that had lined the temple's walls. The nails alone weighed 32,000 ounces!

Local legends attribute the establishment of this temple to the "giants." What is known for certain is that the Incas, adopting the veneration of Pachacamac from the tribes they had overrun, enlarged and embellished the temple. Standing on a mountainside, the Pacific Ocean breaking almost at its feet, the temple rose atop four platforms that supported a terrace five hundred feet above ground level; the four platforms were created by the erection of retaining walls built of immense stone blocks. The topmost terrace extended over several acres. The final structures of the temple complex, aided by sunken plazas, afforded an unimpeded view from the main sanctuary toward the vast ocean.

Not only the living came to pray and to worship here. The dead too were brought to the Rímac valley and the coastal plains to its south, to spend their afterlife in the shadow of the oracle gods; perhaps even for an eventual resurrection, for there was a belief that Rímac could resurrect the dead. At sites known nowadays as Lurin, Pisco, Nazca, Paracas, Ancon, Ica, archaeologists have found in "cities of the dead" innumerable graves and subterranean vaults in which the mummified bodies of noblemen and priests were buried. The mummies, in a seated position with hands and legs bent in, were tied up and fitted into sacklike bags; but within the bag, the deceased were fully clothed in their finest garments. The dry climate and the outer sack protected the superbly woven garments, shawls, turbans, and ponchos, and their incredibly bright colors. The textiles, whose exquisite weaving reminded archaeologists of Europe's finest Gobelin tapestries, were embroidered with religious and cosmological symbols.

The central figure, on the textiles as well as on ceramics, was

always that of a god holding a wand in one hand and a thunderbolt in the other and wearing a horned or rayed crown (Fig.
65); the Indians called him *Rímac,* like the river's name.

Were Rímac and Pachacamac one and the same deity, or two
separate ones? Scholars disagree, for the evidence is inconclu-
sive. They do agree that the nearby mountain ranges were dedicated exclusively to Rímac. His name meant "The Thunderer,"
and thus in meaning and phonetically is akin to the nickname
Raman by which Adad was known to the Semitic peoples—an
epithet stemming from the verb meaning "to thunder."

According to the chronicler Garcilaso, it was in these mountains that "an idol, in the shape of a man," had stood in a shrine
dedicated to Rímac. He may have been referring to any one of
several sites in the mountains flanking the Rímac valley. There,
ruins of what archaeologists believe were step pyramids (artist's
conception, Fig. 66) dominate the scenery to this very day, fool-
ing the viewer to imagine he is seeing a seven-step ziggurat in
ancient Mesopotamia.

Was Rímac the god sometimes called "Kon" or "Ira-Ya," the
one called *Viracocha* in Inca lore? Though no one can say for
certain, what is beyond doubt is that Viracocha was depicted
exactly as the deity shown on the coastal pottery—holding in
one hand the forked weapon and in the other the magical wand.

It was with that wand—a wand of gold—that all Andean
legends of Beginnings commence; on the shores of Lake Titicaca, at a place called Tiahuanacu.

When the Spaniards came, the lands of the Andes were the
lands of the Inca empire, ruled from the highland capital Cuzco.

Figure 65

Figure 66

And Cuzco, Inca tales related, was established by the Children of the Sun who had been created and instructed at Lake Titicaca by the Creator God, Viracocha.

Viracocha, according to the Andean legends, was a great God of Heaven who had come to Earth in great antiquity, choosing the Andes as his creative arena. As one Spanish chronicler, Father Cristoval de Molina, put it, "they say that the Creator was at Tiahuanaco and that there was his chief abode. Hence the superb edifices, worthy of admiration, in that place."

One of the first padres to record the native tales of their history and prehistory was Blas Valera; unfortunately, only fragments of his writings are known from mentions by others, for his original manuscript was burnt in the sack of Cadiz by the English in 1587. He recorded the Inca version that their first monarch, Manco Capac, exited from Lake Titicaca through a subterranean way. He was the son of the Sun and was given by the Sun a golden wand with which to find Cuzco. When his mother went into labor, the world was in darkness. When he was born, there was light and trumpets sounded, and the god Pachacamac declared that "the beautiful day of Manco Capac had dawned."

But Blas Valera also recored other versions that suggested that the Incas appropriated to their dynasty the person and tale of Manco Capac, and that their true ancestors were immigrants from somewhere else who had arrived in Peru by sea. According to this, the monarch called by the Incas "Manco Capac" was the son of a king called Atau who had arrived on the Peruvian coast with two hundred men and women and disembarked at Rímac. From there they went to Ica, and from there they marched to Lake Titicaca, the place from which the Sons of the Sun had governed the Earth. Manco Capac sent his followers in two directions to find those legendary Sons of the Sun. He himself wandered many days until he came to a place that had a sacred cave. The cave was artificially hewed out and was adorned with gold and silver. Manco Capac left the sacred cave and went to a window called *Capac Toco,* meaning "Royal Window." As he came out, he was dressed in golden garments he had obtained in the cave; and by putting on these royal garments he was invested with the kingship of Peru.

From these and other chronicles it is evident that various versions were memorized by the Andean peoples. They recalled a creative Beginning at Lake Titicaca, and the start of kingship at a place of a sacred cave and a royal window; and as the Incas had it, the events were concurrent and formed the basis of their dynasty. Other versions, however, separated the events and the periods.

One of the versions regarding the Beginning was that the great god, Creator of All, Viracocha, arranged for four brothers and four sisters to roam the land and bring civilization to its primitive peoples; and one of these brother-sister/husband-wife couples began kingship in Cuzco. The other version was that the Great God, at his base in Lake Titicaca, created this first royal couple as his children and gave them an object made of gold. He told them to go north and build a city where the golden object would sink into the earth; the place where the miracle had happened was Cuzco. And that is why the Inca kings—providing they had been born of a succession of brother-sister royal couples—could claim direct descent of the Sun God.

Recollections of the Deluge featured in almost all versions of Beginning. According to Father Molina (*Relacion de las fabulas y ritos de los Yngas*) it was already "in the time of Manco Capac, who was the first Ynca and from whom they began to be called Children of the Sun . . . that they had a full account of the Deluge. They say that all people and all created things perished in it, the waters having risen above all the highest mountains in the world. No living thing survived except a man and a woman who remained in a box; and when the waters subsided, the wind carried them to Huanaco, which will be over seventy leagues from Cuzco, a little more or less. The Creator of All Things commanded them to remain there as *Mitimas,* and there in Tiahuanaco the Creator began to raise up the people and nations that are in that region." The repopulation of the Earth began by the Creator first fashioning out of clay the image of one person of each nation; "then he gave life and a soul to each one, men as well as women, and directed them to their designated places on Earth." Those who failed to obey the commandments regarding worship and behavior were turned into stones.

The Creator also had with him on the island of Titicaca the Moon and the Sun, whence they had come on his orders. When all that was needed to replenish the Earth was done, the Moon and the Sun rose up to heaven.

The two divine assistants of the Creator of All are presented in another version as his two sons. "Having created the tribes and nations, and assigned dresses and languages to them," Father Molina wrote, "the Creator ordered his two sons to go in different directions and introduce civilization." The old son, Ymaymana Viracocha (meaning "in whose power all things are placed"), went to give civilization to the mountain peoples; the younger son, Topaco Viracocha ("maker of things"), was ordered to go by way of the coastal plains. When the two brothers completed their work they met at the seashore, "whence they ascended to heaven."

Garcilaso de la Vega, who was born in Cuzco to a Spanish father and an Inca mother soon after the conquest, recorded two legends. According to one the Great God came down from the heavens to Earth to instruct mankind, giving it laws and precepts. He "placed his two children at lake Titicaca," gave them a "wedge of gold," and instructed them to settle where it would sink into the ground, which was at Cuzco. The other legend related that "after the waters of the deluge had subsided, a certain man appeared in the country of Tiahuanacu, which is to the south of Cuzco. This man was so powerful that he divided the world into four parts, and gave them to four men whom he honored with the title of king." One of them, whose epithet-name was *Manco Capac* ("king and lord" in the Quechua language of the Incas), began kingship in Cuzco.

The various versions speak of two phases of creation by Viracocha. Juan de Betanzos (*Suma y Narracion de los Incas*) recorded a Quechua tale wherein the Creator god, "on the first occasion, made the heavens and the earth"; he also created people—Mankind. But "this people did some sort of wrong to Viracocha, and he was angered by it . . . and those first people and their chief he converted into stones in punishment." Then, after a period of darkness, he made at Tiahuanacu new men and women, out of stones. He gave them tasks and abilities and told them where to go. Remaining with only two aides, he sent one southward and one northward, while he himself went in the direction of Cuzco. There he caused a chief to come forth; and having thus established kingship at Cuzco, Viracocha continued his journey "as far as the coast of Ecuador, where his two companions joined him. There they all began to walk together on the waters of the sea, and disappeared."

Some of the tales of the highland peoples focused on how there had come to be a settlement at Cuzco, and how Cuzco had been divinely ordained to become the capital. According to one version what Manco Capac was given (in order to find the site for the city) was a staff or wand made of pure gold; it was called *Tupac-yauri,* meaning "splenderous scepter." He went in search of the designated place in the company of brothers and sisters. Reaching a certain stone, his companions were struck with a feebleness. When Manco Capac struck the stone with the magical staff, it spoke up and told him of his selection as ruler of a kingdom. A descendent of an Indian chief who had converted to Christianity after the Spaniards had landed claimed in his memoirs that the Indians were showing that sacred rock to this very day. "The Ynca Manco Capac married one of his own sisters, named Mama Ocllo... and they began to enact good laws for the government of their people."

This tale, sometimes called the legend of the four Ayar brothers, relates as all other versions of the founding of Cuzco do, that the magical object whereby the monarch and the capital were designated was made of solid gold. It is a clue that we consider vital and central to the unraveling of the enigmas of all American civilizations.

When the Spaniards entered Cuzco, the Inca capital, they found a metropolis with some 100,000 dwelling houses, surrounding a royal-religious center of magnificent temples, palaces, gardens, plazas, and marketplaces. Situated between two streams (the Tullumayo and the Rodadero) at an elevation of some 11,500 feet, Cuzco begins at the foot of the promontory of Sacsahuaman. The city was divided into twelve wards—a number that puzzled the Spaniards—arranged in an oval. The first and oldest ward, appropriately called the Kneeling Terrace, was located on the promontory's slope in the northwest. There the first Incas (and presumably also the legendary Manco Capac) had built their palaces. All the wards bore picturesque names (the Speaking Place, Terrace of Flowers, Sacred Gate, and the like) that in reality described their principal feature.

One of this century's leading scholars on the subject of Cuzco, Stansbury Hagar (*Cuzco, the Celestial City*) stressed the belief that Cuzco was established and laid out in accordance with a plan drawn for Manco Capac at the prehistoric sacred place where the migration of the Founders had begun, at Tiahuanacu on Lake Titicaca. In its name, "Navel of the Earth," and in its division to four parts simulating the four corners of the Earth, he (and others too) saw an expression of terrestrial concepts. In other features of the city's plan, however, he saw aspects of celestial knowledge (hence the title of his book). The streams that flanked the city's center were made to flow through artificial channels that emulated the serpentine Milky Way; and the twelve wards emulated the division of the heavens into twelve houses of the zodiac. Significantly for our own studies of events on Earth and their timing, Hagar concluded that the first and earliest ward represented Aries.

Squier and other nineteenth-century explorers described a Cuzco that was partly all-Hispanic and partly built over the remains of the earlier Inca City. So, for a description of Cuzco as the conquering Spaniards had found it, and for a glimpse as it had been in even earlier times, one must read the words of the early chroniclers. Pedro de Cieza de Leon (*Chronicles of Peru* in the English translation) described the Inca capital, its edifices and squares and bridges in most glowing words, "a nobly adorned city" from whose center four royal roads led to the farthest parts of the empire, and ascribed its riches not only to the custom of keeping intact the palaces of the deceased kings, but also to the law that required gold and silver to be brought into the city in homage and offerings but prohibited to take any out on pain of death. "Cuzco," he wrote in its praise, "was grand and stately, and must have been founded by a people of great intelligence. It had fine streets, except that they were narrow, and the houses were built of solid stones, beautifully joined. These stones were very large and well cut. The other parts of the houses were of wood and straw; there are no remains of tiles, bricks, or lime amongst them."

Garcilaso de la Vega (who bore his Spanish father's name but also the royal title "Inca," for his mother was of the royal Inca dynasty) after describing the twelve wards, related that except for the palace of the first Inca in the First Ward, on the slope of Sacsahuaman, the other Inca palaces were clustered around the city's center near the great temple. Still extant in his time were the palaces of the second, sixth, ninth, tenth, eleventh and twelfth Incas. Some of them flanked the main square of the capital, called Huacay-Pata. There the ruling Inca, seated on a grand dais, his family, court hierarchy, and priests witnessed and conducted the festivals and religious ceremonies, four of which were connected with the winter and summer solstices and the spring and autumn equinoxes.

As the early chroniclers attest, the most famous and superb structure of pre-Hispanic Cuzco was the Cori-Cancha ("Golden Enclosure"), the city's and the empire's most important temple. The Spaniards called it Temple of the Sun, having believed that the Sun was the supreme deity of the Incas. Those who had seen the temple before it was vandalized, demolished, and built over by the Spaniards, reported that it was made up of several parts. The main temple was dedicated to Viracocha; adjoining or auxiliary chapels were devoted to the Moon (*Quilla*), Venus (*Chasca*), a mysterious star called *Coyllor,* and to *Illa-pa,* the god of Thunder and Lightning. There was also a shrine devoted to the Rainbow. It was there, at the Coricancha, that the Spaniards had plundered the golden riches.

Adjoining the Coricancha was the enclosure that was called *Aclla-Huasi*—"The Chosen Women's House." Consisting of dwellings surrounding gardens and orchards as well as workshops for spinning, weaving, and sewing the royal and priestly garments, it was a secluded enclave where virgins dedicated to the Great God lived; one of their tasks was to preserve the Eternal Fire attributed to the god.

The conquering Spaniards, having plundered the city's riches, set out to appropriate to themselves the city itself, dividing among themselves by drawing lots its various edifices. Most were dismantled for their masonry; here and there a gateway or part of a wall was incorporated into new Spanish buildings. Major shrines were used as sites for churches and monasteries. The Dominicans, first on the scene, took over the Temple of the Sun, demolishing its outer structure but incorporating the ancient layout and some wall portions into their church-monastery. One of the most interesting sections thus used and therefore still intact is a semicircular outer wall of what used to be the enclosure of the Inca temple's High Altar (Fig. 67). It was there that the Spaniards found a great golden disk representing (they assumed) the Sun; it fell by lot to the conquistador Leguizano, who gambled it away the following night. The winner had the venerated object melted and cast into ingots.

After the Dominicans came the Franciscans, the Augustines, the Mercedarios, the Jesuits; they all built their shrines, including Cuzco's great cathedral, where Inca shrines had stood. After the priests came the nuns; not surprisingly, their convent stands upon the Inca's convent of the House of the Chosen Women. Governors and Spanish dignitaries followed suit, building their edifices and homes upon and with parts of Inca stone houses.

Figure 67

Some believe that *Cuzco,* meaning "Navel, Omphalus," was so named because it was the capital, a place chosen for a command post. Another theory held by many is that the name means "Place of Raised Stones." If so, the name suits Cuzco's main attraction—its astounding megalithic stones.

While most of Cuzco's Inca dwellings were built of undressed fieldstones held together with mortar, or stones roughly cut to simulate bricks or ashlars, some of the older edifices were built of perfectly cut, dressed, and shaped stones ("ashlars") as those found in the remaining semicircular wall of the Coricancha. The beauty and craftsmanship of this wall and some others contemporary with it have amazed and thrilled countless travelers. Sir Clemens Markham wrote: "In contemplating this unequalled piece of masonry, one is lost in admiration at the extreme beauty of its formation . . . and above all at the untiring perseverence and skill that was required to form each stone with such unerring precision."

Squier, less the architect and more the antiquarian, was more impressed by Cuzco's other stones, those of great size and the oddest shapes that fitted one into another's angles with amazing precision and without mortar. Being of brown trachtyte *Anda-huaylillas*, they must have been specifically selected, he surmised, because of their grain, which "being rough, causes greater adhesion between the blocks than would be effected by the use of any other kinds of stone." He confirmed that the polygonal (many-sided) stones, as Spanish chroniclers had stated, indeed were fitted together with such accuracy "that it was impossible to introduce the thinnest knife-blade or finest needle between them" (Fig. 68a). One such stone, a tourist favorite, has twelve sides and angles (Fig. 68b).

All these heavy blocks of the hardest stone have been brought over to Cuzco and cut by unknown masons with apparent ease, as if they were shaping putty. Each stone face has been

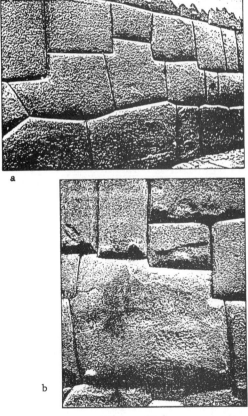

Figure 68

dressed to a smooth and slightly concave surface; how, no one can tell, for there are no grooves or ridges or hammer marks to be seen. How were these heavy stones raised and placed one upon the other, one angled to fit the odd angles below and beside it, is also a mystery. To compound the mystery, all these stones are tightly held together without mortar, withstanding not only human destructiveness but also the frequent earthquakes in the area.

All are agreed by now that while the beautiful ashlars represent a "classical" Inca phase, the cyclopean walls belong to an earlier time. For want of clearer answers, scholars simply call it the Megalithic Age.

It is a puzzle that still seeks a solution. It is also a mystery that only deepens as one ascends the promontory of Sacsahuaman. There, what is assumed to have been an Inca fortress thrusts an even greater enigma at the visitor.

The promontory's name means Falcon's Place. Shaped like a triangle with its base to the northwest, its peak rises some eight hundred feet above the city below. Its sides are formed by gorges that separate it from the mountain chain to which it belongs and which it rejoins at its base.

The promontory can be divided into three parts. Its wide base is dominated by huge rock outcroppings that someone cut and shaped into giant steps or platforms and perforated with tunnels, niches, and grooves. The promontory's middle is taken up by a flattened-out area hundreds of feet wide and long. And the narrower edge, elevated above the rest of the promontory, contains evidence of circular and rectangular structures under which there run passages, tunnels, and other openings in a bewildering maze cut into the natural rock.

Separating or protecting this "developed" area from the rest of the promontory are three massive walls that run parallel to each other in a zigzag (Fig. 69).

The three lines of zigzagging walls are constructed of massive stones and rise one behind the other, each one somewhat higher than the one in front of it, to a combined height of about sixty feet. Earth-fills behind each wall have created terraces that, it is presumed, were meant to serve the promontory's defenders as parapets. Of the three, especially the lowest (first) wall is built of colossal boulders, weighing between ten to twenty tons. In one instance a boulder twenty-seven feet high weighs over 300 tons (Fig. 70). Many stones are fifteen feet high and are from ten to fourteen feet in width and thickness. As in the city below, the faces of these boulders have been artificially dressed to per-

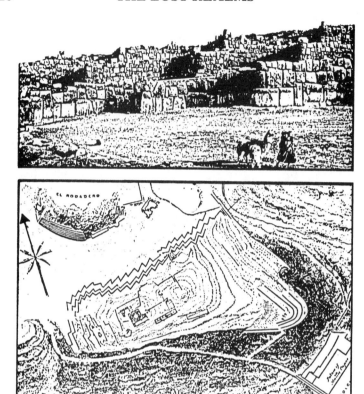

Figure 69

fect smoothness and are beveled at the edges, which means that
they are not fieldstones found lying about and used as nature
had shaped them, but rather the work of expert masons.

The massive stone blocks lie one atop the other, sometimes
separated for an unknown structural reason by a thin stone slab.
Everywhere the stones are of a polygonal shape, the odd sides
and angles fitting without mortar into the odd and matching
shapes of the adjoining stone blocks. The style and the period
are clearly of the same cyclopean construction as that of the
Megalithic Age remains in Cuzco, but here they are substantially more massive.

All over the flattened areas between the walls there are remains of structures that were built of the regularly fashioned
"Inca style" stones. As clearing work on the ground and aerial
photographs show, there had been various structures atop the
promontory. All has crumbled or was destroyed in the wars that

Figure 70

ensued between the Incas and the Spaniards after the conquest. Only the colossal walls remain unscathed, mute witnesses that bespeak an enigmatic age and mysterious builders; for as all studies have shown, the gigantic stone blocks were quarried miles away and had to be transported to the site over mountains, valleys, gorges, and gushing streams.

How and by whom—and why?

Chroniclers from Spanish conquest times, travelers in recent centuries, and contemporary researchers all arrive at the same conclusion: not the Incas, but enigmatic predecessors with some supernatural powers. . . . But no one even has a theory Why.

Garcilaso de la Vega wrote of these fortifications that one had no choice but to believe that they were "erected by magic, by demons and not by men, because of the number and size of the stones placed in the three walls . . . which it is impossible to believe were cut out of quarries, since the Indians had neither iron nor steel wherewith to extract and shape them. And how they were brought together is a thing equally wonderous, since the Indians had neither carts nor oxen nor ropes wherewith to drag them by manual force. Nor were there level roads over which to transport them; on the contrary, steep mountains and abrupt declivities to overcome.

"Many of the stones," Garcilaso wrote, "were brought from ten to fifteen leagues, and especially the stone or rather the rock called *Saycusa* or the Tired Stone, because it never reached the structure, and which, it is known, was brought a distance of fifteen leagues from beyond the river of Yucay...The stones obtained the nearest were from Muyna, five leagues from Cuzco. It defies imagination to conceive how so many and so great stones could be so accurately fitted together as scarcely to admit the insertion of a point of a knife between them. Many are indeed so well fitted that the joint can hardly be discovered. And all this is the more wonderous as they had no squares or levels to place on the stones and ascertain if they would fit together. . . . Nor had they cranes or pulleys or other machinery whatever." He then went on to quote a number of Catholic priests who had suggested that "one cannot conceive how such stones were cut, carried and set in their places . . . unless by diabolic art."

Squier, who said of the stones composing the three walls that they represented "without doubt the grandest specimen of the style called Cyclopean extant in America," was enthralled and puzzled by many other features of these stone colossi and of the other rock faces in the area. One such feature was the three gateways through the rows of walls, one of which was called the Gate of Viracocha. This gateway was a marvel of engineering sophistication: at about the center of the front wall the stone blocks were so placed as to form a rectangular area that led to an opening of about four feet in the wall. Steps then led to a terrace between the first and second walls, from which an intricate passage opened against a transverse wall at a right angle, leading to a second terrace. There, two entrances placed at an angle to each other led to and through the third wall.

All chroniclers related that this central gateway, like the other two at the walls' extremes, could be blocked by lowering large, specially fitted stone blocks into the openings. These stone blockers and the mechanisms for their raising and lowering (to open and block the gateways) were removed at some ancient time, but the channels and grooves for them can still be discerned. On the nearby plateau, where rocks have been carved into precise geometric shapes that make no sense to the modern viewer (Fig. 71a), there is one instance (Fig. 71b)

a

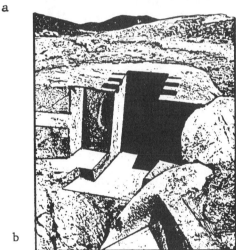

b

Figure 71

where the cut rock appears to have been shaped to hold some
mechanical contraption. H. Ubbelohde-Doering (*Kunst im
Reiche der Inca*) said of these enigmatic carved rocks that they
are "like a model in which every corner has a significance."

Behind the line of walls the promontory was the site of an
agglomeration of structures, some undoubtedly built in Inca
times. That they were built on the remains of earlier structures
is probable; that they had nothing to do with a maze of subter-

ranean tunnels is certain. Underground passages in a labyrinthine pattern begin and end abruptly. One leads to a cavern forty
feet deep; others end in rock faces cut and dressed to resemble
steps that do not seem to lead anywhere.

Facing the cyclopean walls across the wide open flat area are
rock outcroppings that bear descriptive names: the *Rodadero*
("Slide") whose back side is used by children as a slide; the
Piedra Lisa ("Smooth Stone"), which Squier had described to
be "grooved as if the rock had been squeezed up in a plastic
state"—like playing clay—"then hardened into shape, with a
smooth and glossy surface"; and near them the *Chingana* ("Labyrinth"), a cliff whose natural fissures have been artificially enlarged into passages, low corridors, small chambers, niches, and
other hollowed-out spaces. Indeed, rocks dressed and shaped
into horizontal, vertical, and inclined faces, openings, grooves,
niches—all cut in precise angles and geometrical shapes—are
found everywhere behind these cliffs.

The modern visitor cannot describe the scene any better than
Squier did last century: "The rocks all over the plateau back of
the fortress, chiefly limestone, are cut and carved in a thousand
forms. Here is a niche, or a series of them; anon a broad seat
like a sofa, or a series of small seats; next a flight of steps; then
a cluster of square or round or octagonal basins; long lines of
grooves; occasional holes drilled down . . . fissures in the rock
widened artificially into a chamber—and all these cut with the
accuracy and finish of the most skilful worker."

That the Incas used the promontory for a last stand against
the Spaniards is a matter of historical record. That they had put
up structures atop it is also evident from the remaining masonry.
But that they were not the original builders at the site is further
evidenced by their recorded inability to transport even one megalithic stone.

The attempt-that-failed is reported by Garcilaso in regard to
the Tired Stone. According to him, one of the Inca master-
masons who wished to enhance his fame decided to haul up the
stone from where the original builders had dropped it and use it
in his defensive structure. "More than 20,000 Indians brought
this stone up, dragging it with great cables. Their progress was
very slow, for the road up which they came is rough and has
many steep slopes to climb and descend. . . . On one of these
slopes, as a result of carelessness on the part of the bearers who
failed to pull evenly, the weight of the rock proved too much for
the strength of those controlling it, and it rolled over down the
slope and killed three or four thousand Indians."

According to this tale, then, the only time the Incas attempted to haul up and lift into place a cyclopean stone—they failed. Obviously, then, they were not the ones who had brought up, cut and shaped and lifted into place, with a mortarless fitting, the hundreds of the other cyclopean stones.

It is no wonder that Erich von Däniken, who has popularized the theory of Ancient Astronauts, wrote after his visit to the site in 1980 (*Reise Nach Kiribati*, or *Pathways to the Gods* in the English translation) that neither "mother nature" nor the Incas —but only ancient astronauts—could have been responsible for these monumental structures and odd-shaped cliffs. An earlier traveler, W. Bryford Jones (*Four Faces of Peru*, 1967), stated in amazement of the massive stone blocks: "They could only have been moved, I felt, by a race of giants from another world." And writing several years before that, Hans Helfritz (*Die alten Kulturen der Neuen Welt*) said of the incredible cyclopean walls of Sacsahuaman: "The impression is created that they have stood there from the very beginning of the world."

Long before them Hiram Bingham (*Across South America*) recorded one of the native speculations regarding the manner in which these incredible rock sculptures and walls had been created. "One of the favorite stories," he wrote, "is that the Incas knew of a plant whose juices rendered the surface of a block so soft that the marvellous fitting was accomplished by rubbing the stones together for a few moments with this magical plant juice." But who was it that could lift and hold up such cyclopean stones to rub them against each other?

Obviously, Bingham did not accept the natives' explanation and the enigma continued to nag him. "I have visited Sacsahuaman repeatedly," he wrote in *Inca Land*. "Each time it invariably overwhelms and astounds. To a superstitious Indian who sees these walls for the first time, they must seem to have been built by the gods." Why did Bingham make this statement, if not to express a "superstition" harbored within his own heart?

And so we come full circle back to the Andean legends; only they explain the megalithic builders by claiming that there had been gods and giants in these lands, and an Old Empire, and kingship that began with a divine golden wand.

7

THE DAY THE SUN
STOOD STILL

The initial Spanish avarice for gold and treasure obscured their amazement at encountering in Peru, this unknown land at the world's end, an advanced civilization with cities and roads, palaces and temples, kings and priests—and religions. The first wave of priests accompanying the conquerors was bent on destroying everything that had to do with the Indians' "idolatry." But the priests that followed—at that time their country's scholars—found themselves exposed to explanations of the natives' rites and beliefs through Indian noblemen who had converted to Christianity.

The realization that the Andean Indians believed in a Supreme Creator and that their legends recalled a Deluge, increased the curiosity of the Spanish priests. It then transpired that many details of those local tales were uncannily similar to the biblical tales of Genesis. It was therefore inevitable that among the early theories regarding the origin of the "Indians" and their beliefs, an association with the lands and the people of the Bible emerged as the leading theory.

As in Mexico, after various other ancient peoples have been considered, the Israelites of the Ten Lost Tribes seemed the most plausible explanation not only for the similarity of native legends to biblical tales, but also to such customs among the Peruvian Indians as the offering of the first fruits, an Expiation Feast at the end of September that corresponded to the nature and time of the Jewish Day of Atonement, and other biblical commandments such as the rite of circumcision, abstaining from the blood of animal meat, and the prohibition against the eating of fish without scales. In the Feast of First Fruits, the Indians chanted the mystic words *Yo Meshica, He Meshica, Va Meshica*; and some of the Spanish savants discerned in the word *Meshica* the Hebrew term "Mashi'ach"—the Messiah.

(Modern scholars now believe that the component *Ira* in Andean divine names is comparable to the Mesopotamian *Ira/Illa,* from which the biblical *El* stems; that the name *Malquis* by which the Incas venerated their idol is equivalent to that of the Canaanite deity *Molekh* ("Lord"); and that likewise the royal Inca title *Manco* derives from the same Semitic root, meaning "king.")

It was in view of such theories of Israelite-biblical origins that the Catholic hierarchy in Peru, after the initial wave of obliteration, moved to record and preserve the Indian heritage. Local clergymen, such as Father Blas Valera (son of a Spaniard and an Indian woman), were encouraged to write down what they knew and heard. Before the sixteenth century was over, a concerted effort sponsored by the Bishop of Quito was made to compile the local histories, evaluate all known ancient sites, and assemble in one library all the relevant manuscripts. Much that has been learned since is based on what was learned then.

Intrigued by the theories and availing himself of the assembled manuscripts, a Spaniard by name of Fernando Montesinos arrived in Peru in 1628 and devoted the rest of his life to the compilation of a comprehensive and chronological history and prehistory of the Peruvians. Some twenty years later he completed a master work titled *Memorias Antiguas Historiales del Peru* and deposited it in the library of the convent of San Jose de Sevilla. There it lay unpublished and forgotten for two centuries, when extracts from it were included in a French history of the Americas. The full Spanish text saw light only in 1882 (an English translation by P. A. Means was published by the Hakluyt Society in London, England, in 1920).

Picking up a common point of departure in biblical and Andean recollections—the tale of the Deluge—Montesinos employed the event as his starting point. In line with the biblical record he followed the repopulation of Earth after the Deluge from Mount Ararat in Armenia through the Table of Nations in Chapter 10 of the Book of Genesis. He saw in the name *Peru* (or *Piru/Pirua* in the Indian tongue) a phonetic rendering of the biblical name *Ophir,* the grandson of Eber (the forebear of the Hebrews) who himself was the great-grandson of Shem. Ophir was also the name of the famed Land of Gold from which the Phoenicians had brought gold for the temple in Jerusalem that King Solomon was building. Ophir's name in the biblical Table of Nations is listed next to that of his brother Havilah—a name after which the famed land of gold was called in the biblical tale of the four rivers of Paradise:

And the name of one was Pishon;
It is the river which encompasses the whole
land of Havilah, where the gold is

It was much before the time of the kingdoms of Judah and
Israel, much before the Ten Tribes were exiled by the Assyrians,
that people from the lands of the Bible had come to the Andes,
Montesinos theorized. It was none other than Ophir himself,
Montesinos suggested, who had led the earliest settlers into
Peru when mankind began to spread upon the Earth after the
Deluge.

The Inca tales Montesinos assembled attested that long before the latest Inca dynasty there had been an ancient empire.
After a period of growth and prosperity upheavals suddenly befell the land: comets appeared in the skies, the ground shook
with earthquakes, wars broke out. The king reigning at the time
left Cuzco and led his followers to a secluded refuge place in the
mountains called Tampu-Tocco; only a few priests remained in
Cuzco to maintain its shrine. It was during that calamitous time
that the art of writing was lost.

Centuries passed. The kings went periodically from Tampu-
Tocco to Cuzco to consult divine oracles. Then one day a
woman of noble birth announced that her son Rocca had been
carried off by the Sun God. Days later the youth reappeared
clothed in golden garments. He reported that the time of for-
giveness had come, but the people must adhere to certain commandments: royal succession would go to a son born to the king
by a half sister, even if not the firstborn; and writing was not to
be resumed. The people agreed and returned to Cuzco, with
Rocca as the new king; he was given the title *Inca*—sovereign.

By giving this first Inca the name Manco Capac, Inca historians likened him to the legendary founder of Cuzco, Manco
Capac of the four Ayar brothers. Montesinos correctly separated and distanced the Spaniards' contemporary Inca dynasty
(which began to reign only in the eleventh century A.D.) from its
predecessors. His conclusion, that the Inca dynasty consisted of
fourteen kings, including Huayna Capac who had died when the
Spaniards arrived and his two warring sons, has since been confirmed by all scholars.

He concluded that indeed Cuzco had been abandoned before
that Inca dynasty had reinstated kingship in the capital. During
the abandonment of Cuzco, he wrote, twenty-eight kings
reigned from a hidden mountain refuge called Tampu-Tocco.
And before that there had indeed been an ancient empire with
Cuzco as its capital. There, sixty-two kings sat on the throne; of

them, forty-six were priest-kings and sixteen were semidivine rulers who were Sons of the Sun God. And, before all that, the gods themselves lorded over the land.

It is believed that Montesinos had found a copy of the Blas Valera manuscript in La Paz, and was allowed by the Jesuit priests there to copy from it. He also relied heavily on the writings of Father Miguel Cabello de Balboa, whose version related that the first sovereign, Manco Capac, had come to Cuzco not directly from Lake Titicaca but by way of a hidden place called "Tampo-Toco" ("Restplace of the Windows"). It was there that Manco Capac "abused his sister Mama Occllo" and begot a son by her.

Montesinos, having confirmed this by all his other available sources, accepted this information as factual. He thus began the chronicles of kingship in Peru with the journey of the four Ayar brothers and their four sisters who were sent to find Cuzco with the aid of the golden object. But he recorded a version whereby the first to be chosen as a leader was a brother that bore the name of the ancestor who had led the people to the Andes, Pirua Manco (and thus the name Peru). It was he who, having arrived at the chosen site, announced that he had decided to build there a city. He came there accompanied by wives and sisters (or sister-wives); one of them bore him a son who was called Manco Capac. It was this son who built in Cuzco the Temple to the Great God, Viracocha; and therefore it is from that time that the establishment of the ancient empire is counted and the chronicles of the dynasties begin. Manco Capac was acclaimed as Son of the Sun, and was the first of sixteen rulers so deemed. In his time other deities were venerated, one of whom was Mother Earth and another a god whose name meant Fire; he was represented by a stone that spoke oracles.

The principal science at that time, Montesinos wrote, was that of astrology; and the art of writing, on processed leaves of the plantain tree and on stones, was known. The fifth Capac "renewed the computation of time" and began to record the passage of time and the reigns of his ancestors. It was he who introduced the count of a thousand years as a Great Period, and of centuries and periods of fifty years, equivalent to the biblical Jubilee. It was the Capac who had installed this calendar and chronology, Inti Capac Yupanqui, who completed the temple and introduced in it the worship of the great god *Illa Tici Vira Cocha,* meaning "Bright Beginner, Creator of the Waters."

In the reign of the twelfth Capac, news reached Cuzco of the disembarking on the coast of "some men of great stature... giants who were settling on the whole coast" and, possessing metal implements, were despoiling the land. After a time they began to go into the mountains; fortunately, they provoked the wrath of the Great God and he destroyed them with a heavenly fire.

Relieved of the dangers, the people forgot the commandments and the rites of worship. "Good laws and customs" were abandoned, and this did not go unnoticed by the Creator. In punishment, he hid the sun from the land; "there was no dawn for twenty hours." There was a great outcry among the people and prayers and sacrifices were offered at the temple, until (after twenty hours) the sun reappeared. The king immediately thereafter reintroduced laws of conduct and rites of worship.

The fortieth Capac on the throne of Cuzco established an academy for the study of astronomy and astrology and determined the equinoxes. The fifth year of his reign, Montesinos calculated, was the twenty-five hundredth year from Point Zero which, he assumed, was the Deluge. It was also the two thousandth year since kingship had begun at Cuzco; in celebration whereof the king was granted a new title, *Pachacuti* (Reformer). His successors also promoted the study of astronomy; one of them introduced a leap year of one extra day every four years and one extra year every four hundred years.

In the reign of the fifty-eighth monarch, "when the Fourth Sun was completed," the count was 2,900 years since the "Deluge." It was, Montesinos calculated, the year in which Jesus Christ was born.

That first Cuzco empire, begun by the Sons of the Sun and continued by priest-kings, came to a bitter end in the reign of the sixty-second monarch. In his time there occurred "marvels and portents." The earth shook with endless earthquakes, the skies were filled with comets, omens of a coming destruction. Tribes and peoples began to rush to and fro, clashing with their neighbors. Invaders came from the coast, even from across the Andes. Great battles ensued; in one of them the king was felled by an arrow and his army fled in panic; only five hundred warriors survived the battles.

"Thus was the government of the Peruvian monarchy lost and destroyed," Montesinos wrote, "and the knowledge of letters was lost."

The few remaining followers left Cuzco, leaving behind only a handful of priests to take care of the temple. They took along with them the dead king's young son, just a boy, and found refuge in a mountain hideaway called Tampu-Tocco; it was the place where, from a cave, the first semidivine couple exited to establish the Andean kingdom. When the boy came of age, he was proclaimed the first monarch of the Tampu-Tocco dynasty. It lasted almost a thousand years, from the beginning of the second to the eleventh centuries A.D.

During those many centuries of exile, knowledge dwindled and writing was forgotten. In the reign of the seventy-eighth monarch, when the milestone of 3,500 years since the Beginning was reached, a certain person began to revive the art of writing. It was then that the king received a warning from the priests concerning the invention of letters. It was the knowledge of writing, their message explained, that was the cause of the pestilences and accursations that had brought kingship in Cuzco to an end. The god's wish was "that no one ought to use the letters or resuscicate them, for from their employment great harm would come [again]." Therefore the king commanded "by law, under the pain of death, that no one should traffic in *quilcas*, which were the parchments and leaves of trees on which they used to write, nor should use any sort of letters." Instead,he introduced the use of *quipos*, the strands of colored cords that had served since then for chronological purposes.

In the reign of the ninetieth monarch, the fourth millennium from Point Zero was completed. By then the monarchy at Tampu-Tocco was weak and ineffective. The tribes loyal to it were subject to raids and invasions by neighbors. Tribal chiefs ceased paying homage to the central authority. Customs were corrupted, abominations proliferated. In such circumstances a princess of the original blood of the Sons of the Sun, one Mama Ciboca, rose to the occasion. She announced that her young son, who was so handsome that his admirers nicknamed him *Inca,* was destined to regain the throne at the old capital, Cuzco. In a miraculous way he disappeared and returned clothed in golden robes, claiming that the Sun God had taken him aloft, instructed him in secret knowledge, and told him to lead the people back to Cuzco. His name was Rocca; he was the first of the Inca dynasty that came to an ignomious end in the hands of the Spaniards.

Attempting to put these events in an orderly time frame, Montesinos stated at certain intervals that a period called "Sun" had passed or begun. While what length of a period (in years) he was considering is not at all certain, it would appear that he had in mind Andean legends of several "Suns" in the people's past.

Although scholars had held—less so nowadays—that there had been no contact whatsoever between the Mesoamerican and South American civilizations, the latter sound hardly differ-

ent from the Aztec and Maya notions of five Suns. Indeed, all
the Old World civilizations had recollections of past ages, of
eras when the gods reigned alone, followed by demigods and
heroes, and then just mortals. Sumerian texts called King Lists
recorded a line of divine lords followed by demigods who
reigned a total of 432,000 years before the Deluge, then listed
the kings that reigned thereafter through times that are by now
considered historical and whose data has been verified and
found accurate. The Egyptian king lists, as composed by the
priest-historian Manetho, listed a dynasty of twelve gods that
began some 10,000 years before the Deluge; it was followed by
gods and demigods until, circa 3100 B.C., the pharaohs ascended
the throne of Egypt. Again, where his data could be verified
against historical records, it was found to be accurate.

Montesinos found such notions in the Peruvian collective
lore, confirming the reports of other chroniclers that the Incas
believed that theirs was the Fifth Age or Sun. The First Age was
that of Viracochas, gods who were white and bearded. The Second age was that of the giants; some of them were not benevolent, and there had been conflicts between the gods and the
giants. Then followed the Age of Primitive Man, of uncultured
human beings. The Fourth Age was the age of heroes, men who
were demigods. And then there was the Fifth Age, the age of
human kings, of whom the Incas were last in line.

Montesinos also placed the Andean chronology in the European frame by relating it to a certain Point Zero (he thought it
had to be the Deluge) and—most clearly—to the birth of
Christ. The two time sequences, he wrote, coincided in the
reign of the fifty-eighth monarch: the twenty-nine hundredth
year from Point Zero was the "first year of Jesus Christ." The
Peruvian monarchies, he wrote, began 500 years after Point
Zero, i.e., in 2400 B.C.

The problem scholars have with the history and chronology
of Montesinos is thus not lack of clarity, but its conclusion that
kingship and urban civilization began—at Cuzco—almost 3,500
years before the Incas. That civilization, according to the information amassed by Montesinos and those on whose work he
had relied, possessed writing, included astronomy among its
sciences, and had a calendar long enough to require its periodic
reform. All this (and more) was possessed by the Sumerian civilization that blossomed out circa 3800 B.C. and by the Egyptian
civilization that followed circa 3100 B.C. Another offshoot of the
Sumerian civilization, that of the Indus Valley, came about circa
2900 B.C.

Why was it not possible for such trifold developments to

occur a fourth time, in the Andes? Impossible—if there had been no contacts between the Old and New Worlds. Possible, if the same grantors of all knowledge, the gods, were the same and were present all over the Earth.

Incredible as our conclusion must sound, happily it can be proven.

The first test of the veracity of the events and chronologies compiled by Montesinos had already taken place.

A key element in the Montesinos presentation is the existence of an ancient empire, of a line of kings at Cuzco who were finally forced to leave the capital and seek refuge in a secluded mountain place called Tampu-Tocco. The interregnum lasted a thousand years; finally a young man of noble birth was chosen to lead the people back to Cuzco and establish the Inca dynasty.

Was there a Tampu-Tocco, and was it a place identifiable by the landmarks given by Montesinos? The question intrigued many. In 1911, searching for lost Inca cities, Hiram Bingham of Yale University found the place; it is now called Machu Picchu.

Bingham was not looking for Tampu-Tocco when he set out on his first expedition; but after repeatedly going back and exhaustive excavations over more than two decades, he concluded that Machu Picchu was indeed the lost interim capital of the Old Empire. His descriptions of the place, still the most comprehensive, are in his books *Machu Picchu, a Citadel of the Incas* and *The Lost City of the Incas.*

The principal reason for believing that Machu Picchu is the legendary Tampu-Tocco is the clue of the Three Windows. Montesinos recorded that "at the place of his birth Inca Rocca ordered works to be executed, consisting of a masonry wall with three windows, which were the emblem of the house of his fathers, of whom he descended." The name of the place to which the royal house had gone from the stricken capital Cuzco meant "Haven of the Three Windows."

That a place should become known for its windows should not be surprising, since no house in Cuzco, from the humblest to the grandest, had windows. That a place should become known for a specific number of windows—three—could only be the result of the uniqueness, antiquity, or sanctity of the actual existence of such a structure. This was true of Tampu-Tocco, where according to the legends a structure with three windows played a role in the emergence of tribes and the ancient empire in Peru's beginning, a structure that had therefore become "the emblem of the house of his fathers of whom [Inca Rocca] had descended."

The legend, and the legendary place, featured in the tale of the Ayar brothers. As told by Pedro Sarmiento de Gamboa (*Historia General Llamada Yndica*) and other early chroniclers, the four Ayar brothers and their four sisters, having been created by the god Viracocha at Lake Titicaca, reached or were placed by the god in Tampu-Tocco, whence "they came out of said window by order of Tici-Viracocha, declaring that Viracocha created them to be lords."

The oldest of the brothers, Manco Capac, carried with him a sacred emblem in the image of a falcon, and also bore a golden rod that the god had given him with which to locate the right place for the future capital, Cuzco. The journey of the four brother-sister couples began peacefully; but soon jealousies developed. On the pretext that certain treasures were left behind in a cave in Tampu-Tocco, the second brother, Ayar Cachi, was sent back to retrieve them. This however was only a ruse by the three brothers to imprison him in the cave, where he was turned into a stone.

According to these tales, then, Tampu-Tocco dates from the very early times; "the myth of the Ayars," H. B. Alexander wrote in *Latin American Mythology,* "hearkens back to the Megalithic Age and to the cosmogonies associated with Titicaca." When the exiles left Cuzco, they went to a place already in existence, a place where a structure with three windows had already played a role in even earlier events. It is with this understanding that we can now proceed to visit Machu Picchu, for a structure whose wall has three windows has indeed been found there, and nowhere else.

"Machu Picchu, or Great Picchu, is the Quichua name of a sharp peak which rises ten thousand feet above the sea and four thousand feet above the roaring rapids of the Urubamba River near the bridge of San Miguel, two hard days' journey north of Cuzco," Bingham wrote. "Northwest of Machu Picchu is another beautiful peak surrounded by magnificent precipices, called Huayna Picchu, or Lesser Picchu. On the narrow ridge between the two peaks are the ruins of an Inca city whose name has been lost in the shadows of the past.... It is possible that they represent two ancient sites, Tampu-Tocco, the birthplace of the first Inca, and Vilcabamba Viejo."

Nowadays the journey from Cuzco to Machu Picchu, a distance of some seventy-five miles as the crow flies, does not require the two days' hard journey described by Bingham just to get there. A train that chugs its way up then down mountains, passing through tunnels and over bridges and hugging the mountainsides flanking the Urubamba river, gets there in under four hours. Another half-hour cliffhanger bus ride up from the railway station, and the city is reached. The breathtaking view is exactly as Bingham described it. In the saddle between the two peaks, houses, palaces, temples—all roofless now—stand surrounded by terraces that cling to the mountainsides, ready for cultivation. The peak of Huayna Picchu rises on the northwest as a sentinel (Fig. 72); beyond it and all around, peak competes with peak as far as the eye can see. Down below the Urubamba river forms a horseshoe gorge half encircling the city's perch, its gushing waters cutting a whitish path among the jungle's emerald green.

As befits a city that, we believe, at first served as a model for Cuzco and then emulated it, Machu Picchu too consisted of twelve wards or groups of structures. The royal-priestly groupings are on the west and the residential-functional ones (occupied mostly by the Virgins and clan hierarchies) on the east, separated by a series of wide terraces. The common people who tilled and cultivated the terraced mountainsides lived outside the city and in the surrounding countryside (many such hamlets have been found since the initial discovery by Bingham).

Figure 72

Several construction styles, as at Cuzco and other archaeological sites, suggest different phases of occupation. The dwelling houses are built mostly of fieldstones held together with mortar. The royal residences are built of ashlars laid in courses, as finely cut and dressed as any in Cuzco. Then there is one structure where the workmanship is so perfect as to be unmatched; and there are the polygonal megalithic stone blocks. In many instances, the remains from the earlier Megalithic Age and Ancient Empire times have remained as was; in others, later construction atop earlier courses is obvious.

While the eastern wards occupied every available square foot of mountaintop and extended from the city's wall in the south as far north as the terrain permitted and eastward into the agricultural and burial terraces, the western group of wards, that also began at the wall, extended northward only to the border of a Sacred Plaza—as though an unseen line marked off hallowed ground that could not be encroached upon.

Beyond that unseen demarcation line, and facing the great terraced plaza to the east, stand the remains of what Bingham has identified as the Sacred Plaza, mainly "because on two sides of it are the largest temples," one of them with the crucial three windows. It is here, in the construction of what Bingham had named the Temple of the Three Windows and, adjoining it in the Sacred Plaza, the Principal Temple, that cyclopean polygonal stone blocks have been used at the site. The manner in which they were cut, shaped, dressed, and fitted together without mortar puts them in a class with the cyclopean stone blocks and megalithic structures of Sacsahuaman; and, surpassing the polygonality of anything seen in Cuzco, one of the stone blocks here has thirty-two angles.

The Temple of the Three Windows stands at the eastern edge of the Sacred Plaza; the cyclopean stone blocks of its eastern wall raise it well above the terraced level to its west (Fig. 73), affording an unimpeded eastward view through the three windows (Fig. 74). Trapezoid in shape, their sills are cut out of the cyclopean stones that form the wall itself. As at Sacsahuaman and Cuzco, this cutting, shaping, and angling of the hard granite stones was done as though they were soft putty; here too, the white granite stone blocks had to be brought from great distances, through rough terrain and rivers, down valleys and up mountains.

The Temple of the Three Windows has only three walls, its western side being completely open; there it faces a stone pillar, about seven feet high (see Fig. 74). Bingham surmised that it might have supported a roof, which (he admitted) would have

Figure 73

been "a device not found in any other building." It is our opinion that the pillar, in conjunction with the three windows, served astronomical sighting purposes.

Facing the Sacred Plaza on the north is the structure Bingham had named the Principal Temple; it too has only three walls, some twelve feet high. They rest upon or are constructed of cyclopean stone blocks; the western wall, for example, is constructed of just two giant stone blocks held together by a T-shaped stone. A huge monolith, measuring fourteen by five by three feet, rests against the central north wall in which seven niches imitate (but are not) trapezoid windows (Fig. 75).

Winding steps lead from the northern edge of the Sacred

Figure 74

Figure 75

Plaza up a hill whose top was flattened to serve as a platform for the *Intihuatana,* a stone cut with great precision to observe and measure the movements of the Sun (Fig. 76). The name meant "That Which Binds the Sun," and it is assumed that it helped determine the solstices, when the Sun moves farthest away to the north or south, at which time rites were held to "bind the Sun" and make it return, lest it keep going away and disappear, returning the Earth to a darkness that had occurred once before according to the legends.

At the opposite end of the sacred-royal western part of Machu Picchu, just south of the royal ward, rises the other magnificent (and unusual) edifice of the city. Called the *Torreon* for its semicircular shape, it is built of ashlars—cut, shaped, and dressed stones—of rarely seen perfection, matched in a way only by the ashlars of the semicircular wall that embraced the Holy of Holies in Cuzco. The semicircular wall, which is

Figure 76

reached by seven steps (Fig. 77), creates its own sacred enclosure at the center of which there is a rock that has been cut and
shaped and incised with grooves. Bingham found evidence that
this rock and the masonry walls near it were subjected to periodic fires, and concluded that the rock and the enclosure were
used for sacrifices and other rituals connected with the veneration of the rock.

(This sacred rock within a special structure brings to mind
the sacred rock that forms the heart of the Temple Mount in
Jerusalem, as well as the Qua'abah, the black stone that is hidden within the holiest Moslem enclosure in Mecca.)

The sanctity of the rock in Machu Picchu stems not from its
protruding top, but from what lies below. It is a huge natural
rock inside of which there is a cave that has been enlarged and
shaped artificially to precise geometric forms that look like (but
are not) stairs, seats, ledges, and posts (Fig. 78). Additionally,
the interior has been improved with masonry of white granite
ashlars of the purest color and grain. Niches and stone nobbins

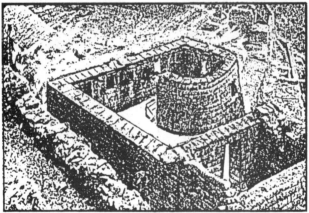

Figure 77

add to the interior complexity. Bingham surmised that the original natural cave was enlarged and enhanced to hold royal mummies, brought there because the place was sacred. But why was it sacred, and important for depositing the deceased kings, to begin with?

The question takes us back to the legend of the Ayar brothers, one of whom was imprisoned in a cave at the Haven of the Three Windows. If the Temple of the Three Windows was the legendary one, and the cave so too, then the legends con-

Figure 78

firm the site and the site is confirmed as the legendary Tampu-Tocco.

Sarmiento, one of the Spanish chroniclers who was himself a conquistador, reported in his *History of the Incas* a local tradition that the ninth Inca (circa A.D. 1340), "being curious about the things of antiquity and wishing to perpetuate his name, went personally to the mountain of Tampu-Tocco... and there entered the cave whence it is held for certain that Manco Capac and his brethren came when they marched into Cuzco for the very first time.... After he had made a thorough inspection, he venerated the place by rituals and sacrifices, and placed doors of gold on the window of Capac Tocco, and ordered that from that time onward the locality should be venerated by all, making it a sacred prayer place for sacrifices and oracles. Having done this, he returned to Cuzco."

The subject of this report, the ninth Inca, was called Titu Manco Capac; he was given the additional title *Pachacutec* ("Reformer") because, after his return from Tampu-Tocco, he reformed the calendar. So, like the Three Windows and the Intihuatana, the Sacred Rock and the *Torreon* affirm the existence of Tampu-Tocco, the tale of the Ayar brothers, the pre-Inca reigns during the ancient empire, and the knowledge of astronomy and the calendar—key elements in the history and chronology put together by Montesinos.

The veracity of Montesinos's data can be additionally enchanced if he was right regarding the existence of writing in ancient empire times. We find that Cieza de Leon held the same view, stating that "in the epoch preceding the Inca emperors there had been writing in Peru . . . on leaves, skins, cloth and stones."

Many South American scholars now join the early chroniclers in believing that the natives of those lands had one or more forms of writing in antiquity.

Numerous studies report petroglyphs ("stone writings") found throughout these lands that display, to varying degrees, pictographic or glyphic writing. Rafael Larco Hoyle, for example (*La Escritura Peruana Pre-Incana*), suggested with the aid of depictions that coastal people as far as Paracas possessed glyphic writing akin to that of the Maya. Arthur Posnansky, the leading explorer of Tiahuanacu, produced voluminous studies showing that the carvings on the monuments there were pictographic-ideographic writing—a step before phonetic script. And a well-known find, the Stone of Calango now on display at the Lima Museum (Fig. 79), suggests a combination of pictographs with a phonetic, perhaps even alphabetic, script.

Figure 79

One of the greatest early explorers of South America, Alexander de Humboldt, dealt with the subject in his major work *Vues des Cordilléres et Monumens des Peuples Indigenes de l'Amerique* (1824). "It has been recently put in doubt," he wrote, "that the Peruvians had, besides *Quippus,* knowledge of a sign script. A passage in *L'Origin de los Indios del Nuevo Mundo* (Valencia, 1610), page 91, leaves no doubt in this regard." After speaking of the Mexican hieroglyphs, Father Garcia adds: "at the start of the conquest, the Indians of Peru confessed themselves by painting characters that listed the Ten Commandments and the transgressions committed against them." It is possible to conclude that the Peruvians possessed the use of a picture script, but that their symbols were coarser than the Mexican heiroglyphs, and that generally the people availed themselves of the *quippus.*

Humboldt also reported that when he was in Lima, he heard of a missionary named Narcisse Gilbar who had found, among the Panos Indians of the Ucayale river north of Lima, a book of folded leaves, similar to such as had been used by the Aztecs in Mexico; but no one in Lima could read it. "It was said that the Indians told the Missionary that the book recorded ancient wars and voyages."

Writing in 1855, Ribero and von Tschudi reported various other discoveries and concluded that there had indeed been another method of writing in Peru besides the quipos. Writing separately about his own travels, von Tschudi (in *Reisen durch Südamerika*) describes his excitement at being shown a photograph of a skin-parchment with hieroglyphic markings. He found the actual parchment in the museum of La Paz, Bolivia, and made a copy of the writing on it (Fig. 80a). "These symbols made on me the greatest astonishing effect," he wrote, "and I stayed in front of this skin for hours," trying to decipher "the labyrinth" of this writing. He determined that the writing started at left, then continued on the second line from the right, then resumed in the third line from the left again, and so on in a serpentine manner. He also concluded that it was written at the time when the Sun was worshiped; but that was as far as he got.

He traced the inscription to its place of origin on the shores of Lake Titicaca. The padre at the Mission Church at the lakeside village Copacabana confirmed that such writing was known in the area, but attributed it to a post-Conquest period. The explanation was clearly unsatisfactory, since if the Indians would not have had their own script, they would have adopted the Spaniards' Latin script to express themselves. Even if this hieroglyphic writing evolved after the Conquest, Jorge Cornejo

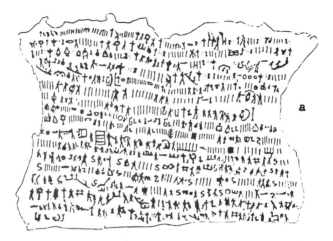

Figure 80

Bouroncle wrote (*La Idolatria en el antiguo Peru*), "its origin must have been more remote."

Arthur Posansky (*Guia general Illustrada de Tiahuanacu*) found additional inscriptions in this script on rocks on the two sacred islands of Lake Titicaca. He pointed out that it was of a kind with enigmatic inscriptions found on Easter Island (Fig. 80b)—a conclusion with which scholars now generally agree. But the Easter Island script is known to belong to the family of Indo-European scripts of the Indus Valley *and of the Hittites*. A common feature to all of them (including the Lake Titicaca inscriptions) is their "as the ox ploughs" system: the writing on the first line begins on the left and ends on the right; it continues on the second line beginning on the right, ending on the left; the third line then begins on the left, and so on.

Without going now into the question of how did a script emulating that of the Hittites (Fig. 80c) reach Lake Titicaca, it seems that the existence of one or more forms of writing in ancient Peru has been confirmed. On this count too, the information provided by Montesinos proves correct.

If in spite of all this the reader still finds it difficult to accept the inevitable conclusion, that there had indeed been an Old World type civilization in the Andes circa 2400 B.C., there is additional evidence.

Completely ignored by scholars as a valid clue has been the repeated statement in the Andean legends that there occurred a frightening darkness in long-ago times. No one has wondered whether this was the same darkness—the nonappearance of the sun when it was due—of which the Mexican legends speak in the tale of Teotihuacan and its pyramids. For if there had indeed been such a phenomenon, that the sun failed to rise and the night was endless, then it would have been observed throughout the Americas.

The Mexican collective recollections and the Andean ones seem to corroborate each other on this point, and thus uphold the veracity of each other, as two witnesses to the same event.

But if even this is not convincing enough, we will call upon the Bible in evidence, and upon none other than Joshua to be the witness.

According to Montesinos and other chroniclers, the most unusual event took place in the reign of Titu Yupanqui Pachacuti II, the fifteenth monarch in Ancient Empire times. It was in the third year of his reign, when "good customs were forgotten and people were given to all manner of vice," that "there was no dawn for twenty hours." In other words, the night did not end when it usually does and sunrise was delayed for twenty hours. After a great outcry, confessions of sins, sacrifices, and prayers, the sun finally rose.

This could not have been an eclipse: it was not that the shining sun was obscured by a shadow. Besides, no eclipse lasts so long, and the Peruvians were cognizant of such periodic events. The tale does not say that the sun disappeared; it says that it did not rise—"there was no dawn"—for twenty hours.

It was as though the sun, wherever it was hiding, suddenly stood still.

If the Andean recollection is true, then somewhere else—on the opposite side of the world—the DAY had to last just as long, not ending when it should have ended but lasting some twenty hours longer.

Incredibly, such an event is recorded, and in no better place than in the Bible itself. It was as the Israelites, under the leadership of Joshua, had crossed the Jordan River into their Promised Land and had successfullly taken the fortified cities of Jericho and Ai. It was then that all the Amorite kings formed an alliance to put up a combined force against the Israelites. A great battle ensued in the valley of Ajalon, near the city of Gibeon. It began with an Israelite night attack that put the Canaanites into flight. By sunrise, as the Canaanite forces regrouped near Beth-Horon, the Lord God "cast down great stones from heaven upon them . . . and they died; there were more of them who had died from the hailstones than those whom the Israelites slew with the sword."

Then Joshua spoke unto Yahweh,
on the day when Yahweh delivered the Amorites
unto the Children of Israel, saying:
"In the sight of the Israelites,
let the Sun stand still in Gibeon
and the Moon in the valley of Ajalon."

And the Sun stood still, and the Moon stayed,
until the people had avenged themselves of the enemies.
Indeed it is all written in the Book of Jashar:
The Sun stood still in the midst of the skies
and it hastened not to go down
about a whole day.

Scholars have struggled for generations with this tale in Chapter 10 of the Book of Joshua. Some discount it as mere fiction; others see in it echoes of a myth; still others seek to explain it in terms of an unusually prolonged eclipse of the sun. But not only are such long eclipses unknown; the tale does not speak of the disappearance of the sun. On the contrary, it relates to an event when the sun continued to be seen, to hang on in the skies, for "about a whole day"—say, twenty hours?

The incident, whose uniqueness is recognized in the Bible ("There was no day like that before or after"), taking place on the opposite side of the Earth relative to the Andes, thus describes a phenomenon that was the opposite of what had happened in the Andes. In Canaan the sun did not set for some twenty hours; in the Andes, the sun did not rise for the same length of time.

Do not the two tales, then, describe the same event, and by coming from different sides of the Earth attest to its factuality?

What the occurrence was is still a puzzle. The only biblical clue is the mention of the great stones falling from the skies. Since we know that the tales describe not a standstill by the sun (and moon) but a disruption of Earth's rotation on its axis, a possible explanation is that a comet had come too close to Earth, disintegrating in the process. Since some comets orbit the sun in a clockwise direction that is opposite to the orbital direction of the Earth and the other planets, such a kinetic force could have conceivably counteracted temporarily the Earth's rotation and slowed it down.

Whatever the precise cause of the phenomenon, what we are concerned with here is its timing. The generally accepted date for the Exodus has been the thirteenth century B.C. (circa 1230 B.C.), and scholars who argued for a date earlier by some two centuries found themselves in a minority. Still, we have concluded in our previous writings (see *The Wars of Gods and Men*) that a date of 1433 B.C. would fit the event, as well as the biblical tales of the Hebrew patriarchs, perfectly into known contemporary events and chronologies of Mesopotamia and Egypt. Subsequent to the publication of our conclusions (in 1985), two eminent biblical scholars and archaeologists, John J. Bimson and David Livingston, reached after an exhaustive study (*Biblical Archaeology Review,* September/October 1987) the conclusion that the Exodus took place about 1460 B.C. Apart from their own archaeological findings and an analysis of the Bronze Age periods in the ancient Near East, the biblical data and calculation process that they have employed was the very same process we had used two years earlier. (We had also explained then why we had chosen to reconcile two lines of biblical data by dating the Exodus in 1433 B.C. rather than 1460 B.C.).

Since the Israelites wandered in the deserts of Sinai for forty years, the entry into Canaan took place in 1393 B.C.; the occurrence observed by Joshua happened soon thereafter.

The question now is: did the opposite phenomenon, the prolonged night, occur in the Andes at the same time?

Unfortunately, the shape in which the writings of Montesinos have reached modern scholars leaves some gaps in the data concerning lengths of reign of each monarch, and we will have to obtain the answer in a roundabout way. The event, Montesinos advises, occurred in the third year of the reign of Titu Yupanqui Pachacuti II. To pinpoint his time we will have to calculate from both ends. We are told that the first 1,000 years from Point Zero were completed in the reign of the fourth monarch, i.e., in 1900 B.C.; and that the thirty-second king reigned 2,070 years from Point Zero, i.e., in 830 B.C.

When did the fifteenth monarch reign? The available data suggests that the nine kings that separated the fourth and fifteenth monarch reigned a total of about 500 years, placing Titu Yupanqui Pachacuti II at about 1400 B.C. Calculating backward from the thirty-second monarch (830 B.C.), we arrive at 564 as the number of intervening years, giving us a date of 1394 B.C. for Titu Yupanqui Pachacuti II.

Either way, we arrive at a date for the Andean event that coincidences with the biblical date and the event's date at Teoti-huacan.

The hard-hitting conclusion is clear:

THE DAY THE SUN STOOD STILL IN CANAAN WAS THE NIGHT WITHOUT SUNRISE IN THE AMERICAS.

The occurrence, thus verified, stands out as irrefutable proof of the veracity of Andean recollections of an Ancient Empire that began when the gods granted Mankind the golden wand at Lake Titicaca.

8

THE WAYS OF HEAVEN

The heavens bespeak the glory of the Lord
and the vault of heaven reveals his handiwork.
One day uttereth to another,
night unto night imparts knowledge—
without words, without speaking,
without their voice being heard.
Throughout the Earth their line has gone,
to the ends of the world is their message;
in them He hath made the Sun pitch its tent.

Thus did the biblical Psalmist describe the marvels of the heavens and the miracle of days and nights following each other, as the Earth rotates on its axis (the biblical "line" that goes through the Earth) and orbits the Sun that sits at the center of all (as a potentate in his tent). "The day is thine and the night too; thou hast established the luminary and the Sun ... Summer and winter by thee were created."

For millennia, ever since Man acquired civilization, astronomer-priests looked to the heavens for guidance to Man on Earth—from the ziggurats of Sumer and Babylon, the temples of Egypt, the stone circle of Stonehenge or the Caracol at Chichén Itzá. Complex celestial motions of the stars and planets have been observed, calculated, recorded; and to make that possible, the ziggurats and temples and observatories were aligned to precise celestial orientations and provided with apertures and other structural features that let the light of the Sun or another star enter as a beam at equinox or solstice times.

Why did Man go to such lengths?—to see what, to determine what?

It is customary among scholars to attribute ancient man's astronomical endeavors to the needs of an agricultural society for a calendar telling it when to sow and when to reap. This expla-

155

nation has been taken for granted far too long. A farmer tilling the land year after year can judge the change of seasons and the coming of rains better than an astronomer, and has the ground-hog to tell him a thing or two. The fact is that wherever pockets of primitive societies (subsisting on agriculture) have been found in remote parts of the world, they have lived and fed themselves for generations without astronomers and a precise calendar. It is also an established fact that the calendar was de-vised in antiquity by an urban, not an agricultural, society.

A simple sun clock, a gnomon, can provide enough daily and seasonal information if one could not have survived without it. Yet ancient man studied the heavens and aligned his temples toward stars and planets, and linked his calendar and festivals not to the ground upon which he stood but to the ways of heaven. Why? Because the calendar was devised not for agricul-tural but for religious purposes. Not to benefit mankind, but to venerate the gods. And the gods, according to the first-ever religion and the people who gave us the calendar, came from the heavens.

One ought to read and reread the Pslamist's verses to realize that the observation of the wonders of the celestial phenomena had nothing to do with tilling the land or herding the cattle; it had to do with the veneration of the Lord of All. And there is no way to understand that better than to go back to Sumer; for it was there, some 6,000 years ago, that astronomy, the calen-dar, and a religion linking Earth with the Heavens had their beginning. It was knowledge, the Sumerians asserted, that was given them by the Anunnaki ("Those Who from Heaven to Earth Came") who had come to Earth from their planet, Ni-biru. Nibiru, they said, was the twelfth member of the Solar System, and that is why the celestial band was divided into twelve houses, the year into twelve months. Earth was the sev-enth planet (counting from the outside in); and therefore as twelve was a hallowed celestial number, seven was a sacred ter-restrial one.

The Anunnaki, the Sumerians wrote upon numerous clay tablets, had come to Earth long before the Deluge. In *The 12th Planet* we determined that it happened 432,000 years before the Deluge—a period equivalent to 120 orbits of Nibiru, orbits that though to the Anunnaki represent but a single year of theirs are equivalent to 3,600 Earth-years. They came and went between Nibiru and Earth each time their planet came closer to the Sun (and Earth) as it passed between Jupiter and Mars; and there is no doubt whatsoever that the Sumerians began to observe the heavens not to know when to sow, but in order to see and celebrate the return of the celestial Lord.

This, we believe, is why Man became an astronomer. This is why, as time passed and Nibiru itself could no longer be observed, Man sought signs and omens in the phenomena that could be seen, and astronomy bred astrology. And if the astronomical orientations and alignments and celestial divisions that began in Sumer could also be found in the Andes, an irrefutable link would be proven.

Some time early in the fourth millennium B.C., according to Sumerian texts, the ruler of Nibiru, Anu, and his spouse Antu paid a visit to Earth. A brand-new sacred precinct with a temple-tower was built in their honor at a place that later came to be known as Uruk (the biblical Erech). A text has been preserved on clay tablets describing their night there. In the evening a ceremonial meal began with a ritual washing of the hands on a celestial signal—the appearance of Jupiter, Venus, Mercury, Saturn, Mars, and the Moon. Then the first part of the meal was served, followed by a pause. While a group of priests began to chant the hymn *Kakkab Anu Etellu Shamame* ("The Planet of Anu Rises in the Skies"), an astronomer-priest, at the "topmost stage of the tower of the temple" watched for the appearance of the Planet of Anu, Nibiru. When the planet was sighted, the priests broke out in singing the composition "To the One Who Grows Bright, the Heavenly Planet of the Lord Anu," and the psalm "The Creator's Image Has Arisen." A bonfire was lit to signal the moment and to pass the news to neighboring towns. Before the night was over the whole land was ablaze with bonfires; and in the morning, prayers of thanksgiving were recited.

The care and great astronomical knowledge that were required for building temples in Sumer are evident from the inscriptions of the Sumerian King Gudea (circa 2200 B.C.). First there appeared to him "a man who shone like the heaven," who was standing beside a "divine bird." This being, Gudea wrote, "who by the crown on his head was obviously a god," turned out to have been the god Ningirsu. He was accompanied by a goddess who "held the tablet of her favorable star of the heavens." In her other hand she held "a holy stylus" with which she pointed out to the king "the favorable planet." A third human-looking god held in his hands a tablet made of precious stone, on which the plan of the temple was drawn. One of Gudea's statues shows him seated with this tablet on his knees. The divine drawing can be clearly seen; it provides the floor plan of the temple and a scale by which to erect the seven stages, one shorter than the other as they rise. And it was, the text indicates, not a Solar but a Start + Planet Temple.

The sophisticated astronomical knowledge displayed by the Sumerians was not limited to the building of temples. As we have brought out in our previous volumes and as is now generally acknowledged, it was in Sumer that all the concepts and principles of modern spherical astronomy were laid out. The list can begin with the division of a circle into 360 degrees, the devising of zenith, horizon, and other astronomical concepts and terminologies, and end with the grouping of stars into constellations, the devising, naming, and pictorial depiction of the zodiac and its twelve houses, and the recognition of the phenomenon of Precession—the retardation, by about one degree every seventy-two years, of Earth's motion around the sun.

Whereas the Planet of the Gods, Nibiru, appeared and disappeared in the course of its 3,600 Earth-years orbit, Mankind on Earth could count the passage of time only in terms of its own orbit around the Sun. After the phenomenon of day and night the easiest to recognize are the seasons. As the simplest and abundant stone circles attest, it was easy to establish markers delineating the four points in the Earth/Sun relationship: the Sun's apparent rising higher in the skies and lingering longer as winter gives way to spring; a point when day and night appear equal; then the gradual distancing of the Sun as days grow shorter and the temperature begins to drop. As cold and darkness increase and it seems that the Sun may vanish altogether, it hesitates, stops, and begins to come back; and the whole cycle is repeated—a new year has begun. Thus were the four occurrences in the Earth/Sun cycle established: the summer and winter solstices ("solar standstills") when the Sun reaches its outermost positions north and south, and the spring and autumn equinoxes (when day and night are equal).

To relate this apparent movement of the sun in relation to Earth when it is actually Earth that orbits around the Sun—a fact known to and depicted by the Sumerians—it was necessary to provide the observer on Earth with a celestial point of reference. This was achieved by dividing the heavens, the great circle formed by the Earth around the Sun, into twelve parts—the twelve houses of the Zodiac, each with its own group of discernible stars (the constellations). A point was chosen—the spring equinox—and the zodiac house in which the Sun was seen at that moment was declared the first day of the first month of the new year. This, all research of the earliest records show, was in the zodiac house or Age of Taurus.

But then came Precession to spoil the arrangement. Because Earth's axis is inclined in relation to its orbital plane around the Sun (23.5 degrees nowadays) and it spins as a top, the axis points to a shifting celestial spot, forming a great imaginary circle in the heavens that takes 25,920 years to complete. That means that the selected "fixed point," shifting one degree every 72 years, shifts completely from one zodiac house to another every 2,160 years. Some two millennia after the calendar was begun in Sumer, it was necessary to order a reform of the calendar and select as the fixed point the House of Aries. Our astrologers still chart their horoscopes based on the First Point of Aries, although our astronomers know that we have been almost two thousand years in the Age of Pisces (and are about to enter the Age of Aquarius).

The division of the grand celestial circle into twelve parts, in honor of the twelve members of the solar system and the matching pantheon of twelve "Olympian" gods, also brought the solar year into a close correlation with the periodicity of the Moon. But, since the lunar month falls short of filling the solar year exactly twelve times, complex intercalary methods were devised by which to add days once in a while so as to bring the twelve lunar months into alignment with the solar year.

By Babylonian times, in the second millennium B.C., temples required a triple alignment: to the new zodiac (Aries), to the matching four solar points (the most important of which, in Babylon, was the spring equinox), and to the lunar period. The principal temple of Babylon honoring its national god Marduk, the remains of which have been found in relatively good preservation, exemplifies all these astronomical principles. Texts have also been found that describe in architectural terms its twelve gates and seven stages, enabling scholars to reconstruct its serviceability as a sophisticated solar, lunar, planetary, and stellar observatory (Fig. 81).

That astronomy, combined with archaeology, can help date monuments, explain historical events, and define the celestial origins of religious beliefs, has been recongized fully only in recent years. It took almost a century for this realization to reach the level of a discipline called archaeoastronomy, for it was in 1894 that Sir Norman Lockyer (*The Dawn of Astronomy*) showed convincingly that at all times and almost everywhere— from the earliest shrines to the greatest cathedrals—the temples have been oriented astronomically. It is noteworthy that the idea had occurred to him due to "a remarkable thing: in Babylon, from the beginning of things, the sign for God was a star"; likewise, in Egypt, "in the hieroglyphic texts, three stars repre-

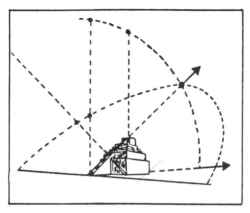

Figure 81

sented the plural 'gods.'" He also noted that in the Hindu pantheon, the most venerated temple gods were *Indra* ("The Day
Brought by the Sun") and *Ushas* ("Dawn"), gods related to the
rising of the Sun.

Focusing on Egypt, where ancient temples still stand and
their architecture and orientation can be studied in detail,
Lockyer recognized that temples in antiquity were either Sun
Temples or Star Temples. The former were temples whose axis
and ritual or calendric functions aligned them with either the
solstices of the equinoxes; the latter were temples not connected
with any of the four Sun points, but designed to observe and
venerate the appearance of a certain star on a certain day at a
certain point on the horizon. Lockyer found it amazing that the
older the temples were, the more sophisticated their astronomy
had been. Thus, at the beginning of their civilization, the Egyptians were able to combine a stellar aspect (the brightest star
then, Sirius) with a solar event (the summer solstice) and with
the annual rising of the Nile. Lockyer calculated that the triple
coincidence could happen only once in about 1,460 years, and
that the Egyptian Point Zero, when their calendrical count
began, was circa 3200 B.C.

But Lockyer's principal contribution to what (after almost a
century!) had evolved into archaeoastronomy was the realization that the orientation of ancient temples could be a clue to
the exact time of their construction. His major example was the
complex of temples at Thebes in Upper Egypt (Karnak). There
the older, more sophisticated orientation of the earliest sacred
cities (to the equinoxes) had given way to the easier orientation
toward the solstices. At Karnak the Great Temple to Amon-Ra

consisted of two rectangular structures built back-to-back on an east–west axis with a southern tilt (Fig. 82). The orientation was such that at solstice time a beam of sunlight would travel the whole length of a corridor (some five hundred feet long), passing from one part of the temple to the other between two obelisks. And, for a couple of minutes, the sunbeam would strike the Holy of Holies with a flash of light at the far end of the corridor, thereby signaling the moment when the first day of the first month began the new year.

But that precise moment was not constant; it kept shifting, resulting in the construction of subsequent temples with modified orientations. When the orientation was based on the equinoxes, the shifting was the varying stellar background against which the Sun was seen—the shift in zodiacal "ages" due to precession. But there appeared to be another and more profound shift affecting the solstices: the angle between the extremes to which the sun seemed to wander kept diminishing! Over time, the Sun's movements seemed subject to yet another phenomenon in the Earth/Sun relationship. This was the discov-

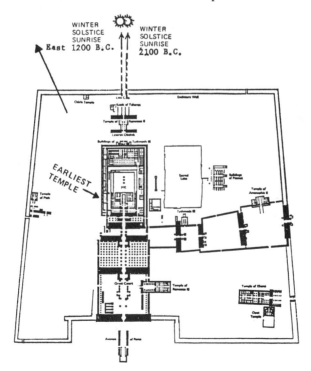

Figure 82

ery by astronomers that the Earth's obliquity, the tilt of its axis against its orbital path around the sun, has not always been its present one (somewhat under 23.5 degrees). The Earth's wobble changes this tilt by about 1 degree over 7,000 years or so, decreasing to perhaps 21 degrees before it starts to increase again to well over 24 degrees. Rolf Müller, who applied this fact to Andean archaeology (*Der Himmel über dem Menschen der Steinzeit* and other studies) calculated that if archaeological remains were oriented to a tilt of 24 degrees, it means they were built at least 4,000 years ago.

The application of this sophisticated and independent dating method is as important as the innovation of radiocarbon dating —perhaps even more so, since radiocarbon tests can be made only on organic materials (such as wood or charcoal) found in or near buildings, which does not preclude an unknown earlier age for the building; but archaeoastronomy can date the building itself and even the times when different parts were constructed.

Professor Müller, whose work we shall examine more closely, concluded that the perfect ashlar structures at Machu Picchu and Cuzco (as distant from the polygonal megalithic ones) are over 4,000 years old, thereby confirming the chronology of Montesinos. Such application of archaeoastronomy to Andean remains, as we shall see, has upset even more notions regarding the antiquity of civilization in the Americas.

Modern astronomers were slow to come to Machu Picchu, but eventually they did. It was in the 1930s that Rolf Müller, a professor of astronomy at the University of Potsdam, published his first studies dealing with the astronomical aspects of the ruins of Tiahuanacu, Cuzco, and Machu Picchu. His conclusions, establishing the great antiquity of these remains, and especially of the monuments of Tiahuanacu, nearly ruined his career.

At Machu Picchu Müller focused his attention on the Intihuatana atop the hill in the city's northwest and on the structure atop the sacred rock, for in both places he saw precise features that enabled him to figure out their purposes and use (*Die Intiwatana (Sonnenwarten) im Alten Peru* and other writings).

The Intihuatana, he realized, was placed atop the highest point of the city. It could command a view of the horizon in all directions; but walls of megalithic ashlars confined the view to only certain directions, ones that were in the mind of the builders. The Intihuatana and its base were carved out of a single natural rock, raising the pillar or stub of the artifact to the desired height. Both the stub and the base were carved and oriented in a precise manner (see Fig. 76). Müller determined that the various inclined surfaces and angled sides were so devised as to enable the determination of sunset at the summer solstice, sunrise at the winter solstice, and of the spring and autumn equinoxes.

Before his investigations at Machu Picchu Müller had researched at length the archaeoastronomical aspects of Tiahuanacu and at Cuzco. An old Spanish woodcut (Fig. 83a) suggested to him that the great Temple of the Sun at Cuzco was so constructed as to allow the sun's rays to shine directly into the Holy of Holies at the moment of sunrise on the day of the winter solstice. Applying the theories of Lockyer to the Coricancha, Müller was able to calculate and show how the pre-Columbian walls together with the circular Holy of Holies were able to serve the same purpose as the temples of Egypt (Fig. 83b).

The first aspect of the structure atop the sacred rock in

a

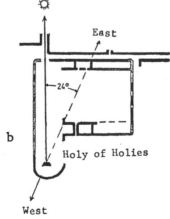

b

Figure 83

Machu Picchu that is obvious is its semicircular shape and the perfect ashlars of which it is built. These are obvious similarities to the semicircular Holy of Holies in Cuzco (we have already stated our opinion, that the one at Machu Picchu preceded that of Cuzco); and to Müller that suggested at once a similar function—that of determining the winter solstice. After establishing that the straight walls of this structure were oriented by its architects according to the geographic location and elevation above sea level of the site, he determined that the two trapezoid windows in the circular portion (Fig. 84) enabled an observer to see through them sunrise at the summer and winter solstices—4,000 years ago!

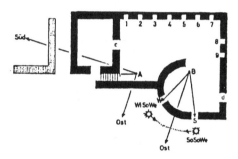

Figure 84

In the 1980s two astronomers from the Steward Observatory, University of Arizona, D. S. Dearborn and R. E. White (*Archaeoastronomy at Machu Picchu*) went over the same ground with more precise instruments. They confirmed the astronomical orientations of the Intihuatana and the two windows in the Torreon (where the viewing takes place from the protruding sacred rock along its grooves and edges). They did not join, however, in Müller's discussion of the structure's age. Neither they nor Müller attempted to trace back, to millennia ago, the lines of observation through the most ancient megalithic structure, the legendary Three Windows. There, we believe, the results would have been even more astounding.

Müller did, however, study the orientation of the megalithic walls in Cuzco. His conclusion, whose far-reaching implications have been ignored, was that "they are positioned for the era of 4000 B.C. to 2000 B.C." (*Sonne, Mond und Sterne über dem Reich der Inka*). This puts the age of the megalithic structures (at Cuzco, Sacsahuaman, and Machu Picchu, at least) in the 2,000-year period preceding the 2000 B.C. of the Torreon and

Intihuatana at Machu Picchu. In other words, Müller concluded that the structures from the pre-Inca period stretch over two zodiac ages: the megalithic ones belonging to the Age of Taurus, the ones from the time of the Ancient Empire and the hiatus at Tampu-Tocco being from the Age of Aries.

In the ancient Near East the shift caused by precession required periodic reform of the original Sumerian calendar. A major change, accompanied by major religious upheavals, took place circa 2000 B.C. with the transition from the zodiac of the Bull to that of the Ram. To others' (but not our own) amazement, such changeovers and reforms are also evidenced in the Andes.

That the ancient Andean people had a calendar should have been a foregone conclusion from the writings of Montesinos and other chroniclers who referred to repeated reforms of the calendar by various monarchs. It took however several studies, beginning in the 1930s, to confirm that these people not only had a calendar but also recorded it (though they were supposed to have no writing). A pioneer in the field, Fritz Buck (*Inscripciones Calendarias del Peru Preincaico* and other writings) produced archaeological evidence to support such conclusions, such as a mace that was a time-reckoning instrument and a vase, found in the ruins of the temple of Pachacamac, that denoted four periods of twelve with the aid of line and dot markings akin to those of the Maya and Olmecs.

According to Father Molina, the Incas "commenced to count the year in the middle of May, a few days more or less, on the first of the moon. They went to the Coricancha in the morning, at noon, and at night, bringing the sheep that were to be sacrificed that day." During the sacrifices, the priests chanted hymns, saying "O Creator, O Sun, O Thunder, be forever young and do not grow old; let all things be at peace; let the people multiply and their food and all things continue to be abundant."

Because the Gregorian calendar was introduced in Cuzco only after Molina's time, the day of the New Year related by him corresponds to May 25 or thereabouts. Observation towers that had been described by Garcilaso have been discovered in recent years by astronomers from the universities of Texas and Illinois; they found that the sighting lines were proper for May 25. According to the chroniclers the Incas considered their year to begin at the winter solstice (equivalent to the summer solstice in the northern hemisphere). But this event occurs not in May, but on June 21 . . . a difference of a full month!

The only plausible explanation for this can come from a recognition that the calendar and the system for observation on which it was based were bequeathed to the Incas from an earlier Age: a retardation by one month results from the precessional shift that lasts 2,160 years per zodiac house.

The Intihuatana at Machu Picchu, as we have mentioned, served to determine not only the solstices but also the equinoxes (when daylight and nighttime are equal when the Sun is over the Equator, in March and September). Both the chroniclers and modern researchers (such as L. E. Valcarel, *The Andean Calendar*) report that the Incas went to great lengths to determine the precise days of the equinoxes and venerated them. This custom must have also stemmed from earlier times, for we read in the early reports that the monarchs of the Ancient Empire were preoccupied with the need to determine the equinoxes.

Montesinos informs us that the fortieth monarch of the Ancient Empire established an academy for the study of astronomy and astrology and determined the equinoxes. The fact that he was given the title *Pachacutec* indicates that the calendar was at that time so much out of synchronization with the celestial phenomena that its reform became imperative. This is a most interesting bit of information that has been totally neglected. According to Montesinos, it was in the fifth year of this monarch's reign that 2500 years from Point Zero had been completed—and 2,000 years from the beginning of the ancient empire.

What was happening circa 400 B.C. that required a reform of the calendar? The length of the time span, 2000 years, parallels the time spans of zodiacal shifts due to precession. In the ancient Near East, when the calendar was begun at Nippur circa 4000 B.C., the spring equinox occurred in the House or Age of Taurus. It retarded to that of Aries circa 2000 B.C. and to Pisces by Christ's time.

The Andean reform circa 400 B.C. confirms that the ancient empire and its calendar indeed began circa 2500 B.C. It also suggests that those monarchs were familiar with the zodiac; but the zodiac was a purely artificial and arbitrary division of the celestial band around the Sun into twelve parts; a Sumerian invention that had been adopted in the Old World by all the peoples who had succeeded them (to this very day). Was this possible? The answer is yes.

One of the pioneers in the field, S. Hagar, in a lecture delivered to the fourteenth Congress of Americanists in 1904, titled "The Peruvian Asterisms and their Relation to the Ritual," showed that the Incas not only were familiar with the zodiac houses (and their parallel months) but also had distinct names for them. The names, to scholars' surprise but not to ours, bear an uncanny resemblance to the ones with which we are all familiar and which originated in Sumer. Thus, January, the month of Aquarius, was dedicated to *Mama Cocha* and *Capac Cocha,* Mother Water and Lord Water. March, the month of Aries when the first moon signified in antiquity New Year's eve, was called *Katu Quilla,* Market Moon. April, Taurus, was named *Tupa Taruca,* Pasturing Stag (there were no bulls in South America). Virgo was *Sara Mama* (Maize Mother) and its symbol was the female member; and so on.

Indeed, Cuzco itself was a testimonial in stone both to the familiarity with the twelve-house zodiac and the antiquity of that knowledge. We have already mentioned the division of Cuzco into twelve wards and their association with the zodiac houses. It is significant that he first ward, on the slopes of Sacsahuaman, was associated with Aries. For Aries to have been associated with the spring equinox, as we have shown, we have to turn the clock back more than 4,000 years.

One must wonder whether the knowledge required for such astronomical information and calendar reforms could have been retained and passed along over so many millennia without some kind of record-keeping, without being written down in some form. The Maya codices contained, as we have seen, astronomical data copied and obtained from earlier sources. Archaeologists have determined that oblong bars held by Maya rulers (as depicted on their stelae) were actually "sky bars" that spelled out the glyphs for certain constellations of the zodiac (as was the series of glyphs framing the image of Pacal on the lid of his coffin, at Palenque). Were these artful depictions from the classic period copied from earlier, perhaps less artistically refined, calendrical records? This is suggested by a round stone found at Tikal (Fig. 85a) on which the image of the Sun God (with beard and tongue out) is surrounded by celestial glyphs.

Such "primitive" calendar-zodiac circular stones must have preceded the perfected Aztec "calendar stones," several of which have been found and a golden one of which, the most hallowed of all, was presented to Cortés by Moctezuma when the latter believed that he was only returning to the God of the Plumed Serpent what was his.

Were there such records—in gold—in existence in ancient Peru? In spite of the treatment meted out by the Spaniards to anything connected with the "idols," and especially if the object was made of gold (which was quickly melted down, as had happened to the Image of the sun from the Coricancha), at least one such relic remains.

It is a golden disk, about 5½ inches in diameter (Fig. 85b).

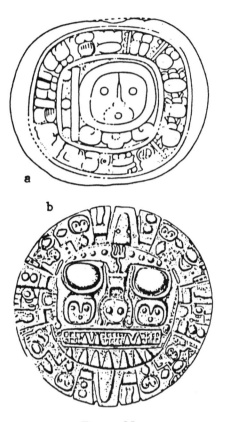

Figure 85

Discovered in Cuzco and now lodged in the Museum of the American Indian in New York, it was described over a century ago by Sir Clemens Markham (*Cuzco and Lima; The Incas of Peru*). He concluded that the disk represented the sun in the center and had twenty distinct symbols around it; he took them to stand for months, akin to the Maya calendar of twenty months. W. Bollaert, in a lecture before the Royal Society of Antiquarians in 1860 and subsequent writings, considered the disk to be "a lunar calendar or a zodiac." M. H. Saville (*A Golden Breastplate from Cuzco,* in the Museum's 1921 publication) pointed out that six of the encircling signs are repeated twice and two are repeated four times (he marked them from A to H) and therefore doubted the validity of Markham's twenty-month theory.

The simple fact that six times two is twelve leads us to agree with Bollaert, and to suggest that this is a zodiacal tablet rather than one of months. All scholars agree that this artifact is from pre-Inca times. None have shown, however, how similar it is to the calendar stone discovered at Tikal—perhaps because it would add another nail to the coffin in which the notion that there had been no contact, no "diffusion" between Mesoamerica and South America, must be laid to rest.

It was early in 1533 that a small band of soldiers from Pizarro's landing party had entered Cuzco, the Inca capital. The main body of Pizarro's force was still at Cajamarca, where they held the pretender, Atahualpa, prisoner; and the mission of the band sent to Cuzco was to get the capital's contribution to the golden ransom demanded by the Spaniards in exchange for Atahualpa's freedom.

In Cuzco, Atahualpa's general Quizquiz allowed them to enter and examine several important buildings, including the Temple of the Sun; the Incas, as we have mentioned, called it the *Coricancha,* the Golden Enclosure, for its walls were covered with golden plates and within the walls there had been wondrous artifacts of gold, silver, and precious stones. The few Spaniards who had entered Cuzco removed seven hundred gold plates and helped themselves to other treasure and returned to Cajamarca.

The main Spanish force entered Cuzco at the end of that year; and we have already described the fate that befell the city, its edifices, and its shrines, including the desecration of the Holy of Holies and the looting, then melting down, of the Golden Emblem of the sun that hung above the Great Altar.

But the physical destruction could not eradicate what the Incas retained in their memories. The Coricancha was built, the Incas recalled, by the very first monarch; it began as a hut with a thatched roof. Later monarchs enlarged and enhanced it, until it assumed the final dimensions and shape as seen by the Spaniards. In the Holy of Holies, they related, the walls were covered from floor to ceiling with plates of gold. "Over what was called the High Altar," Garcilaso wrote, "was the image of the Sun on a gold plate twice the thickness of the rest of the wall plates. The image showed it with a round face and beams and flames of fire, all in one piece."

That indeed was the golden object that the Spaniards had seen and removed. But it was not the original image that had dominated the wall, facing the sun's beam at sunrise on the designated day.

The most detailed description of the centerpiece and its accompanying images was provided by Don Juan de Santa Cruz Pachacuti-Yumqui Salcamayhua, the son of a royal Inca princess and a Spanish nobleman (which is why he is sometimes referred to as Santa Cruz and sometimes as Salcamayhua). The account was included in his *Relacion* (English translation by Sir Clemens Markham) in which he set out to glorify the royal Inca dynasty in the eyes of the Spanish. It was the first king of the Inca dynasty, Salcamayhua stated, who had "ordered the smiths to make a flat plate of gold which signified that there was a creator of heaven and earth." Salcamayhua illustrated his text with a drawing: it was the unusual and rare shape of an oval.

That first image was replaced by a round plate when a certain monarch later declared the Sun supreme. It was changed back to an oval image by a subsequent Inca, "a great enemy of idols; he ordered his people not to pay honors to the Sun and Moon"; rather, to the celestial body represented by the oval shape; it was he who had "caused images to be put around the plate." Referring to the oval shape as "The Creator," Salcamayhua made it clear that it did not mean the Sun, for the images of the sun and the Moon had flanked the oval. To illustrate what he meant, Salcamayhua drew a large oval flanked by two smaller circles.

The centerpiece stayed that way, with the oval as the superior image, until the time of the Inca Huascar, one of the two half brothers involved in the struggle for the throne when the Spaniards arrived. He removed the oval image and replaced it "with a round plate, like the Sun with rays." "Huascar Inca had placed an image of the Sun in the place where the Creator had been." Thereby, the alternating religious tenets changed back to a pantheon in which the Sun, not Viracocha, was supreme. To signify that he was the proper successor to the throne, Huascar added to his name the epithet *Inti* ("Sun"), meaning that it was he, and not his half brother, who was a true offspring of the original Sons of the Sun.

Explaining that the gabled wall with the oval as its principal image represented "what the heathens thought" regarding the heavens and the earth, Salcamayhua drew a large sketch showing how the wall had looked before Huascar replaced the oval shape with the Sun's image. The sketch has survived because Francisco de Avila, who had questioned Salcamayhua and others about the meaning of the depictions, kept it among his papers. He also scribbled on and around the sketch notations explaining the images, using the Quechus and Aymara terms given by the natives and his own Castilian Spanish: When these notations are removed (Fig. 86) one gets a clear picture of what had been depicted above the altar (the long crisscrossed object at the bottom): terrestrial symbols (people, an animal, a river, mountains, a lake, etc.) in the bottom part; celestial images (Sun, Moon, stars, the enigmatic oval, etc.) in the upper part.

Scholars have both agreed and disagreed regarding the interpretation of the individual symbols, but not about the overall meaning of the sacred wall. Markham saw in the upper part "a stellar chart which is a veritable key to the symbolical cosmogony and astronomy of ancient Peru," and was certain that the gabled triangular tip was a hieroglyph for "sky." S. K. Lothrop (*Inca Treasure*) stated that the images above the great altar "formed a cosmogonic tale of the creation of heaven and earth, the Sun and Moon, the first Man and Woman." All are agreed that, as Salcamayhua had stated, it represented "what the heathens thought"—the sum total of their religious beliefs and legendary tales; a saga of Heaven and Earth and the bond between them.

The celestial assembly of images clearly depicts the Sun and the Moon flanking the golden oval plate, and groups of heavenly bodies above and below the oval. That the two flanking star symbols stand for the Sun and Moon is clarified by the conventional faces drawn above them plus the notations in the native tongue, *Inti* (Sun) and *Quilla* (Moon).

Figure 86

Since the Sun was thus depicted, what did the central image, the great oval, represent? The tales describe how this symbol alternated with the Sun in being worshiped and venerated in Inca times. Its identity is clearly explained by a notation that reads, *"Illa Ticci Uuiracocha, Pachac Acachi. Quiere decir imagen del Hacedor del cielo y de la tierra."* Translated, it means "Illa Ticci Viracocha, Maker of All; that is to say, image of the Creator of Heaven and Earth."

But why was Viracocha depicted as an oval?

One of the principal researchers of the subject, R. Lehmann-Nitsche (*Coricancha—El Templo del Sol en el Cuzco y las Imagenes de su Altar Mayor*) developed the thesis that the oval shape represented the "Cosmic Egg," a theogonic idea that is echoed in Greek legends, in Hindu religions, "even in Genesis." It is "the oldest theogony whose details have not been grasped by white authors." It had been represented in the sanctuaries of the Indo-European deity Mithra as an egg surrounded by the constellations of the zodiac. "Perhaps one day Indianologists will see the similarities in the details and cult of Viracocha, Brahma with the seven eyes, and the Israelite Yahweh...In the classic antiquity and in the Orphic cult there were sacred images of the Mystic Egg; why shouldn't the same happen in the great sanctuary of Cuzco?"

Lehmann-Nitsche thought of a Cosmic Egg as the only explanation for the unusual use of an oval shape, for apart from its similarity to the outline of an egg, the elliptical shape (which is difficult to draw or fashion accurately) is not found naturally on the face of the Earth. But he and others seemed to ignore the fact that the elliptical shape has superimposed on it (at the bottom) a star symbol. If, as it seems, the elliptical or oval shape applies to one more celestial body (besides the five above and four below), it spells to us the "oval" that is found in nature—not on Earth, but in the heavens: it is the natural curve of a planet's orbit around its sun. It is, we suggest, the orbital path of a planet in our Solar System.

What the sacred wall depicted, we must conclude, was not distant or mysterious constellations, but our own Solar System, with the Sun, the Moon, and ten planets, adding up to a total of twelve. We see the planets of our Solar System divided into two groups. In our view, these are the five outer planets on the distant side—Pluto, Neptune, Uranus, Saturn and Jupiter (counting from the outside inward). The lower or nearer group represents the four inner planets—Mars, Earth, Venus, Mercury. The two groups are divided by the vast elliptical orbit of the twelfth member of the Solar System. To the Incas, it represented the celestial Viracocha.

Should we be surprised to find that this was exactly the Sumerian view of our Solar System?

As the depictions descend from the heavens toward Earth, a starry sky is shown on the wall's right and clouds on the left. Scholars agree with the original notations, "summer" (bright starry skies) and "winter clouds." In considering the seasons part of the creative act, the Inca depiction again follows the Near Eastern pattern. The earth's tilt (causing the seasons) was attributed in Sumer to Nibiru and in Babylon to Marduk. The concept was echoed when the Psalmist sang of the biblical Lord, "Thou hast made summer and winter."

Below "summer" there appears a star symbol; a fierce animal is shown below "winter." It is generally agreed that these images represent the constellations associated (in the southern hemisphere) with these seasons, the one for winter representing Leo (the Lion). This is amazing in more than one way. First, because there are no lions in South America. Second, because when the calendar was begun in Sumer in the fourth millennium B.C. the summer solstice there occurred when the Sun was seen in the zodiac constellation of the Lion (UR.GULA in Sumerian). But in the southern hemisphere that time of year would have been *winter*. So that the Inca depiction borrowed not only the idea of twelve zodiac constellations, but also their seasonal order in Mesopotamia!

We now arrive at the symbols that—as in the *Enuma Elish* and in the Book of Genesis—transfer the tales of creation from the heavens to Earth: the first Man and Woman, Eden, a large river, a serpent, mountains, a sacred lake. An Incan "panorama of the world," in the words of Lehmann-Nitsche. It would be more accurate to say, the Pictorial Bible of the Andes.

The analogy is actual, not just figurative. The elements in this part of the pictorial composition could well serve to illustrate the Mesopotamian-biblical tales of Adam and Eve in the Garden of Eden, complete with the serpent (on the wall's right) and the Tree of Life (on the wall's left). The Sumerian E.DIN (from which *Eden* stems) was the valley of the great river Euphrates, emanating from the high mountains in the north. This geography is clearly depicted on the wall's right, where a globe representing Earth bears the notation "Pacha Mama"— Mother Earth. Even the Rainbow, which featured in the Near Eastern tales of the Deluge, is shown here.

(While all accept that the globe or circle marked Pacha

Mama represents the Earth, none have stopped to wonder how the Incas knew that the Earth was round. The Sumerians, however, were aware of the fact and depicted the Earth and all the other planets accordingly.)

The group of seven dots below the Earth symbol has given scholars endless problems. Adhering to the erroneous notion that the ancients conceived of the Pleiades as numbering seven stars, some have suggested that the symbol represents that portion of the constellation Taurus. But if so, the symbol belongs in the upper, celestial portion of the panel, not at its bottom. Lehmann-Nitsche and others interpreted the seven-symbol as "the seven eyes of the supreme god." But we have already shown that the seven dots, the number seven, was the designation of Earth itself in the Sumerian enumeration of the planets. The symbol "seven" is thus exactly where it belongs, as a caption for the globe of the Earth.

The last image on the sacred wall is that of a great lake connected by a waterway to a smaller body of water. The notation on its states, "Mama Cocha," Mother Water. All are agreed that this represents the Andean sacred lake, Lake Titicaca. By depicting it, the Incas had taken the story of Creation from the Heavens to Earth and from the Garden of Eden to the Andes.

Lehmann-Nitsche summed up the meaning and message of the composite depiction on the wall above the Great Altar by saying, "it takes man from the ground to the stars." It is doubly amazing that it takes the Incas to the other side of the Earth.

9

CITIES LOST AND FOUND

The discovery of the story of Genesis, in its original Mesopotamian version, depicted on the Inca temple's Holy of Holies, raises a host of questions. The first obvious one is, How—how did the Incas come to know these tales, not just in the general manner in which they have become known universally (the creation of the first couple, the Deluge), but in a manner that follows the Epic of Creation including knowledge of the complete Solar System and the orbit of Nibiru?

One possible answer is that the Incas had possessed this knowledge from time immemorial, bringing it with them to the Andes. The other possibility is that they had heard it from others whom they met in these lands.

In the absence of written records as one finds in the ancient Near East, the choice of an answer depends to some extent on how one answers another question: Who, indeed, were the Incas?

The *Relacion* of Salcamayhua is a good example of the Incas' attempt to perpetuate an exercise in state propaganda: the attribution of the revered named *Manco Capac* to the first Inca monarch, Inca Rocca, in order to make the people they had subjugated believe that the first Inca was the original "Son of the Sun," fresh out of the sacred Lake Titicaca. In fact, the Inca dynasty began some 3,500 years after that hallowed beginning. Also, the language that the Incas spoke was Quechua, the language of the people of the central-north Andes, whereas in the highlands of Lake Titicaca the people spoke Aymara. That, and other considerations, have led some scholars to speculate that the Incas were latecomers who had arrived from the east, settling in the Cuzco valley that borders on the great Amazon plain.

175

That, in itself, does not rule out a Near Eastern origin or link for the Incas. While attention has been focused on the depiction on the wall above the High Altar, no one has wondered why, in the midst of peoples who had made images of their gods and who placed their idols in shrines and temples, there was no idol whatsoever in the great Inca temple, nor in any other Inca shrine.

The chroniclers related that an "idol" was carried during some celebrations, but it was the image of Manco Capac, not of a god. They also relate that on a certain holy day a priest would go to a distant mountain upon which there stood a large idol of a god, and would sacrifice there a llama. But the mountain and its idol were from pre-Inca times, and the reference could well be to the temple of Pachacamac on the coast (regarding which we have already written).

Interestingly, the two customs are in line with biblical commandments from the time of the Exodus. The prohibition against making and worshiping idols was included in the Ten Commandments. And on the eve of the Day of Atonement, a priest had to sacrifice a "sin-goat" in the desert. No one has ever pointed out that the *quipos* used by the Incas to recall events— strings of different colors that had to be of wool, with knots at different positions—were in make and purpose akin to the *tzit-zit,* "fringes on the corner of a blue thread," that the Israelites were commanded to attach to their garments as a way to re-member the Lord's commandments. There is the matter of the rules of succession, by which the legal heir was the son by a half sister—a Sumerian custom followed by the Hebrew patriarchs. And there was the custom of circumcision in the Inca royal family.

Peruvian archaeologists have reported intriguing finds in the Amazonian provinces of Peru, including the apparent remains of stone-built cities, especially in the valleys of the Utcubamba and Marañón rivers. There are undoubtedly "lost cities" in the tropical zones; but in some instances the announced discoveries are really expeditions to known sites. Such was the case of headline news from Gran Patajen in 1985—a site visited by the Peruvian archaeologist F. Kauffmann-Doig and the American Gene Savoy twenty years earlier. There have been reports of aerial sightings of "pyramids" on the Brazilian side of the border, of lost cities such as Akakor, and Indians' tales of ruins holding untold treasures. A document in the national archives in Rio de Janeiro is purportedly an eighteenth-century report recording a lost city in the Amazon jungles seen by Europeans in 1591; the document even transcribes a script found there. It was the main reason for an expedition by Colonel Percy Fawcett whose mysterious disappearance in the jungles is still a subject of popular-science articles.

All this is not to say that there are no ancient ruins in the Amazon basin that remain from a trail across the South American continent from Guiana/Venezuela to Ecuador/Peru. Humboldt's reports of his travels across the continent mention a tradition that people from across the sea landed in Venezuela and proceeded inland; and the principal river of the Cuzco valley, the Urubamba, is but a tributary of the Amazon. Official Brazilian teams have visited many sites (without, however, conducting sustained excavations). At one site near the mouth of the Amazon, pottery urns decorated with incised patterns that remind one of the designs on earthenware jars from Ur (the Sumerian birthplace of Abraham) have been found. An islet called Pacoval appeared to have been artificially created, and served as a base for a number of mounds (which were not excavated). According to L. Netto, *Investigacioes sobre a Archaeologia Braziliera,* similarly decorated urns and vases "of superior quality" have been found farther up the Amazon. And, we believe, an equally important route connecting the Andes with the Atlantic Ocean did exist farther to the south.

Still, it is uncertain that the Incas themselves came this way. One of their ancestry versions attributes their beginnings to a landing on the Peruvian coast. Their language, Quechua, bears Far Eastern resemblances both in word meanings and dialect. And they clearly belong to the Amerindian stock—the fourth branch of mankind that, we have ventured to suggest, stemmed from the line of Cain. (A guide in Cuzco, hearing of our biblical expertise, asked whether *In-ca* might have stemmed from *Ca-in* by reversing the syllables. One wonders!)

The evidence at hand, we believe, indicates that the Near Eastern tales and beliefs, including knowledge of the story of Nibiru and the Anunnaki who had come from there to Earth— the pantheon of twelve—were brought to the predecessors of the Incas from overseas. It took place in the days of the Ancient Empire; and the bearers of these tales and beliefs were also Strangers From Across the Seas, but not necessarily the same ones who brought similar tales, beliefs, and civilization to Mesoamerica.

In addition to all the facts and evidence that we had already provided, let us return to Izapa, a site near the Pacific coast where Mexico and Guatemala meet and where the Olmecs and the Maya rubbed shoulders. Recognized only belatedly as the largest site along the Pacific coast of North or Central America, it spans 2500 years of continuous occupation, from 1500 B.C. (a date confirmed by carbon dating) to A.D. 1000. It had the customary pyramids and ball courts; but it has mostly amazed archaeologists by its carved stone monuments. The style, imagination, mythical content and artistic perfection of these carvings have come to be called "Izapan style," and it is now recognized that it was the source from which the style spread to other sites along the Pacific slopes of Mexico and Guatemala. It was art belonging to the Early and Middle Preclassic Olmec, adopted by the Maya as the site changed hands.

Archaeologists from the New World Archaeological Foundation of Brigham Young University, who have devoted decades to the excavation and study of the site, have no doubt that it was oriented toward the solstices at the time of its foundation and that even the various monuments were placed "on deliberate alignments with planetary movements" (V. G. Norman, *Izapa Sculpture*). Religious, cosmological, and mythological themes intermingled with historical subjects are expressed in the stone carvings. We have already seen (Fig. 51b) one of the many and varied depictions of winged deities. Of particular interest here is a large carved stone whose face measures some thirty square feet, designated by the archaeologists Izapa Stela 5, found in conjunction with a major stone altar. The complicated scene (Fig. 87) has been recognized by various scholars as a "fantastic

Figure 87

Figure 88

visual myth" concerning the "genesis of humanity" at a Tree of Life that grows by a river. The mythical-historical tale is told by an old bearded man seated on the left, and is retold by a Maya-looking man on the right (of the stela's observer).

The scene is filled with diverse vegetation, birds, and fish as well as human figures. Interestingly, two central figures represent men that have the face and feet of elephants—an animal completely unknown in the Americas. The one on the left is shown in association with a helmeted Olmec man, which reinforces our contention that the colossal stone heads and the Olmecs they portrayed were Africans.

The left-hand panel, when enlarged (Fig. 88a), clearly reveals details which we consider extremely important clues. The bearded man tells his story over an altar that bears the symbol of the umbilical cutter; this was the symbol (Fig. 88b) by which Ninti (the Sumerian goddess who had helped Enki create Man) was identified on cylinder seals and on monuments. When the Earth was divided among the gods she was given dominion over the Sinai peninsula, the Egyptians' source of their cherished blue-green turquoise; they called her Hathor and depicted her with cow's horns, as on this Creation of Man scene (Fig. 88c). These "coincidences" reinforce the conclusion that the Izapa stela illustrates none other than the Old World tales of the Creation of Man and the Garden of Eden.

And finally there are portrayals of pyramids, smooth sided as at Giza on the Nile, depicted here at the bottom of the panel beside a flowing river. Indeed, as one examines and reexamines this millennia-old panel, one must agree that a picture is worth a thousand words.

Legends and archaeological evidence indicate that the Olmecs and the Bearded Ones did not stop at the edge of the ocean, but pushed on southward into Central America and the northern lands of South America. They may have advanced overland, for they certainly left traces of their presence at inland sites. In all probability they journeyed southward the easier way, by boats.

The legends in the equatorial and northern parts of the Andes recalled not only the arrival by sea of their own ancestors (such as Naymlap), but also two separate ones by "giants." One had occurred in ancient empire times, the other in Mochica times. Cieza de Leon described the latter thus: "There arrived on the coast, in boats made of reeds as big as large ships, a party of men of such size that, from the knee downward their height was as great as the entire height of an ordinary man." They had metal tools with which they dug wells in the lving rock, but for food they raided the natives' provisions. They also violated the natives' women, for there were no women among the landing giants. The Mochica depicted these giants who had enslaved them on their pottery, painting their faces in black (Fig. 89) while that of the Mochicas was painted white. Also found in Mochica remains are clay portrayals of older men with white beards.

It is our guess that these unwanted visitors were Olmecs and their bearded Near Eastern companions who were fleeing the uprisings in Mesoamerica, circa 400 B.C. They left behind them a trail of dreaded veneration as they passed through Central America to the equatorial lands farther down in South America. Archaeological expeditions to the equatorial areas of the Pacific coast have found enigmatic monoliths that stem from that fearsome period. The George C. Heye expedition found in Ecuador giant stone heads with humanlike features but with fangs as though they were ferocious jaguars. Another expedition found at San Agustin, a site closer to the Colombian border, stone

Figure 89

statues portraying giants, sometimes shown holding tools or weapons; their facial features are those of the African Olmecs (Fig. 90a, b).

These invaders may have been the source of the legends current also in these lands of how Man was created, of a Deluge, and of a serpent god who demanded an annual tribute of gold. One of the ceremonies recorded by the Spaniards was a ritual dance performed by twelve men dressed in red; it was performed on the shores of a lake connected with the legend of El Dorado.

The equatorial natives worshiped a pantheon of twelve, a number of great significance and an important clue. It was headed by a triad consisting of the Creation God, the Evil God, and the Mother Goddess; and it included the gods of the Moon, the Sun, and the Rain-Thunder. Significantly too, the Moon God ranked higher than the Sun God. The deities' names changed from locality to locality, retaining however the celestial affinity. Among the strange-sounding names, though, two stand out. The head of the pantheon was called in the Chibcha dialect *Abira*—remarkably similar to the Mesopotamian divine epithet *Abir,* which meant Strong, Mighty; and the Moon God, as we have noted, was called "Si" or "Sian," which parallels the Mesopotamian name *Sin* for that deity.

The pantheon of these South American natives therefore brings inevitably to mind the pantheon of the ancient Near East and the eastern Mediterranean—of the Greeks and the Egyptians, the Hittites and the Canaanites and Phoenicians, the Assyrians and the Babylonians—all the way back to where it all

Figure 90

began: to the Sumerians of southern Mesopotamia from whom all others had obtained the gods and their mythologies.

The Sumerian pantheon was headed by an "Olympian Circle" of twelve, for each of these supreme gods had to have a celestial counterpart, one of the twelve members of the Solar System. Indeed, the names of the gods and their planets were one and the same (except when a variety of epithets were used to describe the planet or the god's attributes). Heading the pantheon was the ruler of Nibiru, ANU whose name was synonymous with "Heaven," for he resided on Nibiru. His spouse, also a member of the Twelve, was called ANTU. Included in this group were the two principal sons of ANU: E.A ("Whose House Is Water"), Anu's Firstborn but not by Antu; and EN.LIL ("Lord of the Command") who was the Heir Apparent because his mother was Antu, a half sister of Anu. Ea was also called in Sumerian texts EN.KI ("Lord Earth"), for he had led the first mission of the Anunnaki from Nibiru to Earth and established on Earth their first colonies in the E.DIN ("Home of the Righteous Ones")—the biblical Eden.

His mission was to obtain gold, for which Earth was a unique source. Not for ornamentation or because of vanity, but as a way to save the atmosphere of Nibiru by suspending gold dust in that planet's stratosphere. As recorded in the Sumerian texts (and related by us in *The 12th Planet* and subsequent books of *The Earth Chronicles*), Enlil was sent to Earth to take over the command when the initial extraction methods used by Enki proved unsatisfactory. This laid the groundwork for an ongoing feud between the two half brothers and their descendants, a feud that led to Wars of the Gods; it ended with a peace treaty worked out by their sister Ninti (thereafter renamed Ninharsag). The inhabited Earth was divided between the warring clans. The three sons of Enlil—Ninurta, Sin, Adad—together with Sin's twin children, Shamash (the Sun) and Ishtar (Venus), were given the lands of Shem and Japhet, the lands of the Semites and Indo-Europeans: Sin (the Moon) lowland Mesopotamia; Ninurta, ("Enlil's Warrior," Mars) the highlands of Elam and Assyria; Adad ("The Thunderer," Mercury) Asia Minor (the land of the Hittites) and Lebanon. Ishtar was granted dominion as the goddess of the Indus Valley civilization; Shamash was given command of the spaceport in the Sinai peninsula.

This division, which did not go uncontested, gave Enki and his sons the lands of Ham—the brown/black people—of Africa: the civilization of the Nile Valley and the gold mines of southern and western Africa—a vital and cherished prize. A great scientist and metallurgist, Enki's Egyptian name was *Ptah* ("The Developer"; a title that translated into *Hephaestus* by the Greeks and *Vulcan* by the Romans). He shared the continent with his sons; among them was the firstborn MAR.DUK ("Son of the Bright Mound") whom the Egyptians called *Ra,* and NIN.GISH.ZI.DA ("Lord of the Tree of Life") whom the Egyptians called Thoth (Hermes to the Greeks)—a god of secret knowledge including astronomy, mathematics, and the building of pyramids.

It was the knowledge imparted by this pantheon, the needs of the gods who had come to Earth, and the leadership of Thoth, that directed the African Olmecs and the bearded Near Easterners to the other side of the world.

And having arrived in Mesoamerica on the Gulf coast—just as the Spaniards, aided by the same sea currents, did millennia later—they cut across the Mesoamerican isthmus at its narrowest neck and—just like the Spaniards due to the same geography—sailed down from the Pacific coast of Mesoamerica southward, to the lands of Central America and beyond.

For that is where the gold was, in Spanish times and before.

* * *

Before the Incas and the Chimu and the Mochica, a culture named by scholars Chavin flourished in the mountains that lie in northern Peru between the coast and the Amazon basin. One of its first explorers, Julio C. Tello (*Chavin* and other works) called it "the matrix of Andean civilization." It takes us back to at least 1500 B.C.; and like that of the Olmec civilization in Mexico at the same time, it arose suddenly and with no apparent prior gradual development.

Encompassing a vast area whose dimensions are constantly expanded as new finds are made, the Chavin Culture appeared to have been centered at a site called Chavin de Huantar, near the village of Chavin (and hence the culture's name). It is situated at an elevation of 10,000 feet in the Cordillera Blanca range of the northwestern Andes. There, in a mountain valley where tributaries of the Marañón river form a triangle, an area of some 300,000 square feet was flattened and terraced and made suitable for the construction of complex structures, carefully and precisely laid out according to a preconceived plan that took into consideration the contours and features of the site (Fig. 91a). Not only do the buildings and plazas form precise rectangulars and squares; they have also been precisely aligned with the cardinal points, with east–west as the major axis. The three main buildings stood upon terraces that elevated them and leaned against the outer western wall that ran for some 500 feet. The wall that apparently encompassed the complex on three sides, leaving it open to the river that flowed on the east, rose to about forty feet.

The largest building was at the southwest corner, measured about 240 by 250 feet, and consisted of at least three floors (see an artist's bird's-eye-view reconstruction, Fig. 91b). It was built of masonry stone blocks, well shaped but not dressed, laid out in regular and level courses. As some remaining slabs indicate, the walls were faced outside with smooth, marblelike stone slabs; some still retain their incised decorations. From a terrace on the east a monumental stairway led through an imposing gate up toward the main building; the gate was flanked by two cylindrical columns—a most unusual feature in South America— that together with adjoining vertical stone blocks supported a thirty-foot horizontal lintel made of a single monolith. Farther up, a double monumental stairway led to the building's top. This stairway was built of perfectly cut and shaped stones that remind one of the great Egyptian pyramids. The two stairways led to the building's top, where archaeologists have found the remains of two towers; the rest of the uppermost platform remained unbuilt.

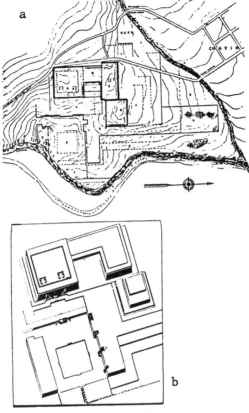

Figure 91

The eastern terrace, forming part of the platform on which this edifice was built, led to (or from) a sunken plaza reached by ceremonial steps and surrounded on three sides by rectangular plazas or platforms. Just outside the southwestern corner of the sunken plaza, and perfectly aligned with the staircases of the main edifice and its terrace, there stood a large flat boulder; it had in it seven grind holes and a rectangular niche.

The exterior's precision was exceeded by the interior complexity. Within the three structures there ran corridors and mazelike passages, intermingled with connecting galleries, rooms, and staircases, or leading to dead ends and therefore nicknamed labyrinths. Some of the galleries have been faced with smooth slabs, here and there delicately decorated; all the passages are roofed with carefully selected stone slabs that have been placed with great ingenuity that prevented their collapse

a   b

Figure 92

over the millennia. There are niches and protrusions for no apparent purpose; and vertical or sloping shafts that the archaeologists thought might have served for ventilation.

What was Chavin de Huantar built for? The only plausible purpose that its discoverers could see was that of a religious center, a kind of ancient "Mecca." This notion was strengthened by the three fascinating and most enigmatic relics found at the site. One that baffles by its complex imagery was discovered by Tello in the main building and is called the Tello Obelisk (Fig. 92a,b shows the front and back). It is engraved with an agglomeration of human bodies and faces but with feline hands with fangs or wings. There are animals, birds, trees; gods emitting rocketlike rays; and a variety of geometric designs. Was this a totem pole that served for worship, or an attempt by an ancient "Picasso" to convey all the myths and legends on one column? No one has yet come up with a plausible answer.

A second carved stone is called the Raimondi Monolith (Fig. 93), after the archaeologist who found it at a nearby estate; it is believed that it originally stood atop the grooved stone at the

Figure 93

southwestern edge of the sunken plaza, aligned with the monumental stairway. It is now on exhibit in Lima.

The ancient artist carved upon this seven-foot-high granite column the image of a deity holding a weapon—a thunderbolt, some believe—in each hand. While the deity's body and limbs are essentially though not entirely anthropomorphic, the face is not. This face has puzzled scholars because it does not represent or stylize a local creature (such as a jaguar); rather, it appears to be the artist's conception of what scholars conveniently called "a mythological animal," namely one of which the artist had heard but had not actually seen.

To our eyes, however, the deity's face is that of a bull—an animal completely absent in South America but one that featured considerably in the lore and iconography of the ancient Near East. Significantly (in our opinion) it was the "cult animal" of Adad, and the mountain range in his domain, in Asia Minor, is still called to this very day the Taurus Mountains.

A third unusual and enigmatic carved stone column at Chavin de Huantar is called *El Lanzon* because of its lancelike shape (Fig. 94). It was discovered in the middle building and has remained there because its height (twelve feet) exceeds the

Figure 94

ten-foot height of the gallery where it stands; the monolith's top therefore protrudes into the floor above it through a carefully cut square opening. The image on this monolith has been the subject of much speculation; to our eyes, again, it seems to depict an anthropomorphized face of a bull. Does it mean, then, that whoever erected this monument—obviously *before* the building was constructed, for the latter was built to accommodate the statue—worshiped the Bull God?

It was by and large the high artistic level of the artifacts rather than the complex and unusual structures that so impressed scholars and led them to consider Chavin the "matrix culture" of north-central Peru, and to believe that the site was a religious center. But that the purpose was not religious but rather utilitarian seems to be indicated by recent finds at Chavin de Huantar. These latest excavations revealed a network of subterranean tunnels hewed out of the native rock; they honeycombed the whole site, both under built as well as unbuilt parts, and served to connect several series of underground compartments arranged in a chainlike manner (Fig. 95).

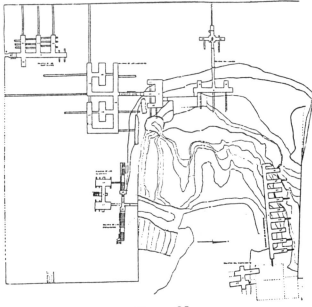

Figure 95

The openings of the tunnels perplexed their discoverers, for they seemed to connect the two river tributaries that flank the site, one (due to the mountainous terrain) above it and the other in the valley below it. Some explorers have suggested that these tunnels were so built for flood control purposes, to channel the onrushing water from the mountains as the snows melt and let it flow under instead of through the buildings. But if there was a danger of such flooding (after heavy rains rather than from melting snows), why did the otherwise ingenious builders place their structures at such a vulnerable spot?

They did so, we hold, on purpose. They ingeniously used the two levels of the tributaries to create a powerful, controlled flow of water needed for the processes that were carried out at Chavin de Huantar. For there, as at many other sites, such devices of flowing water were used in the panning of gold.

We will encounter more of these ingenious waterworks in the Andes; we have seen them, in more rudimentary forms, at Olmec sites. They were in Mexico part of complex earthworks; they were in the Andes masterpieces in stone—sometimes large sites such as Chavin de Huantar, sometimes lone remains of incredibly cut and shaped rocks, as this one seen by Squier in

Figure 96

the Chavin area (Fig. 96), that seem to have been intended for some ultramodern machinery long gone.

It was indeed the stonework—not of the edifices but of the artistic artifacts—that seems to provide the answer to the question Who was there at Chavin de Huantar? The artistic skills and stone-sculpting styles are surprisingly reminiscent of the Olmec art of Mexico. The enchanting objects include a jaguar-cat receptacle, a feline-bull, an eagle-condor, a turtle basin; a large number of vases and other objects decorated with glyphs created of entwined fangs—a motif decorating wall slabs as well as artifacts (Fig. 97a). There were, however, also stone slabs covered with Egyptian motifs—serpents, pyramids, the sacred Eye of Ra (Fig. 97b). And as though this variety was insufficient, there were fragments of carved stone blocks that depicted Mesopotamian motifs, such as deities within Winged Disks (Fig. 97c) or (engraved on bones) images of gods wearing conical headdresses, the headgear by which Mesopotamian gods were identified (Fig. 97d).

The deities wearing the conical headdresses have facial features that have an "African" look, and having been carved on bones may represent the earliest art depictions at the site. Could it be that Africans—negroid, Egyptian-Nubian—were ever at this South American site at its earliest time? The surprising answer is yes. There were indeed black Africans here and at

Figure 97

nearby sites (especially at one called Sechin), and they left their portraits behind. At all these sites carved stones by the dozens bear depictions of those people; in most instances they are shown holding some kind of tool; in many instances, the "engineer" is depicted as associated with a symbol for waterworks (Fig. 98).

At coastal sites that lead to the Chavin sites in the mountains, archaeologists have found sculpted heads of clay, not stone, that must have represented Semitic visitors (Fig. 99); one was so strikingly similar to Assyrian sculptures that the discoverer, H. Ubbelohde-Doering (*On the Royal Highway of the Incas*) nicknamed it "King of Assyria." But it is not certain that these visitors had made it to the highland sites—at least not alive: sculpted stone heads with Semitic features have been found at Chavin de Huantar—but mostly with grotesque grimaces or mutilations, stuck as trophies in the site's surrounding walls.

The age of Chavin suggests that the first wave of these Old World, both Olmec and Semitic migrants, had arrived there circa 1500 B.C. Indeed, it was in the reign of the 12th monarch of the Ancient Empire that, as Montesinos chronicled, "news reached Cuzco of the disembarking on the coast of some men of great stature...giants who were settling on the whole coast"

Figure 98

and who possessed metal implements. After some time they moved inland into the mountains. The monarch sent runners to investigate and to provide him with reports of the giants' advance, lest they come too close to the capital. But as things turned out, the giants provoked the wrath of the Great God and he destroyed them. These events had taken place about a century before the standstill of the Sun that had occurred circa 1400 B.C.—i.e. circa 1500 B.C., the very time at which Chavin de Huantar's waterworks were built.

Figure 99

Figure 100

This, it must be pointed out, is not the same incident reported by Garcilaso, about giants who despoiled the land and raped the women—an occurrence in Moche times, circa 400 B.C. Indeed, it was at that time, as we have already seen, that the two commingled groups of Olmecs and Semites were fleeing Mesoamerica. Their fate, however, was no different in the northern Andes. Besides the grotesque Semitic stone heads found at Chavin de Huantar, depictions of mutilated negroid bodies are found in the whole area, and especially at Sechin.

Thus it was, after some 1,000 years in the northern Andes and almost 2,000 years in Mesoamerica, that the African-Semitic presence had come to a tragic end.

Although some of the Africans may have gone farther south, as finds at Tiahuanacu attest, the African-Semitic extension into the Andes from Mesoamerica appears to have not gone beyond the Chavin-culture area. The tales of the giants stricken by divine hand may hold more than a kernel of fact; for it is quite possible that there, in the northern Andes, two realms of two gods had met, with an unseen boundary between jurisdictions and human subordinates.

We say this because, in that very zone, other white men had been present. They were portrayed in stone busts (Fig. 100)—nobly clad, wearing turbans or headbands with symbols of authority, and decorated with what scholars call "mythological animals." These bust-statues have been mostly found at a site

Figure 101

near Chavin named Aija. Their facial features, especially the
straight noses, identify them as Indo-Europeans. Their origin
could have been only the land of Asia Minor and Elam to its
southeast, and in time the Indus Valley farther east.

Is it possible that people from those distant lands had crossed
the Pacific and come to the Andes in prehistoric times? The link
that evidently existed is confirmed by depictions illustrating the
feats of an ancient Near Eastern hero whose tales were told and
retold. He was Gilgamesh, ruler of Uruk (the biblical Erech)
who had reigned circa 2900 B.C.; he went in search of the hero
of the Deluge story whom the gods had granted (according to
the Mesopotamian version) immortality. His adventures were
told in the *Epic of Gilgamesh,* which was translated in antiquity
from Sumerian into the other languages of the Near East. One
of his heroic deeds, the wrestling with and defeat of two lions
with his bare hands, was a favorite pictorial depiction by ancient
artists, as this one on a Hittite monument (Fig. 101a).

Amazingly, the same depiction appears on stone tablets from
Aija (Fig. 101b) and a nearby site, Callejon de Huaylus (Fig.
l01c) in the northern Andes!

These Indo-Europeans have not been traced in Mesoamerica
or Central America, and we must assume that they came across
the Pacific straight to South America. If legends be the guide,
they preceded the two waves of African "giants" and Mediterra-

nean Bearded Ones, and could have been the earliest settlers of which the tale of Naymlap recounts. The traditional landing site for that arrival has been the peninsula of Santa Elena (now Ecuador) which, with its nearby La Plata island, juts out into the Pacific. Archaeological excavations have confirmed early settlements there, beginning with what is called a Valdivian Phase circa 2500 B.C. Among the finds reported by the renowned Ecuadorian archaeologist Emilio Estrada (*Ultimas Civilizaciones Pre-Historicas*) were stone statuettes with the same straight-nose features (Fig. 102a) as well as a symbol on pottery (Fig. 102b) that was the Hittite hieroglyph for "gods" (Fig. 102c).

It is noteworthy that the megalithic structures in the Andes, as we have already seen at Cuzco, Sacsahuaman, and Machu Picchu, all lie south of the unseen demarcation line between the two divine realms. The handiwork of the megalithic builders—Indo-Europeans guided by their gods?—which began south of Chavin (Fig. 96) has left its mark all the way south into the valley of the Urubamba river and beyond—everywhere, indeed, where gold was collected and panned. Everywhere, rocks were fashioned as though they were soft putty into channels, compartments, niches, and platforms that from a distance look

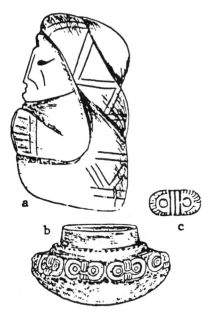

Figure 102

like stairways to nowhere; tunnels lead into mountainsides; fissures have been enlarged into corridors whose walls have been smoothed or shaped in precise angles. Everywhere, even at sites where the inhabitants could obtain all their water needs from the river below, elaborate water funneling and channeling were created higher up to make water from spring, tributary, or rain sources flow in a desired direction.

West-southwest of Cuzco, on the way to the town of Abancay, lie the ruins of Sayhuiti-Rumihuasi. As at other such sites it is situtuated near the junction of a river and a smaller stream. There are remain of a retaining wall, the remnant of large-sized structures that had once stood there; as Luis A. Pardo has pointed out in a study devoted to the site (*Los Grandes Monolitos de Sayhuiti*) the name means in the native tongue "Truncated Pyramid."

The site is known for its several monoliths and especially one called the Great Monolith. The name is appropriate since this huge rock, which from a distance appears as an immense bright egg resting on the hillside, measures about fourteen by ten by nine feet. While its bottom part has been carefully shaped as half an ovoid, the upper part has been carved out to represent in all probability a scale model of some unknown area. Discernible are miniature walls, platforms, stairways, channels, tunnels, rivers, canals; diverse structures, some representing edifices with niches and steps between them; images of various animals indigenous to Peru; and human figures of what look like warriors and, some say, gods.

Some see in this scale model a religious artifact, honoring the deities that they discern upon it. Others believe it represents a section of Peru that encompasses three districts, extending to the south to Lake Titicaca (which they identify with a lake carved on the stone) and the very ancient site of Tiahuanaco. Was this, then, a map carved in stone—or perhaps a scale model of a grand artificer who planned the layout and structures to be erected?

The answer may lie in the fact that, winding through this scale model, are grooves, an inch to two inches wide. They all originate in a "dish" located at the monolith's highest point and slope down, winding and zigzagging, to the lowest edge of the sculptured model, reaching there round discharge holes. Some consider these grooves to have served for the pouring by priests of potions (coca juices) as offerings to the gods represented on the rock. But if it was the gods themselves who were the architects, what was their purpose?

Figure 103

The telltale grooves are also a feature of another immense rock outcropping that has also been cut and shaped with geometric precision (Fig. 103), its surface and sides made into steps, platforms, and cascading niches. One side has been cut to form small "dishes" on the upper level; they are connected to a larger receptacle from which a deep channel leads down, separating midway into two grooves. Whatever liquid they carried poured into the rock, which was hollowed out and could be entered through an entryway in the back.

Other remains on the site, probably broken off from larger slabs, puzzle by the complex and geometrically precise grooves and hollows cut into them; they can be best likened to dies or matrixes for the casting of some ultramodern instruments.

One of the better known sites, just east of Sacsahuaman, is called Kenko—a name which in the native tongue means "Twisting Channels." The main tourist attraction there is a huge monolith standing on a podium that may have represented a lion or other large animal standing on its hind legs. In front of the monolith is a six-foot-high wall built of beautiful ashlars, surrounding the monolith in a circle. The monolith stands in front of an immense natural rock and the circular wall reaches and ends at the rock as a pincer. In the back, the rock has been cut, carved, and shaped into several levels connected by staggered platforms. Zigzagging channels have been cut on the rock's artificially sloping sides and the rock's interior has been hewed out to create labyrinthine tunnels and chambers. Nearby, a cleft in the rock leads to a cavelike opening that has been hollowed out with geometric precision to form stone features that some describe as thrones and altars.

There are more of these sites around Cuzco-Sacsahuaman, all along the Sacred Valley and reaching to the southeast, where a lake bears the name Golden Lake. A site named Torontoy includes among its precisely cut, megalithic stone blocks one that has thirty-two angles. Some fifty miles from Cuzco, near Torontoy, an artificial waterflow was made to cascade between two walls and over fifty-four "steps," all cut out of the living rock; significantly, the site is called Cori-Huairachina, "Where Gold is Purified."

Cuzco meant "The Navel" and indeed Sacsahuaman appears to have been the largest, most colossal and central of all these sites. One aspect of this centrality may be evidenced by a place called Pampa de Anta, some ten miles west of Sacsahuaman. There, the sheer rock has been carved into a series of steps that form a large crescent (hence the rock's name *Quillarumi*, "Moon Stone"). Since there is nothing to view from there except the eastern skies, Rolf Müller (*Sonne, Mond und Steiner über dem Reich der Inka*) concluded that it was some kind of observatory, situated so as to reflect astronomical data to the promontory at Sacsahuaman.

But what was Sacsahuaman itself, now that the notion of its having been built by the Incas as a fortress is completely discredited? The perplexing labyrinthine channels and other seemingly haphazard cutouts into which the natural rocks were shaped begin to make sense as a result of new archaeological excavations begun several years ago. Though far from uncovering more than a small part of the extensive stone structures in the plateau that extends behind the smooth Rodadero rock, they have already revealed two major aspects of the site. One is the fact that walls, conduits, receptacles, channels, and the like have been created both out of the living rock and with the aid of perfectly shaped large ashlars, many of the polygonal kind of the Megalithic Age, to form a series of water-channeling structures one above the other; rain or spring waters could thus be made to flow in a regulated manner from level to level.

The other aspect is the uncovering of a huge circular area enclosed by megalithic ashlars, that by all opinions served as a reservoir. Also uncovered was a sluice-chamber built of megalithic ashlars, that lies underground at a level permitting the running off of the water from the circular reservoir. As children who come to play there have demonstrated, the channel leading away from this sluice-chamber leads to the *Chingana* or "Labyrinth" carved out of the native rock behind and below this circular area.

Even before the whole complex that had been built on this promontory is uncovered, it is by now clear that some mineral or chemical compounds had been poured down the Rodadero, giving its back smooth side the discoloration resulting from such use. Whatever it was—gold-bearing soil?—was poured down into the large circular reservoir. From the other side, water was force-flowed. It all looks like a large-scale gold-panning facility. The water was finally flowed off through the sluice-chamber, and out and away through the labyrinth. In the stone vats, what remained was gold.

What then did the megalithic, colossal zigzagging walls, at the edge of the promontory, protect or support? To this question there is still no clear answer, except to surmise that some kind of massive platform was required for the vehicles—airborne, we must presume—that were used to haul in the ores and take away the nuggets.

One site that may have served, or was intended to serve, a similar transportation function, located some sixty miles northwest of Sacsahuaman, is Ollantaytambu. The archaeological remains are atop a steep mountain spur; they overlook an opening between the mountains that rise where the Urubamba-Vilcanota and Patcancha rivers meet. A village that gave its name to the ruins is situated at the bottom of the mountain; the name, meaning "Restplace of Ollantay," stems from the time an Inca hero prepared there a stand against the Spaniards.

Several hundred stone steps of crude construction connect a series of terraces of Inca make and lead to the principal ruins on the summit. There, in what has been presumed to have served as a fortress, there are indeed remains of Inca-walled structures built of fieldstones. They look primitive and ugly beside pre-Inca structures from the Megalithic Age.

The megalithic structures begin with a retaining wall built of the beautifully fashioned polygonal stones as one finds at the previously described megalithic remains. Passing through a gateway cut of a single stone block one reaches a platform supported by a second retaining wall, similarly constructed of polygonal stones but of a larger size. On one side an extension of this wall becomes an enclosure with twelve trapezoid openings—two serving as doorways and ten being false windows; perhaps this is why Luis Pardo (*Ollamtaitampu, Una ciudad megalitica*) called this structure "the central temple." On the other

Figure 104

side of the wall there stands a massive and perfectly shaped gate (Fig. 104) that in its time (though not now) served as the way up to the main structures.

The greatest mystery of Ollantaytambu is there: a row of six colossal monoliths that stand on the topmost terrace. The gigantic stone blocks are from eleven to almost fourteen feet high, average six or more feet in width and vary in thickness from about three to over six feet (Fig. 105). They stand joined together, without mortar or any other bonding material, with the aid of long dressed stones that had been inserted between the colossal blocks. Where the thickness of the blocks fell short of the greatest thickness (of over six feet), large polygonal stones fitted together, as at Cuzco and Sacsahuaman, to create an even thickness. In front, however, the megaliths stand as a single wall, oriented exactly southeast, with faces that have been carefully smoothed to obtain a slight curvature. At least two of the monoliths bear the weathered remains of relief decorations; on the fourth one (counting from the left) the design is clearly that of the Stairway symbol; all archaeologists agree that the symbol, which had its origin at Tiahuanacu at Lake Titicaca, signified the ascent from Earth to Heaven or, in reverse, a descent from Heaven to Earth.

Jambs and protrusions on the sides and faces of the monoliths and steplike cuts at the top of the sixth one suggest that the construction was not completed. Indeed, stone blocks of various shapes and sizes lie strewn about. Some have been cut and

Figure 105

shaped and given perfect corners, grooves and angles. One provides a most significant clue: a deep T shape has been cut into it (Fig. 106). All the scholars, having found such cuts in gigantic stone blocks at Tiahuanacu, had to agree that this groove was intended to hold together two stone blocks with a *metal* clamp; as a precaution against earthquakes.

One must therefore wonder how scholars can continue to attribute these remains to the Incas, who did not possess any metal except gold, which is too soft and thus totally unsuitable to hold together colossal stone blocks shaken by an earthquake. Naive too is the explanation that Inca rulers built this colossal place as a gigantic bathhouse, for bathing was one of their cherished pleasures. With two rivers running just at the foothills, why haul immense blocks—some weighing as much as 250 tons

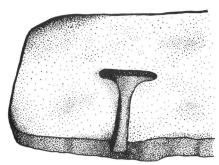

Figure 106

—to build a bathtub up the hill? And all that, without iron tools?

More serious is the explanation for the row of six monoliths that they were part of a planned retaining wall, probably to support a large platform atop the mountain. If so, the size and the massivity of the stone blocks bring to mind the colossal stone blocks used to construct the unique platform at Baalbek, in the Lebanon mountains. In *The Stairway to Heaven* we described and examined at length that megalithic platform, and concluded that it was the "landing place" that had been the first destination of Gilgamesh—a landing place for the "aerial ships" of the Anunnaki.

The many similarities we find between Ollantaytambu and Baalbek include the origin of the megaliths. The colossal stone blocks of Baalbek were quarried miles away in a valley, then incredibly lifted, transported, and put in place to fit with other stones of the platform. At Ollantaytambu too the giant stone blocks were quarried on the mountainside on the opposite side of the valley. The heavy blocks of red granite, after they had been quarried, hewed, and shaped, were then transported from the mountainside, across two streams, and up the Ollantaytambu site; then carefully raised, put precisely in place, and finally fused together.

Whose handiwork was Ollantaytambu? Garcilaso de la Vega wrote that it was "from the very first epoch, before the Incas." Blas Valera stated, "from an era that anteceded the epoch of the Incas . . . the era of the pantheon of the gods of pre-Inca times." It is time that modern scholars agree.

It is also time to realize that these gods were the same deities to whom the construction of Baalbek has been attributed by Near Eastern legends.

Was Ollantaytambu intended to be a stronghold, as Sacsahuaman might have been, or a landing place, as Baalbek had been?

In our previous books we have shown that, in determining the site of their spaceport and "landing places," the Anunnaki first anchored a landing corridor on some outstanding geographical feature (such as Mount Ararat). The flight path within this corridor was then inclined at a precise 45 degrees to the equator. In postdiluvial times, when the spaceport was in the Sinai peninsula and the landing place for airborne craft at Baalbek, the grid followed the same pattern.

The *Torreon* at Machu Picchu has, besides the two observation windows in the semicircular section, another enigmatic

Figure 107

window (Fig. 107) that has an inverted stairway opening at its bottom and a wedgelike slit at its top. Our own studies show that a line from the Sacred Rock through the slit to the Intihuatana will run at a precise angle of 45 degrees to the cardinal points, thus establishing for Machu Picchu its principal orientation.

This 45 degree orientation determined not only the layout of Machu Picchu, but also the location of major ancient sites. If one draws on a map of the region a line connecting the legendary stops made by Viracocha from the Island of the Sun in Lake Titicaca, the line will pass Cuzco and continue to Ollantaytambu—precisely at a 45 degree angle to the equator!

A series of studies and lectures by Maria Schulten de D'Ebneth, summed up in her book *La Ruta de Wirakocha*, showed that the 45 degree line on which Machu Picchu is located fits a grid pattern along the sides of a square tilted at 45 degrees (so that the corners, not the sides, point toward the cardinal points). She confessed that she was inspired to search for this

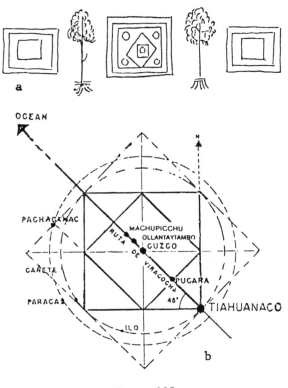

Figure 108

ancient grid by the *Relacion* of Salcamayhua. Relating the tale of the three windows, he drew a sketch (Fig. 108a) to illustrate the narrative, and gave each window a name: Tampu-Tocco, Maras-Tocco, and Sutic-Tocco. Maria Schulten realized that these are place names. When she applied the tilted square to a map of the Cuzco-Urubamba area, with its northwestern corner at Machu Picchu (alias Tampu-Tocco), she discovered that all the other places fell into the correct positions. She drew lines showing that a 45 degree line originating at Tiahuanacu, combined with squares and circles of definite measurements, embraced all the key ancient sites between Tiahuanacu, Cuzco, and Quito in Ecuador, including the all-important Ollantaytambu (Fig. 108b).

No less important is another finding by her. The subangles that she had calculated between the central 45 degree line and sites located away from it, such as Pachacamac's temple, indicated to her that the Earth's tilt ("obliquity") at the time this grid was laid out was close to 24° 08'. This means the grid was planned (according to her) 5,125 years before her measurements were done in 1953; in other words, in 3172 B.C.

It is a determination that confirms our own conclusion that the megalithic structures belong to the Age of Taurus, the era between 4000 B.C. and 2000 B.C. And, by combining modern studies with the data provided by the chroniclers, it affirms what the legends kept reiterating:

It all began at Lake Titicaca.

10

"BAALBEK OF THE NEW WORLD"

Every version of every legend in the Andes points to Lake Titicaca for the Beginning—the place where the great god Viracocha performed his creative feats, where mankind reappeared after the Deluge, where the ancestors of the Incas were granted a golden wand with which to establish Andean civilization. If this be fiction, then it is supported by fact; for it is on the shores of Lake Titicaca that the first and greatest city in all of the Americas had stood.

Its scope, the size of its monoliths, the intricate carvings upon its monuments and its statues have amazed all who have seen Tiahuanacu (as the place has been called) ever since the first chronicler described it for Europeans. Everyone equally wondered who had built this unique city and how, and puzzled over its untold antiquity. Yet the greatest puzzle of all is the location itself: a barren, almost lifeless place some 13,000 feet —four kilometers!—up among the highest Andean peaks that are permanently snow-covered. Why would anyone expend incredible effort to erect colossal edifices out of stone that had to be quarried and brought over from many miles away in this treeless, windswept desolate place?

The thought struck Ephraim George Squier when he reached the lake a century ago. "The islands and promontories of Lake Titicaca," he wrote (*Peru Illustrated*) "are for the most part barren. The waters hide a variety of strange fishes, which contribute to support a population necessarily scanty in a region where barley will not ripen except under very favorable circumstances, and where maize, in its most dimunitive size, has its most precarious development; where the potato, shrunk to its smallest proportions, is bitter; where the only grain is the quinoa; and where the only indigenous animals fit for food are the biscacha, the llama, and the vicuña." Yet in this treeless world, he added, "if tradition be our guide, were developed the germs of Inca civilization" from an earlier, "original civilization which carved its memorials in massive stones, and left them on the plain of Tiahuanaco, and of which no tradition remains except that they are the work of the giants of old, who reared them in a single night."

A different thought, however, struck him as he climbed up a promontory overlooking the lake and the ancient site. Was it perhaps because of the isolation, because of the surrounding peaks, because of the vista between the peaks, that the place had been chosen? From a ridge at the southwestern edge of the plain in which the lake is situated, near where its waters flow out southward through the Desaguadero river, he could see not only the lake with its southern peninsulas and islands, but also the snowy peaks to the east.

"Here," he wrote with words accompanying a sketch he had made, "the great snowy chain of the Andes burst on our sight in all its majesty. Dominating the lake is the massive bulk of Illampu, or Sorata, the crown of the continent, the highest mountain of America, rivaling, if not equaling in height, the monarchs of the Himalayas; observers vary in their estimates and calculations of its altitude from 25,000 to 27,000 feet." Southward from this outstanding landmark the uninterrupted chain of mountains and peaks "terminates in the great mountain of Illimani, 24,500 feet in altitude." Between the western ridge at whose edge Squier had stood and the gigantic mountains to the east, lay the flat depression that was occupied by the lake and its southern shores. "Nowhere else in the world, perhaps," Squier went on, "can a panorama so diversified and grand be obtained from a single point of view. The whole great tableland of Peru and Bolivia, at its widest part, with its own system of waters, its own rivers and lakes, its own plains and mountains, all framed in by the ranges of the Cordilleras and the Andes, is presented like a map" (Fig. 109).

Were these geographical and topographical features the very reason for the selection of the site—at the edge of a great plain basin, with two peaks that stand out not only from the ground but also from the skies—just as the twin peaks of Ararat (17,000 and 13,000 feet) and the two pyramids of Giza had served to mark the landing paths of the Anunnaki?

Unbeknown to Squier, he had raised the analogy, for he had titled the chapter describing the ancient ruins "Tiahuanaco, the Baalbec of the New World"; for that was the only comparison he could think of—a comparison with a place that we have identified as the landing place of the Anunnaki to which Gilgamesh had set his steps five thousand years ago.

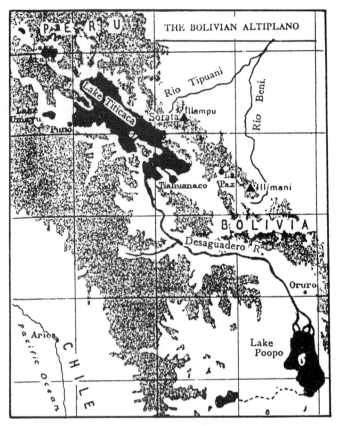

Figure 109

The greatest explorer of Tiahuanacu and its ruins this century has been, without doubt, Arthur Posnansky, a European engineer who moved to Bolivia and devoted his lifetime to unraveling the mysteries of these ruins. As early as 1910 he complained that, from visit to visit, he saw less and less of the artifacts, for the local natives, builders in the capital La Paz, and even the government itself for construction of the railroad, systematically carry off the stone blocks not for their artistic or archaeological value, but as freely available building materials. Half a century earlier Squier voiced the same complaint, noticing that in the nearest town, on the peninsula of Copacabana, the church as well as the villagers' abodes were built of stones taken away from the ancient ruins as if they were a quarry. Even the cathedral in La Paz, he found out, was erected using Tiahuanacu's stones. Yet, the little that remained—mostly because it was too massive to move—impressed him that these were remains of a civilization that disappeared before that of the Incas began, a civilization contemporary with that of Egypt and the Near East. The remains indicate that the structures and the monuments were the work of a people who were capable of a unique, perfect, and harmonious architecture—yet one that "had no infancy and passed through no period of growth." No wonder, then, that the wondering Indians had told the Spaniards that these artifacts were raised overnight by giants.

Pedro de Cieza de Leon, who traveled throughout what is now Peru and Bolivia in the years 1532–1550, reported in his *Chronicles* that, without doubt, the ruins of Tiahuanacu were "the most ancient place of any that I have yet described." Among the edifices that amazed him was a "hill made by the hands of men, on a great foundation of stone" that measured more than 900 feet by 400 feet at its base and rose some 120 feet. Beyond it he saw "two stone idols, of the human shape and figure, the features very skillfully carved, so that they appear to have been done by the hand of some great master. They are so large that they seem like small giants, and it is clear that they have the sort of clothing different from those now worn by the natives of these parts; they seem to have some ornament on their heads."

Nearby he saw the remains of another building, and of a wall "very well built." It all looked very ancient and worn. In another part of the ruins he saw "stones of such enormous size that it causes wonder to think of them, and to reflect how human force can have sufficed to move them to the place where we see them, being so large. Many of these stones are carved in different ways, some of them having the shape of a human body, which must have been their idols."

He noticed near the wall and the large stone blocks "many holes and hollow places in the ground," which puzzled him. More to the west he saw other ancient remains, "among them many doorways, with their jambs, lintels and thresholds all in one stone." He wondered most particularly that "from these great doorways there came out still larger stones upon which the doorways were formed, some of them thirty feet broad, fifteen or more long and six in thickness. The whole of this," he reported with utter amazement—the doorway and its jambs and lintel—"were one single stone." He added that "the work is one of grandeur and magnificence, when all considered," and that "for myself I fail to understand with what instruments or tools it can have been done, for it is very certain that before these great stones could be brought to perfection and left as we see them,

Figure 110

the tools must have been much better than those now used by the Indians."

Of all the artifacts seen by the first Spaniards to arrive on the scene, so sincerely described by Cieza de Leon, these colossal one-piece gateways still lie where they had fallen. The site, about a mile to the southwest of the principal ruins of Tiahuanacu, has been called by the Indians Puma-Punku as though it were a separate site; but it is nowadays certain that it was part of the greater metropolis embraced by Tiahuanacu that measured a mile by almost two miles in size.

The remains there have amazed every traveler who has seen them during the past two centuries, but were first scientifically described by A. Stübel and Max Uhle (*Die Ruinenstaette von Tiahuanaco im Hochland des Alten Peru,* 1892). The photographs and sketches that accompanied their report showed that the gigantic stone blocks lying about were components of several structures of amazing complexity that may have formed the eastern edifice of the site (Fig. 110 is based on the latest studies). The four-part edifice that collapsed (or was overthrown) lies as enormous platforms with or without the parts that formed one piece with them vertically or at other angles (Fig. 111). The

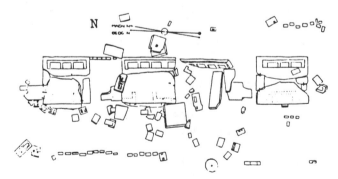

Figure 111

Figure 112

individual, broken-off portions weigh as much as one hundred tons each; they are made of red sandstone, and Posnansky (*Tihuanacu—The Cradle of American Man*) has proved conclusively that the quarry for these blocks, which weighed three or four times as much when they were one unit, was on the western shore of the lake some ten miles away. These stone blocks, some measuring twelve by ten feet and almost two feet thick, are covered with indentations, grooves, precise angles and surfaces that have varying levels. At certain points the blocks have indentations (Fig. 112) that were certainly intended to hold metal clamps, to attach each vertical section to those adjoining it—a technical "gimmick" that we had seen at Ollantaytambu. But whereas there the suggestion was that the clamps were made of gold (the only metal known to the Incas)—an untenable suggestion because of the softness of gold—here the clamps were made of *bronze*. That this was so is known because some of these bronze clamps have actually been found. This is certainly a discovery of immense significance, for bronze is a most difficult alloy to produce, requiring the combination of a certain proportion of copper (about 85–90 percent) with tin; and whereas copper can be found in its natural state, tin must be extracted by difficult metallurgical processes from the ores in which it is contained.

How was this bronze obtained, and was its availability not only part of the puzzle but also a clue to the answers?

Putting aside the customary explanation that the colossal and intricate structures of Puma-Punku were "a temple," what practical purpose did it serve?—what was the function for which such immense effort and sophisticated technologies were expended? The German master architect Edmund Kiss (whose visualization of the way the structures might have originally looked inspired his plans for Nazi monumental buildings) believed that the mounds and remains flanking and fronting on the four-part collapsed section were elements of a harbor, for the lake had certainly extended that far in antiquity. But this leaves open and even reinforces the question, what was going on at Puma-Punku? What did it import and what products did it ship out at this barren altitude?

Ongoing excavations at Puma-Punku have uncovered a series of semisubterranean enclosures constructed of perfectly shaped stone blocks. They remind one of the sunken plazas of Chavin de Huantar, and raise the possibility that these were elements—reservoirs, pools, sluice-chambers—of a similar waterworks system.

More answers may lie in the most puzzling (if that is still possible) finds at the site: blocks of stone, complete by themselves or undoubtedly broken off from larger blocks, that have been shaped, angled, cut, and grooved in an astonishing way with an astounding precision and with tools that are hard to find even today. The best way to describe these technological miracles is to show some of them (Fig. 113).

There is absolutely no plausible explanation for these artifacts except to suggest—based on our own present technology —that these were matrixes, dies for the casting of intricate metal parts; parts for some complex and sophisticated equipment that Man in the Andes, or for that matter anywhere else, was absolutely incapable of possessing in pre-Inca times.

Various archaeologists and researchers had come to Tiahuanacu since the 1930s for brief or sustained work—Wendell C. Bennett, Thor Heyerdahl, and Carlos Ponce Sangines are names best recognized; but by and large, they only used, built upon, accepted, or argued with the conclusions of Arthur Posnansky, who first presented his extraordinary work and insights in the 1914 extensive volumes of *Una Metropoli Prehistorica en la America del Sur* and, after another three decades of devoted research, in the four-volumed *Tihuanacu—Cuna del Hombre de las Americas,* combined with an English translation (in 1945). This edition was honored with an official forword by the Bolivian government (the site ended up in the Bolivian part of the lake after its partition from Peru), and celebrated "the 12,000th year of Tiahuanacu."

For this, when all was said and done, was the most astounding (and controversial) conclusion of Posnansky: That Tiahua-

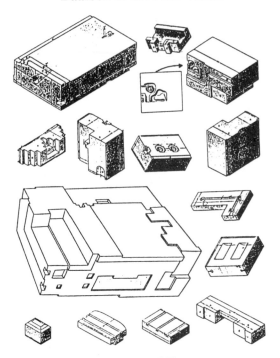

Figure 113

nacu was millennia old; that its first phase was built when the
level of the lake was about one hundred feet higher and before
the whole area had been engulfed by an avalanche of water—
perhaps the famous Great Flood, thousands of years before the
Christian era. Combining the archaeological discoveries with
geological studies, study of flora and fauna, measurements of
skulls found in tombs and portrayed in stone heads, and bringing to bear every facet of his engineering and technological expertise, Posnansky concluded that there had been three phases
in the history of Tiahuanacu; that it was settled by two races—
first the Mongoloid people, then Middle Eastern Caucasians—
and at no time by the negroid people; and that the place had
undergone two catastrophes, first a natural one by an avalanche
of water, and then another sudden upheaval of unknown nature.

Without necessarily agreeing with these hard-hitting conclusions or with their timetable, the geological, topographical, cli-
matic, and all scientific data amassed by Posnansky, and of
course the archaeological discoveries he made, have been accepted and used by all who have followed in the half century
since his monumental endeavors. His map of the site (Fig. 114)

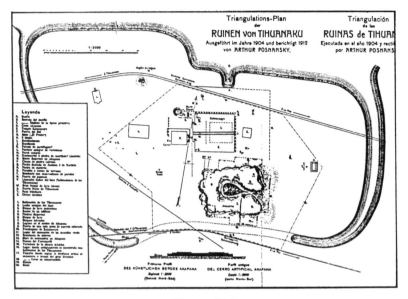

Figure 114

has remained the basic layout plan of the site, of its measurements, orientations, and principal edifices. While some of the sections he pointed to as potentially holding additional remains and artifacts were indeed excavated and profitably so, the main interest was and remains on three major components of the site.

The one at the southeastern part of the ruins is a hill known as the *Akapana*. It was probably given originally the shape of a stage-pyramid, and is presumed to have acted as the fortress guarding the site; the principal reason for that assumption being the fact that at the top of this pyramid-hill the center was excavated to form an oval, lined with ashlars, that acted as a water reservoir. The presumption was that it was intended to collect rainwater and provide the defenders with water as they fell back to this stronghold. Rumors however persisted that it was a place where gold was hidden, and in the eighteenth century a Spaniard named Oyaldeburo was given a mining concession for the Akapana. He cut through the eastern side of the hill to drain off the water, searched the bottom of the reservoir, tore down structures of beautiful ashlars, and dug deep into the hill wherever he found channels and conduits.

The destruction nevertheless revealed that the Akapana was not a natural hill but a very complex structure. Ongoing excavations, still barely scratching the surface, follow the work of Posnansky, who showed that the stone-lined reservoir was provided with masterful sluices that could regulate the flow of water down through channels constructed of ashlars with great precision. The complex inner workings of the Akapana were so built as to lead the water from one level inside the Akapana to another lower one in alternating vertical and horizontal sections, a vertical height of fifty feet but, because of the zigzagging, covering a far larger distance. In the end, some feet below the bottom of the Akapana, the water flowed through a stone outlet into the artificial canal (or moat), some 100 feet wide, that encircled the whole site. It led from there to wharfs at the site's north and thence to the lake. Now, if the purpose were just to drain off excess water to prevent overflow after heavy downpours, a simple straight inclined pipe (as was found at Tula) would have sufficed. But here we have angled channels, built with dressed stones fitted with great ingenuity to regulate the water's flow from one inner level to another. And this indicates to us a processing technique—the use of flowing water for washing ores, perhaps?

That some processing might have taken place in the Akapana is further suggested by the discovery on the surface and in the soil removed from the "reservoir" of large quantities of dark-green rounded "pebbles" that range in size from three-fourths of an inch to two inches. Posnansky determined that they are crystalline, but neither he nor others (to our knowledge) conducted further tests to determine the nature and origin of these globular objects.

A structure more to the center of the site ("K" on Posnansky's map) had so many subterranean and semisubterranean features that Posnansky thought it might represent a section set aside for tombs. All around there were sections of stone blocks cut to act as water conduits; they were in a state of disarray that Posnansky blamed not only on treasure hunters but also on a previous team of explorers, under Count Crequi de Montfort, who during their excavations in 1903 wantonly dug up remains, broke whatever stood in their way (according to Posnansky), and carried off many artifacts. The report on the discoveries and conclusions of this French expedition was given in a book by George Courty and in a lecture to the 1908 International Congress of Americanists by Manuel Gonzales de la Rosa. The essence of their findings was that "there were two Tiahuanacos," one the visible ruins, the other subterranean and invisible.

Posnansky himself described the conduits, channels, and a sluice (as atop the Akapana) that he found among the disturbed sunken portions of this structure, and determined that the conduits ran in several levels, led perhaps to the Akapana, and

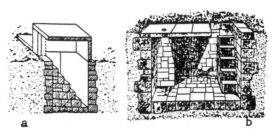

a   b

Figure 115

were linked with other subterranean structures to the west (in the direction of the lake). He described in words and a drawing (Fig. 115a,b) some of the subterranean and semisubterranean compartments, unable to hold back his amazement at the precision of the workmanship, the fact that the ashlars were made of hard andesite and that these compartments were completely waterproof: over all the seams and especially on the large roof slabs there had been spread a layer made of true lime, a couple of inches thick, which rendered the places "absolutely waterproof. This," he noted, "is the first and only time that we find the use of lime in a prehistoric American construction."

What went on in these subterranean chambers and why they were so specifically built, he could not tell. Perhaps they held treasure, but that, he pointed out, would have long disappeared by the hand of treasure seekers. Indeed, no sooner had he uncovered some of these chambers than "the place was stripped and robbed by the iconoclastic half-breeds of modern Tihuanacu." Apart from what he excavated or saw strewn about at the site, large quantities of stone conduits—pieces of all shapes, sizes and diameters—could be seen in the nearby church and in the bridges and culverts of the modern railroad and even in use in La Paz. The indications were of extensive ground and underground waterworks at Tiahuanacu; and Posnansky devoted to them a whole chapter in his ultimate work, titled *Hydraulic Works in Tihuanacu.* Recent excavations have uncovered more stone conduits and water channels, confirming the conclusions of Posnansky.

The second outstanding edifice at Tiahuanacu needed the least excavating, for it stands there majestically for all to see—a colossal stone gateway that rises above the flatness of the site like an *Arc de Triomphe* with no one to parade through it, no one to watch and cheer (Fig. 116, front and back).

Known as the Gate of the Sun, it has been described by Posnansky as "the most perfect and important work . . . a legacy

Figure 116

and elegant testimony of the cultured people and their leaders' knowledge and civilization." All who have seen it agree, for it is amazing not only by dint of having been cut and shaped out of a single block of stone (measuring about ten by twenty feet and weighing over one hundred tons), but also because of the intricate and breathtaking carvings upon it.

There are niches and geometric carved openings and surfaces upon the lower part of the gate's front and on its back side, but

Figure 117

the marveling has been at the carved section on the gate's upper front part (Fig. 117). There a central figure, almost three-dimensional though carved only in relief, is flanked by three rows of winged attendants; a lower row of images depicting only the central figure's face, framed by a meandering line, completes the composition.

There is general agreement that the central and dominant figure is that of Viracocha, holding a scepter or weapon in the right hand and a forked lightning in the other (Fig. 118). This image appears on vases, textiles, and artifacts in southern Peru and adjoining lands, indicating the extent to which what scholars call the Tiahuanacu culture had spread. Flanking this god are winged attendants, arranged in three horizontal rows, eight to a row on each side of the central figure. Posnansky pointed out that only the first five on each side in each row are carved in the same pronounced relief as the deity; the others on the extremes are carved faintly, as an afterthought.

He drew the central figure, the meander under it, and the fifteen original spaces on each side (Fig. 119) and concluded that this was a calendar of a twelve-month year, beginning at the spring equinox (September in the southern hemisphere); and that the central large figure, showing the deity in full body, represented that month and its equinox. Since the "equinox" denotes that time of the year when day and night are equal, he surmised that the segment right under the central figure, which is in the center of the meandering row, stands for the other

Figure 118

equinox month, March. He then assigned the remaining months in succession to the other segments within the meander. Pointing out that the two end segments show a bugler together with the deity's head, he suggested that these were the two extreme months when the Sun moves farthest away, the solstice months of June and December, when the priests would sound the bugle to call the sun back. The Gate of the Sun, in other words, was a calendar in stone.

The calendar, Posnansky surmised, was a solar calendar. Not only was it geared to the spring equinox when it began, but it also marked the other equinox and the solstices. It was a calendar of eleven months of thirty days each (the number of winged attendants above the meander) plus a "great month" of thirty-five days, the Month of Viracocha, making up a solar year of 365 days.

He should have mentioned that a twelve-month solar year beginning at the spring equinox was a Near Eastern calendar begun in Sumer, at Nippur, circa 3800 B.C.

The image of the deity, as well as those of the winged attendants and month-faces, seemingly depicted in natural realism,

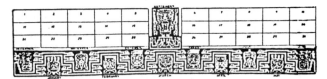

Figure 119

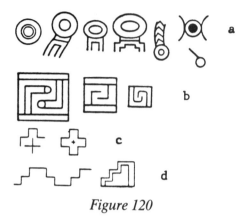

Figure 120

are in fact made up of many components that each have their own, mostly geometric shape. Posnansky devoted considerable study to these various components. They also appear on other monuments and sculptures of stone as well as on ceramic objects. He classified them pictographically according to the object (animal, fish, eye, wing, star, etc.) that they depicted or the idea they represented (Earth, Heaven, movement, and so on). He determined that circles and ovals depicted in a variety of ways and colors represented the Sun, Moon, planets, comets, and other celestial objects (Fig. 120a), that the bond between Earth and Heaven (Fig. 120b) was frequently expressed, and that the dominant symbols were the cross and the stairway signs (Fig. 120c, d). He saw in the latter, the Stairway, the "trademark" of Tiahuanacu, its monuments and its ultimate civilization—the source from which this symbol, he believed, spread throughout the Americas. He acknowledged that it was a glyph based on the Mesopotamian ziggurats, but noted that he did not think therefore that there had been Sumerians at Tiahuanacu.

All that reinforced his growing sense that the Gate of the Sun was part of a larger structural complex at Tiahuanacu whose purpose and function was to serve as an observatory; and this guided him in his most important and, as it turned out, most controversial work and conclusions.

Official records of the Commission for the Destruction and Expiation of Idolatry, established by the Spaniards for that clear purpose (although some suspect it was also a cover for treasure hunting), attest that the commission's men arrived in Tiahuanacu in 1625. A 1621 report by Father Joseph de Arriaga listed over 5,000 "objects of idolatry" that were obliterated by breaking, melting, or burning. What they did at Tiahuanacu is not known. The Gate of the Sun, as early photographs show, was found in the nineteenth century standing broken in two at the top, with the right-hand part leaning dangerously against the other half.

When and by whom it was straightened out and put back together is a mystery. How it was broken in two is also unknown. Posnansky did not think it was the handiwork of the Commission; rather, he thinks that this gate escaped their wrath because it had fallen and was covered by soil and thus hidden from sight when the Commission's zealots arrived. Since it was apparently reerected, some have wondered whether it was put back in its original place; the reason being the realization that the gate was not, originally, a solitary edifice standing alone in the large plain, but was part of the huge structure just east of it. The shape and size of that structure, called the *Kalasasaya*, was delineated by a series of vertical stone pillars (which is what the name meant, "The Standing Pillars"), revealing a somewhat rectangular enclosure measuring about 450 by 400 feet. Since the axis of this structure appeared to be east–west, some wondered whether the gate should not have stood in the center rather than in the northern edge of the enclosure's western wall (as it now does).

Whereas before only the great weight of the monolithic gate argued against notions of its having been moved almost two hundred feet, it is now clear from archaeological evidence that it probably stands where it belonged, for the center of the western wall was taken up by a terrace whose own center was aligned with the east–west axis of the Kalasasaya. Posnansky found along this axis various stones especially carved to permit astronomical observations; and his conclusion that the Kalasasaya was an ingenious celestial observatory is now accepted as a matter of fact.

The most obvious archaeological remains of the Kalasasaya have been the standing pillars that formed a slightly rectangular enclosure. Though not all of the pillars that once had acted as anchors for a continuous wall are still there, their count hints at an association with the number of days in a solar year and in a lunar month. Of particular interest to Posnansky were eleven pillars (Fig. 121) erected alongside the terrace protruding from the center of the western wall. His measurements of the lines of sight along the specially placed observation stones, the orientation of the structure, and the slight and purposely intended deviations from perfect cardinal points, convinced him that the Kalasasaya was built by people with ultramodern knowledge of

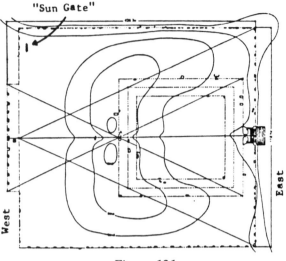

Figure 121

astronomy for the precise fixing of the equinoxes as well as the solstices.

The architectural drawings of Edmund Kiss (*Das Sonnentor von Tihuanaku*), based on Posnansky's work as well as on his own measurements and evaluations, envision (probably correctly) the structure inside the enclosure as a hollow stage-pyramid: a structure whose outer walls rise in stages but only to surround a central open-air square courtyard. The principal monumental stairway was in the center of the eastern wall; the principal observation points were in the centers of the two wider terraces that completed the "pyramid" on the west (Fig. 122).

It was on this point that Posnansky made his most startling discovery with the explosive ramifications. By measuring the distance and angles between the two solstice points, he realized that the obliquity of the Earth against the Sun on which the astronomical aspects of the Kalasasaya were based did not conform to the 23.5 degrees of our present era.

The obliquity of the ecliptic, as the scientific term is, for the orientation of the Kalasasaya's astronomical lines of sight, he found, was 23° 8' 48". *Based on the formulas determined by astronomers at the International Conference of Ephemerides in Paris in 1911, which takes into account the geographical position and elevation of the site, this meant that the Kalasasaya was built circa 15,000 B.C.!*

Announcing that Tiahuanacu was the oldest city in the world, one that was "built before the Flood," Posnansky inevi-

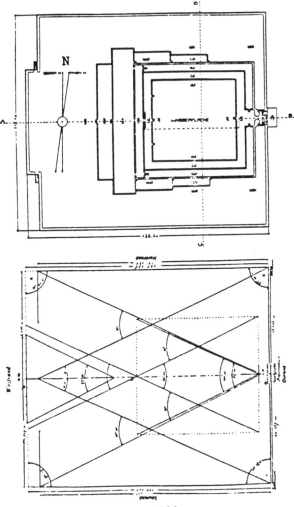

Figure 122

tably aroused the wrath of the scientific community of his time; for it was held then, based on the theories of Max Uhle, that Tiahuanacu was established some time at the beginning of the Christian era.

The obliquity of the ecliptic should not be confused (as some critics of Posnansky did) with the phenomenon of Precession. The latter changes the stellar background (constellation of stars) against which the Sun rises or acts at a certain time, such as the spring equinox; the change, though small, adds up to 1 degree in seventy-two years and to 30 degrees (a full zodiac house) in

2,160 years. The obliquity changes result from the almost imperceptible roll of the Earth as that of a ship, raising and lowering the horizon. This change in the angle at which the Earth is inclined against the Sun may amount to 1 degree in about 7,000 years.

Intrigued by the findings of Posnansky, the German Astronomical Commission sent an expedition to Peru and Bolivia; its members were Professor Dr. Hans Ludendorff, Director of the Astronomical and Astrophysical Observatory at Potsdam, Professor Dr. Arnold Kohlschütter, Director of the Astronomical Observatory in Bonn and the honorary astronomer of the Vatican, and Dr. Rolf Müller, an astronomer from the Potsdam observatory. They made measurements and observations at Tiahuanacu between November 1926 and June 1928.

Their investigations, measurements, and visual observations confirmed, first of all, that the Kalasasaya was indeed an astronomical-calendrical observatory. They found, for example, that the western terrace with the eleven pillars along it, due to the width of the pillars, the distances between them, and their positions, enabled precise measurements of the Sun's seasonal movements that had taken into account the slightly different number of days from solstice to equinox to solstice and back.

Their studies, moreover, confirmed that on the most controversial point Posnansky was essentially correct: the obliquity on which the astronomical features of the Kalasasaya were based did indeed differ substantially from the obliquity's angle in our time. Based on data that presumably throws light on the obliquity observed in ancient China and Greece, astronomers are confident about the applicable curve of the up-and-down motion only to a few thousand years back. The astronomical team concluded that the results could indeed indicate a date circa 15,000 B.C., but also one of 9300 B.C., depending on the curve used.

Needless to say, even the latter date was simply unacceptable to the scientific community. Yielding to the criticism, Rolf Müller conducted further studies in Peru and Bolivia, teaming up with Posnansky at Tiahuanacu. They found that results would change if certain variants were considered. First, if the observation of the solstice points were to be not from where Posnansky had assumed but from a different possible point, the angle between the solstice extremities (and thus the obliquity) would be slightly different; also, one could not say with any knowledge whether the ancient astronomers fixed the moment of solstice when the Sun was above the horizon line, in its midst or had just sunk below it. With all these variants, Müller published a definite report in the leading scientific journal *Baesseler Archiv* (vol. 14) in which he stated all the alternatives and concluded that if the angle of 24° 6' is to be accepted as the most accurate, the obliquity curve would cross this reading at either 10,000 B.C. or 4000 B.C.

Posnansky was invited to address the Twenty-Third International Congress of Americanists on the subject. He accepted the correct angle of obliquity to be 24° 6' 52.8", which left a choice between 10,150 B.C. and 4050 B.C. Conceding that this was "thorny material," he left the matter hanging by agreeing that it needs further study.

Such studies have indeed been conducted, even if not directly at Tiahuanacu. We have already mentioned that the calendar of the Incas indicated a Beginning in the Age of the Bull, not of Aries (the Ram). Müller himself, as we mentioned earlier, arrived at 4000 B.C. as the approximate age of the megalithic remains in Cuzco and Machu Picchu. And we have also referred to the research, along totally different lines of investigation, by Maria Schulten de D'Ebneth which led her to conclude that the Grid of Viracocha conformed to an obliquity of 24° 8' and thus to the date 3172 B.C. (by her calculations).

As the artifacts bearing the image of Viracocha—on textiles, on mummy wrappings, on pottery—were increasingly discovered all over southern Peru and even farther north and south, comparisons with other non-Tiahuanacu data could be made. Based on that, even such stubborn archaeologists as Wendell C. Bennett kept pushing the age of Tiahuanacu back, from the middle of the first millennium A.D. to almost the beginning of the first millennium B.C.

Radiocarbon datings, however, take the generally accepted dates farther and farther back. Beginning in the 1960s CIAT, the Bolivian Centro de Investigaciones Arqueologicas en Tiwanaku, has conducted systematic excavations and preservation work at the site. Its first major undertaking was the complete excavation and restoration of the sunken "small temple" east of the Kalasasaya, where a number of stone statues and stone heads were found. It uncovered a semisubterrenean courtyard, perhaps for ritual offerings, that was surrounded by a stone wall in which stone heads were stuck—in the manner of Chavin de Huantar. The official 1981 report by Carlos Ponce Sangines, Director of Bolivia's National Archaeological Institute (*Description Sumaria del Templete Semisubterraneo de Tiwanaku*), states that samples of organic matter found at this location gave radiocarbon readings of 1580 B.C.; as a result, Ponce Sangines, in his comprehensive study *Panorama de la Arqueologia Boli-*

viana, considered that time as the beginning of the Old Phase of Tiahuanacu.

Such radiocarbon dates indicate the age of the organic remains found at sites, but do not preclude an older age for the stone structures making up the site. Indeed, Ponce Sangines himself revealed in a subsequent study (*Tiwanaku: Space, Time and Culture*) that new dating techniques called Obsidian Hydration gave the earlier date 2134 B.C. for obsidian objects found at the Kalasasaya.

In this connection it is intriguing to read in the writings of Juan de Betanzos (*Suma y Narracion de los Incas,* 1551) that when Tiahuanacu was first settled under the chief called Con-Tici Viracocha, "he had with him a certain number of people . . . And after he had come out of the lagoon he went to a place near it, where today stands a village called Tiaguanaco. They say," Betanzos continued, "that once, when the people of Con-Tici Viracocha were already settled there, there was darkness in the land." But Viracocha "ordered the Sun to move in the course in which it now moves; abruptly, he made the Sun begin the day."

The darkness resulting from the Sun's standstill and the "beginning of the day" when the motion resumed is undoubtedly a recollection of the same event that we had placed, on both sides of the Earth, circa 1400 B.C. Gods and men, according to Betanzos's record of local lore, were already at Tiahuanacu from earlier times—perhaps as early as the archaeoastronomical data indicates?

But why was Tiahuanacu established, at this site, at that early time?

In recent years archaeologists have found similar architectural features between Teotihuacan in Mexico and Tiahuanacu in Bolivia. Jose de Mesa and Teresa Gisbert (*Akapana, la Piramide de Tiwanacu*) have pointed out that the Akapana had a ground plan (square with protruding accessway) like the Pyramid of the Moon in Teotihuacan, about the same base measurements as this pyramid, and the same height (about fifty feet) as the first state of the Pyramid of the Sun and its height-to-width ratio. In view of our own conclusions that the original (and practical) purpose of Teotihuacan and its edifices was expressed by the site's waterworks, within and alongside the two pyramids, the water channels inside the Akapana and throughout Tiahuanacu assume a central role. Was Tiahuanacu established where it was as a processing facility? And if so, of what?

Dick Ibarra Grasso (*The Ruins of Tiahuanaco* and other works) concurred with the envisioning of greater Tiahuanacu, encompassing the Puma-Punku section, as stretching for miles along a major east–west axis not unlike the "Way of the Dead" in Teotihuacan, with several major north–south arteries. At the edge of the lake, where Kiss had envisioned a quay, they see archaeological evidence for massive retaining walls that, built in a meander, created actual deep-water piers at which boats laden with cargo could tie up. But if so, what did Tiahuanacu import and what did it export?

Ibarra Grasso reported the discovery of the "small green pebbles" that Posnansky had found on the Akapana, elsewhere in Tiahuanacu: in the ruins of a small Akapana-like pyramid to the south, where the boulders that served to retain it had turned green; in the area of the subterranean structures west of the Kalasasaya; and in very large quantities among the ruins of Puma-Punku.

Significantly, the boulders in the retaining walls in the piers of Puma-Punku have also turned green. That can mean only one thing: exposure to copper, for it is oxidized copper that gives stone and soil their greenish color (just as the presence of oxidized iron lends a red-brown hue).

Was copper, then, processed at Tiahuanacu? Probably; but then, this could have been done more reasonably at some less forbidding place and closer to copper sources. Copper, it would appear, was brought to Tiahuanacu, not carried away from it.

What Tiahuanacu was the source of should have been clear from the very meaning of the name of its location: *Titicaca*. The name of the lake comes from that of one of two islands that lie just off the Copacabana peninsula. It was there, on the island called Titicaca, the legends tell, that the rays of the Sun had struck *Titikalla*, the sacred rock, as soon as the Sun appeared after the Deluge. (It is therefore also known as Island of the Sun.) It was there, at the sacred rock, that Viracocha granted the divine wand to Manco Capac.

And what do all these names mean? *Titi* in the Aymara language was the name of a metal—either lead or tin, according to linguists.

Titikalla, we suggest, meant the "Rock of Tin." *Titicaca* meant "Stone of Tin." And Lake Titicaca was the lake that was the source of tin.

Tin, and bronze, were the products for which Tiahuanacu was established—right where its ruins still enchant.

11

A LAND OF WHICH THE INGOTS COME

"There was a man in the land of Uz whose name was Job; and that man was perfect and upright and one that feared God and eschewed evil." He was blessed with a large family and thousands of sheep and cattle. He was "the greatest man in the East."

"Then, one day, the song of the gods came to present themselves to Yahweh, and Satan was there among them. And Yahweh asked Satan where he had been; and Satan answered: Ranging over the Earth, roaming all over it."

Thus begins the biblical tale of Job, the righteous man who was put to the test by Satan to the limits of man's faith in God. As one calamity followed another and Job began to question the Lord's ways, three of his friends journeyed from distant lands to give him sympathy and comfort. As Job voiced his plaints and doubts of divine wisdom, the friends pointed out to him the many wonders of the heavens and the earth that were known only to God; among them were the marvels of metals and their sources and the ingenuity of finding them and extracting them from the depths of the earth:

> Surely there is a source for silver
> And a place where gold is refined;
> Where iron is obtained from ores
> and copper is smelted out of stones.
>
> To darkness He puts an end,
> The usefulness he researches
> of stones in depths and obscurity.
> He breaches the brook away from habitation,
> where the forgotten and strange men move about.

There is a land of which the ingots come,
Whose underground is upheavaled as with fire;
A place where the blue-green stones are,
that has the ores of gold.
Even a vulture knows not the way thereto,
And a falcon's eye has not discerned it . . .

There He set His hand to the granite,
He overturned mountains at their roots.
He cut galleries through the rocks,
and all that is precious His eyes had seen,
He dammed up the sources of the streams,
and that which is hidden He brought to light.

Does man know all these places? Job asked, did man by
himself discover all the metallurgical processes? Indeed, he
challenged his three friends, where does this knowledge of minerals and metals come from?

And where shall Knowledge be found?
Where does Comprehension come from?
No man knows its progression;
Its source is not where mortals dwell . . .

Solid gold is not its full measure,
In silver it is priceless.
To the red gold of Ophir it is not confined,
nor by precious cornelian or lapis-lazuli.
Gold and crystal are not its measure,
neither is its value in golden vessels.
Black coral and alabaster need no mention;
Knowledge is beyond mere pearls . . .

Clearly, Job conceded, all this Knowledge comes from God
—the one who had both enriched him and deprived him and
who could restore him:

God alone understands its course
and knows how it is established.
For He can scan the ends of the Earth
and see all that is under the skies.

The inclusion of the marvels of mining in Job's discourse with
his three friends may not have been accidental. Though nothing

is known of the identity of Job himself or of the land where he had lived, the names of the three friends provide some clues. The first one was Elipaz of Teman, from southern Arabia; his name meant "God is my Pure Gold." The second one was Bildad of Shuha, a country believed to have been located south of Carcemish, the Hittite city; the land's name meant "Place of the deep pits." The third one was Zophar of Na'amah, a place named after the sister of Tubal-Cain, "the master of all smiths" according to the Bible. All three, thus, had come from lands associated with mining.

In asking these detailed questions Job (or the author of the Book of Job) displayed considerable knowledge of mineralogy, mining, and metallurgical processes. His time is certainly long after Man's first use of copper by hammering lumps of native copper into useful shapes and well into the period when metals were obtained by mining ores that had to be smelted, refined, and cast. In Classical Greece of the first millennium B.C. the art of mining and metals was also considered a matter for uncovering the secrets of nature; the very word *metal* comes from the Greek *metallao,* which meant "to search, to find hidden things."

Greek poets and philosophers, followed by Roman ones, perpetuated Plato's division of human history according to four metal ages of Gold, Silver, Bronze (copper), and Iron, in which gold represented the ideal age when Man had been closest to his gods. A biblical division included in the vision of Daniel begins with clay before the list of metals and is a more accurate version of Man's progress. After a long Old Stone Age, the Middle Stone Age began in the Near East circa 11,000 B.C.—right after the Deluge. Some 3,600 years later Near Eastern man stepped off the mountain ranges into the fertile valleys, beginning agriculture, animal domestication, and the use of native metals (metals found in riverbeds as nuggets, requiring neither mining nor refining). Scholars have called this the Neolithic (New-Stone) Age, but it was really the age when clay—for pottery and many other uses—replaced stone, just as the sequence in the Book of Daniel holds.

The early use of copper was therefore of copper-stones, and for that reason many scholars prefer to call the transition from the stone ages to the metal ages not a Copper Age but a Chalcolithic, Copper-Stone Age. This copper was processed by hammering it into the desired shape, or by a process called annealing if the copperstone was first softened by fire. Believed to have begun in the highlands surrounding the Fertile Crescent of the Near East, this metalworking of copper (and eventually of gold) was possible due to the circumstances particular to them.

Gold and copper are found in nature in their "natural state," not only as veins deep within the rocks inside the earth, but also in the form of nuggets and lumps (even dust in the case of gold) that the forces of nature—storms, floods, or the persistent flow of streams and rivers—have shaken loose out of the rocks as they became exposed. Such natural lumps of these metals would then be found near and in riverbeds; the metal would be separated from the mud and gravel by washing with water ("panning") or sifting through sieves. Although this does not involve cutting shafts and tunnels, the method is called placer mining. Most authorities believe that such mining was practiced in the highlands surrounding the Fertile Crescent of Mesopotamia and the Mediterranean eastern coasts as early as the fifth millennium B.C., and certainly before 4000 B.C.

(This is a process that has been used throughout the ages; few people realize that the "gold miners" of the renowned nineteenth-century gold rushes were not really miners who cut deep into the depths of the earth in search of gold, as is the case, say, of gold mining in southern Africa. They in fact engaged in placer mining, sifting the gravel washed down into riverbeds for nuggets or gold dust. During the Yukon gold rush in Canada, for example, "miners" using a backhoe, a sluice and a pan reported the collection of more than a million ounces of gold each year during the peak times a century ago; the real production was probably twice as much. It is interesting that even nowadays such placer miners continue to find in the beds of the Yukon and Klondike rivers and their tributaries hundreds of thousands of ounces of gold a year.)

It is noteworthy that although both gold and copper were thus available in their natural state, and gold was even more suitable for use because unlike copper it does not oxidize, Near Eastern man of those early millennia did not utilize gold but limited his use to copper. The phenomenon usually goes without explanation; but it is our opinion that the explanation is to be found in the notions familiar from the New World—that gold was a metal belonging to the gods. When gold came into use, at the beginning of the third millennium B.C. or several centuries earlier, it was for enhancing the temples (literally, "God's House") and for making golden vessels for the service of the gods therein. It was only circa 2500 B.C. that gold came into royal use, indicating a change of attitudes whose reasons are yet to be explored.

Sumerian civilization blossomed out circa 3800 B.C. and it is evident from archaeological discoveries that its beginnings, in both northern and southern Mesopotamia, were in place by 4000 B.C.; that is also the time when real mining, the processing of ores and metallurgical sophistication, appeared on the scene —a complex and advanced body of knowledge that (as in the case of all other sciences) the ancient peoples said was given them by the Anunnaki, the gods who had come to Earth from Nibiru. Reviewing the stages in man's use of metals, L. Aitchison (*A History of Metals*) noted with astonishment that by 3700 B.C. "every culture in Mesopotamia was based on metalworking"; he concluded with obvious admiration that the metallurgical heights then reached "must inevitably be attributed to the technical genius of the Sumerians."

Not only copper and gold, that could be obtained from native nuggets, but also other metals that clearly required extracting from veins inside rocks (as is the case with silver) or smelting and then refining their ores (as, for example, lead) were obtained, processed, and used. The art of alloying—the combining chemically in a furnace of two or more metals—was developed. Primitive hammering gave way to the art of casting; and the very complex process known as *Cire perdue* ("lost wax"), which enabled the casting and making of beautiful and useful objects (such as statuettes of gods or animals or temple utensils) was invented—in Sumer. The progress made there spread worldwide. In the words of *Studies in Ancient Technology* by R. J. Forbes, "by 3500 B.C. metallurgy had been absorbed by the civilization in Mesopotamia" (which began circa 3800 B.C.). "This stage is reached in Egypt some three hundred years later and by 2500 B.C. the entire region between the Nile cataracts and the Indus is metal minded. By this time metallurgy seems to have started in China, but the Chinese did not become true metallurgists until the Lungshan period, 1800–1500 B.C. ... In Europe the earliest metal objects are hardly earlier than 2000 B.C."

Before the Deluge, when the Anunnaki had been mining gold in southern Africa for their own needs on Nibiru, the smelted ores were shipped in submersible boats to their E.DIN. Sailing through what is now the Arabian Sea and up the Persian Gulf, they delivered their cargoes for final processing and refining at BAD.TIBIRA, an antediluvial "Pittsburgh." The name meant "Place Established for Metallurgy." The term was sometimes spelled BAD.TIBILA, in honor of Tibil, the god of metallurgical craftsmen or smiths; and there can be little doubt that the name of the metallurgical craftsman of the line of Cain, *Tubal*, stems from the Sumerian terminology.

After the Deluge the great Tigris-Euphrates plain where the *Edin* had been was buried under impenetrable mud; it took nearly seven millennia for the plain to become dry enough for people to resettle there and launch the Sumerian civilization. Though in this plain of dry mud there were neither stone resources nor minerals, tradition required that Sumerian civilization and its urban centers follow "the olden plan," and the Sumerian metallurgical center was established where Bad-Tibira had once been. The fact that other people in the ancient Near East employed not only Sumerian technologies but also Sumerian terminologies attests to the centrality of Sumer in ancient metallurgy. In no other ancient language have there been found so numerous and precise terms concerning metallurgy. There have been found in Sumerian texts no less than thirty terms for varieties of copper (URU.DU), be it processed or unprocessed. There were numerous terms prefixed by ZAG (sometimes shortened to ZA) to denote the metals' shine, and KU for the purity of the metal or its ores. There were terms for varieties and alloys of gold, silver, and copper—even for iron (which supposedly came into use only a millennium or so after Sumer's primacy); called AN.BAR, it too had more than a dozen terms depending on its and its ores' quality. Some Sumerian texts were virtual lexicons listing terms for "white stones," colored minerals, salts that were obtained by mining, and bituminous substances. It is known from records and finds that Sumerian traders reached out to very distant sources for metals, offering in exchange not only Sumer's staples—grains and woollen garments—but also finished metal products.

While all that could be attributed to Sumerian know-how and acumen, what needs explaining is the fact that theirs was also the terminology and written symbols (initially pictographs) connected with mining—an activity conducted in distant lands and not in Sumer. Thus, the perils of mine working in Africa were mentioned in a text called "Inanna's Descent to the Lower World"; and the ordeal of those punished to work in the mines of the Sinai Peninsula was detailed in the Epic of Gilgamesh when his companion, Enkidu, was sentenced by the gods to end his days there. Sumerian pictographic writing included an impressive array of symbols (Fig. 123) pertaining to mining, many showing varieties of mine shafts according to their structures or the minerals mined therein.

Where all these mines were located—certainly not in Sumer

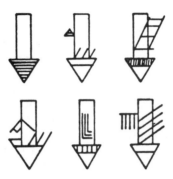

Figure 123

itself—is not always clear, for many place names remain unidentified. But some royal inscriptions indicate far and distant
lands. A good example is this quote from Cylinder A, column
xvi of Gudea, kind of Lagash (third millennium B.C.) in which
he recorded the rare materials used in building the E.NINNU
temple for his god:

> Gudea built the temple bright with metal,
> He made it bright with metal.
> He built the E.ninnu with stone,
> he made it bright with jewels;
> With copper mixed with tin he built it.
> A smith, a priest of the divine lady of the land,
> worked on its facade;
> With two hand-breadths of shining stone
> he cased the brickwork,
> with diorite's hand-breadth of bright stone.

One of the key passages in the text (which Gudea repeated
in Cylinder B, to make sure posterity remembers his pious
achievements), is the use of "copper mixed with tin" to build
the temple. The paucity of stone in Sumer had led there to the
invention of the clay brick, with which the tallest and most imposing edifices had been achieved. But as Gudea informs us, in
this instance specially imported stones were used and even the
brickwork was faced with "a handbreadth of diorite" and two
handbreadths of less rare stone. For this, copper tools were not
good enough; harder tools were needed—tools of the ancient
world's "steel," *bronze.*
As Gudea has correctly stated, bronze was a "mixture" of

copper and tin, not a natural element; it was the product of alloying copper and tin in a furnace, and thus a totally artificial product. The Sumerian rule-of-thumb for the alloy was 1:6, i.e., about 85 percent copper and 15 percent tin, which is indeed an excellent ratio. Bronze, however, was a technological achievement in other ways too. It could be shaped only by casting, not hammering or annealing; and the tin for it must be obtained from its ores through a process called smelting and recovery, for it is very rarely found in nature in its native state. It must be recovered from an ore called cassiterite. This ore is generally found in alluvial deposits that resulted from the washing out of vein or lode tin from its rocks by natural forces such as heavy rains, floods, and avalanches. The tin is recovered from the cassiterite by smelting, usually in combination with limestone in the first phase of recovery. Even this oversimplified description of the metallurgical processes involved will suffice to make clear that bronze was a metal that required advanced metallurgical know-how at every stage of its processing.

To add to the problems, it was also a metal difficult to find. Whatever sources may have been available—which is not certain—near Sumer, were quickly exhausted. Some Sumerian texts mention two "tin mountains" in a far land whose identity is unclear; some (e.g., B. Landsberger in the *Journal of Near Eastern Studies,* vol. xxi) do not shun such faraway places as the tin belt of the Far East (Burma, Thailand, and Malaysia) that is now a major source of tin. It has been ascertained that in their search for this vital metal Sumerian traders, via intermediaries in Asia Minor, reached out to tin-ore sources along the Danube, especially in the provinces known nowadays as Bohemia and Saxony (where the ores have been long exhausted). Forbes has observed that "the finds in the Royal Cemetery of Ur (2500 B.C.) show that the Ur smiths... understood the metallurgy of bronze and copper perfectly. Where the tin ore they used came from, is still a mystery." The mystery, indeed, still persists.

Not only Gudea and other Sumerian kings in whose inscriptions tin is mentioned had to go to great lengths to obtain it (probably already in its recovered state). Even a goddess, the famous Ishtar, had to transverse mountains to find its place. In a text known as *Inanna and Ebih* (Inanna being Ishtar's Sumerian name and Ebih being the name of a distant, unidentified mountain range), Inanna sought permission of the superior gods by saying,

> Let me set out on the road to the tin ores,
> Let me learn about their mines.

For all these reasons, and perhaps because the gods—the Anunnaki—had to teach ancient man how to recover the tin from its ore through smelting, the metal was considered by the Sumerians to be a "divine" metal. Their word for it was AN.NA, literally "Heavenly Stone." (Likewise, when iron that required ore smelting came into use, it was called AN.BAR, "Heavenly Metal.") Bronze, the alloy of copper and tin, was called ZA.BAR, "Gleaming Double Metal."

The term for tin, *Anna*, was borrowed by the Hittites without much change. But in the Akkadian language, the language of the Babylonians and Assyrians and the other Semitic-speaking peoples, the term underwent a slight change to *Anaku*. The term is usually taken to mean "pure tin" *(Anak-ku);* but we wonder whether the change may have reflected a closer, more intimate association of the metal with the Anunnaki gods, for it has also been found spelled *Annakum,* meaning that which belongs to or comes from the Anunnaki.

The term appears in the Bible several times. Ending with a soft *kh,* it meant a tin-plumbline, as in the prophecy of Amos envisioning the Lord holding an *Anakh* to illustrate his promise not to deviate anymore from his people Israel. As *Anak* the term meant "necklace," reflecting the high value put on this bright metal as its rarity increased and it became as precious as silver. And it also meant "giant"—a Hebrew rendering (as we have suggested in a previous volume) of the Mesopotamian "Anunnaki." It is a rendering that raises intriguing associations with the legends of both the Old World and the New World attributing this or that feat to the "giants."

All these associations of tin with the Anunnaki may have stemmed from their original role in granting mankind this metal and the know-how it required. In fact, the slight but significant modification from the Sumerian AN.NA to the Akkadian *Anaku* suggests a certain time frame. It is well documented, from archaeological discoveries as well as texts, that the great surge into the Bronze Age slowed down circa 2500 B.C. The founder of the Akkadian dynasty, Sargon of Akkad, valued the metal so much that he chose it rather than gold or silver for commemorating himself (Fig. 124), circa 2300 B.C.

Metallurgical historians find confirmation of the dwindling supplies of tin in the fact that the percentage of tin in bronze kept being lowered, and in the discovery from texts that most of the new bronze objects were made from old bronze, by melting down earlier objects and mixing the molten alloy with more copper, sometimes reducing the tin content to as little as 2 percent. Then, for unexplained reasons, the situation changed

Figure 124

abruptly. "Only from the Middle Bronze Age onwards, say from 2200 B.C.," Forbes wrote, "are true bronze forms used and higher percentages of tin appear more regularly, and not only for intricate forms as in the earlier period."

Having given mankind bronze with which to launch the great civilizations of the fourth millennium B.C., the Anunnaki seemed to come to the rescue again over a millennium later. But while the unknown sources of tin in the first instance may have been Old World ones, the source in the second instance is a complete mystery.

Here, then, is our daring thought: *The new source was the New World.*

If, as we believe, New World tin had reached the Old World's civilization centers, it could have come from one and only one place: Lake Titicaca.

This not because the name, as we have shown, signifies lake of "the tin stones"; but because this part of Bolivia is still, millennia later, a major source of the world's tin. Tin, though not rare, is considered a scarce mineral, found only at a few places in commercial quantities. Nowadays 90 percent of the world production comes from Malaysia, Thailand, Indonesia, Bolivia, Congo-Brazzaville, Nigeria, and China (in descending order). Some earlier sources, in the Near East or in Europe, have been exhausted. Everywhere, the source of tin is alluvial cassiterite, the oxidized tin ore washed by the forces of nature out of its lodes. In only two places has tin ore been found in its original lodes: Cornwall and Bolivia. The former has been exhausted;

the latter still supplies the world from mountains that seem to be truly "tin mountains" as described in the Sumerian text of Inanna.

These rich but difficult mining sources, at elevations exceeding 12,000 feet, are concentrated primarily southeast of La Paz, the Bolivian capital, and east of Lake Poopo. The much easier to attain alluvial cassiterite in riverbeds has come from the eastern coastal area of Lake Titicaca. There it was that ancient man collected the ores for their highly prized content, and where this kind of production continues today.

Some of the most reliable research concerning Bolivian-Titicaca tin mining in antiquity was done by David Forbes (*Researches on the Mineralogy of South America*); conducted more than a century ago, it was able to provide a picture as close to that found in Conquest times as possible, before the large-scale, mechanized operations of the twentieth century changed the landscape and obscured the ancient evidence. Since pure tin is extremely rare in nature, he was surprised to be shown a sample of pure tin encasing a rock—not encased within the rock, but encasing the rock within the sample. An investigation ascertained that this sample did not come from inside a mine in Oruro, but from rich cassiterite alluvial deposits. He totally rejected the offered explanation that the metallic tin was the result of forest fires caused by lightning "smelting" the cassiterite ore, because the process of recovery of tin from the ore involves more than the mere heating of the ore: a combination first with carbon (to convert the ore, SnO_2 + C to CO_2 + Sn) and as often as not again with limestone to purify the slag.

Forbes was then shown specimens of metallic tin from gold washings on the banks of Tipuani, a tributary of the Beni river flowing eastward from the mountain ranges near the lake. To his astonishment—his own words—he found the source to be rich with gold nuggets, cassiterite, and nuggets and beads of metallic tin; this meant, convincingly, that whoever worked that area for its gold also knew how to process the tin-ore for its tin. Exploring the area just east of Lake Titicaca he was amazed—his words—by the large proportion of reduced (i.e., recovered) and melted tin. He stated that the "mystery" of the occurrence of metallic tin in these areas "cannot be explained by purely natural causes." Near Sorata he found a bronze macehead which on analysis showed the alloy to be over 88 percent copper and just over 11 percent tin, "which is quite identical with many of the ancient bronzes" of Europe and the Near East. The sites appeared to be "from extremely ancient periods."

Forbes was also surprised to realize that the Indians living around Lake Titicaca, descendants of the Aymara tribes, seemed to know where to find all these intriguing sites. In fact, the Spanish chronicler Barba (1640) stated that the Spaniards had found both tin and copper mines worked by the Indians; the tin mines were "near Lake Titicaca." Posnansky found such pre-Inca mines six miles from Tiahuanacu. He and others after him confirmed the overwhelming presence of bronze artifacts at Tiahuanacu and its environs. He argued convincingly that the back of the Gate of the Sun's niches had been fitted with golden panels that could swivel on protruding hinges or "turning prongs" which had to be of bronze to support the weight. He found at Tiahuanacu stone blocks bearing niches that served to hold bronze bolts, as at Puma Punku. At Puma Punku he had seen a piece of metal, undoubtedly bronze, that "with its dentiform prongs looked like a tackle or device for lifting weights." This piece was seen and sketched by him in 1905, but was carried off and gone by his next visit. In view of the systematic plundering of Tiahuanacu, in Inca as well as in modern times, the bronze tools found on the sacred islands of Titicaca and Coati provide a measure of what must have once existed at Tiahuanacu itself. These finds included bronze bars, levers, chisels, knives, and axes—all tools that could have served in construction work, but as likely as not also in mining operations.

Indeed, Posnansky began his four-volume treatise with an introduction dealing with mining in prehistoric times in the Bolivian highland plateau in general and in the environs of Lake Titicaca in particular. "In the mountain range of the Altiplano"—highland plateau—"are found tunnels or caverns, opened by ancient inhabitants with the object of providing themselves with useful metals. These caves are to be distinguished from those opened by the Spaniards in search of precious metals, in that the remains of ancient metallurgical labors long antedate those of the Spaniards . . . in most remote periods an intelligent and enterprising race . . . provided themselves from the depths of this mountain range with useful, if not precious, metals.

"What sort of metal was the prehistoric man of the Andes seeking in the depths of the mountains in so remote a period?" Posnansky asked. "Was it gold or silver? Certainly not! A metal of much more use caused him to ascend to the highest peaks of the Andean mountain range: it was tin." And the tin, he explained, was needed to alloy with copper to create "the noble bronze." That this was the purpose of man at Tiahuanacu, he stated, was confirmed by the discovery, within a radius of thirty leagues from Tiahuanacu, of many tin mines.

But did Andean man require this tin to make his own bronze tools? Apparently not. A major study by the leading metallurgist Erland Nordenskiöld (*The Copper and Bronze Ages in South America*) established that neither age had taken place there: There had been in South America no trace of a developed bronze or even a copper age, and the reluctant conclusion was that whatever bronze tools had been found, were in fact based on Old World shapes and Old World technologies. "Examining all our material of weapons and tools of bronze and copper from S. America," Nordenskiöld wrote, "we must confess that there is not much that is entirely original, and that to the majority of fundamental types there is something to correspond to the Old World." Still voicing his reluctance to subscribe to this conclusion, he went on to admit again that "it must be confessed that there is considerable similarity between the metal technique of the New World and that of the Old during the Bronze Age." Significantly, some of the tools included in his examples had handles shaped as the head of the Sumerian goddess Ninti with her symbol of the twin umbilical cutters, later the Mistress of the Sinai mines.

The history of bronze in the New World is thus linked to the Old World, and the story of tin in the Andes, where New World bronze originated, is inexorably linked to Lake Titicaca. In that, Tiahuanacu had a central role, tied to the minerals surrounding it; otherwise, why was it built there at all?

The three civilization centers of the Old World arose in fertile river valleys: the Sumerian in the plain between the Tigris and Euphrates, the Egyptian-African along the Nile, that of India along the Indus river. Their base was agriculture; trade, made possible by the rivers, provided the industrial raw materials and enabled the export of grains and finished products. Cities sprung up along the rivers, commerce required written records, trade flourished when society was organized and international relations developed.

Tiahuanacu does not fit that pattern. It gives the appearance of being, as the popular saying goes, "all dressed up with nowhere to go." A great metropolis whose culture and art forms influenced almost the whole Andean region—built in the middle of nowhere, on the shores of an inhospitable lake at the top of the world. And even if for the minerals, why there? Geography may provide an answer.

It is customary to begin every description of Lake Titicaca by stating that it is the highest navigable body of water in the world, at an altitude of 13,861 feet. It is a rather large lake, with a surface area of 3,210 square miles. Its depth varies from a thousand feet to a hundred. Elongated in shape, it has a maximum length of 120 miles and a maximal width of 44 miles. Its ragged shoreline, the product of the mountains that surround it, forms numerous peninsulas, capes, isthmuses, and straits, and the lake has more than two score islands. The northwest–southeast layout of the lake (Fig. 109) is dictated by the mountain chains that skirt it. On the east runs the great range of the Cordillera Real of the Bolivian Andes, which includes the towering twin-peaked Mount Illampu in the Sorata group and the imposing Illimani just southeast of La Paz. Except for several small rivers that flow from this range into the lake, most flow eastward, down to the vast Brazilian plain and into the Atlantic Ocean some 2,000 miles away. It is here on the lake's eastern shores and the beds of rivers and streams that flow both ways that great deposits of cassiterite have been found.

No less imposing mountains skirt the lake on the north. There the runoff rainwaters flow mostly northward, feeding rivers, such as the Vilcanota, which some consider the true source of the Amazon; for, gathering tributaries and merging into the Urubamba, they all flow down north and then northeast into the great Amazon basin. It is there, between the mountains bordering the lake and Cuzco, that most of the gold available to the Incas had been found.

The western shore of Lake Titicaca, though bleak and dreary, is the most populated. There, among the mountains and the bays, on the coasts and in the peninsulas, present-day villages and towns share locations with ancient sites—as does Puno, the largest lakeside town and port, with the nearby enigmatic ruins of Sillustani. At that point, as modern railroad engineers have found out, a road or rail line can lead not only north but also through one of the few gaps in the Andes toward the coastal plains and the Pacific Ocean, a bare two hundred miles away.

The maritime and terrestrial geography and topography change considerably as one views the lake's southern portion (which, like most of the lake's eastern shore, belongs not to Peru but to Bolivia). There two of the largest peninsulas, that of Copacabana on the west and of Hachacache on the east, almost meet (Fig. 125) leaving only a narrow strait between the lake's much larger northern portion and its small southern one. That southern portion thus assumes the nature of a lagoon (and was so termed by Spanish chroniclers)—a body of tranquil waters as compared to the windswept northern part. The two main islands

Figure 125

of native legend, the Island of the Sun (actually, the island of
Titicaca) and the Island of the Moon (actually, Coati) lie just off
the northern shore of Copacabana.

It was on these islands that the Creator hid his children, the
Moon and the Sun, during the Deluge. It was from *Titi-kala,* a
sacred rock on the island of Titicaca, that the Sun rose to
heaven after the Deluge, according to one version; it was on the
sacred rock that the Sun's rays first fell when the Deluge was
over, according to another version. And it was from a cave
under the sacred rock that the first couple was sent to repopu-
late the lands—where Manco Capac was given the golden wand
with which to find Cuzco and begin Andean civilization.

The lake's main outflowing river, the Desaguadero, begins its flow at the southwestern corner. It feeds off waters from Lake Titicaca to a satellite lake, Lake Poopo, situated some 260 miles away to the south, in the Bolivian province of Oruro; there is copper and silver all along that way and all the way to the Pacific coast, where Bolivia meets Chile.

It is at the southern shore of the lake that the water-filled cavity between all these mountain ranges continues as dry land, creating the valley or plateau on which Tiahuanacu is situated. Nowhere else all around the lake is there such a level plateau. Nowhere else is there a nearby lagoonlike body of water that connects with the rest of the lake, making waterborne transportation feasible. Nowhere else around the lake is there a site like this, with passes through the mountains in the three landward directions and by water northward.

And nowhere else are the prized metals right at hand—gold and silver, and copper and tin. Tiahuanacu was there because it was the best place for it to be for what it was: the metallurgical capital of South America, of the New World.

All the various spellings that have been employed—Tiahuanacu, Tiahuanaco, Tiwanaku, Tianaku—are only efforts to capture the pronunciation of the name as it has been transmitted and retained by the native population. The original name, we suggest, was TI.ANAKU: the place of *Titi* and *Anaku*—TIN CITY.

Our suggestion that *Anaku* in the place's name stems from the Mesopotamian term which meant tin as the metal granted by the Anunnaki invokes a direct link between Tiahuanacu and Lake Titicaca and the ancient Near East. There is evidence to support such a suggestion.

Bronze accompanied the sprouting of the Near Eastern civilizations and came into full metallurgical utilization there by 3500 B.C. But by 2600 B.C. or so, the supplies of tin dwindled and almost petered out. Then, suddenly, fresh supplies appeared circa 2200 B.C.; the Anunnaki, somehow, had stepped in to end the tin crisis and save the very civilizations they had given Mankind. How was that achieved?

Let us look at some known facts.

Circa 2200 B.C., when tin supplies in the Near East improved so abruptly, an enigmatic people appeared on the Near Eastern scene. Their neighbors called them *Cassites* ("Kosseans" to the Greeks of later times). There is no explanation for the name that scholars know of. But it strikes us as the possible source of the term *cassiterite* by which tin-ores have been known since antiquity; it implies a recognition of the Cassites as the people who could supply the ore or who had come from where the ore is found.

Pliny, the first century A.D. Roman savant, wrote that tin, which the Greeks called "cassiteros," was more valuable than lead. He stated that it was esteemed by the Greeks since the Trojan war (and is indeed mentioned by Homer by the term *cassiteros*). The Trojan war had taken place in the thirteenth century B.C. at the western edge of Asia Minor, where the early Mediterranean Greeks came into contact with the Hittites (or were, perhaps, Indo-European cousins of theirs). "The legends say that men seek this cassiteros in the isles of the Atlantic," Pliny wrote in his *Historia Naturalis,* "and that it is transported in boats made of osier"—a twiggy plant, like a willow—"covered with hides stitched together." The islands that the Greeks call Cassiterites, "in consequence of their abundance of tin," he wrote, are out in the Atlantic facing the cape called the End of Earth; "they are the six Islands of the Gods, which some people have designated as the Isles of Bliss." It is an intriguing statement, for if the Hittites from whom the Greeks had learned all that spoke of the gods as being the Anunnaki, we have here a term with all the connotations of *Anaku.*

The reference, however, is usually taken to mean the Scilly Islands off Cornwall, especially since the Phoenicians are known to have reached that part of the British Isles for its tin in the first millennium B.C.; the Prophet Ezekiel, their contemporary, specifically mentions tin as one of the metals that the Phoenicians of Tyre had imported in their seagoing vessels.

The references in Pliny and Ezekiel are the most conspicuous though not the only pillars upon which quite a number of modern authors have raised theories of Phoenician landings on the American continents at that time. The line of thought has been that after the Assyrians ended the independence of the Phoenician city-states in the eastern Mediterranean in the ninth century B.C., the Phoenicians established a new center, Carthage (*Keret-Hadasha,* "New City") in the western Mediterranean, in North Africa. From that new base they continued their trade in metals, but also began to raid the native Africans for slaves. In 600 B.C. they circumnavigated Africa in search of gold for the Egyptian king Necho (thus emulating a feat performed for King Solomon four centuries earlier); and in 425 B.C. under a leader named Hanno they sailed around West Africa to establish gold and slave supply posts. Hanno's expedition returned safely to Carthage, for he lived to tell the tale of his voyage. But others before him or after him, so the theory goes, were swept off course by the Atlantic currents and shipwrecked on an American coast.

Putting aside the much more speculative discoveries of artifacts that point to Mediterranean presences in North America, the evidence for such presences in Middle and South America is more compelling. One of the few academicians who has stuck his neck out in this direction is Professor Cyrus H. Gordon (*Before Columbus* and *Riddles in History*). Reminding his readers of earlier mention of the identity of the name Brazil with the Semitic term *Barzel* for iron, he gave considerable credence to the so-called Paraiba Inscription that turned up in that north Brazilian site in 1872. Its disappearance soon thereafter and the vague circumstances of its discovery have induced most scholars to consider it a forgery, especially as its acceptance as authentic would undermine the notion that there had been no contacts between the Old and New Worlds. But Gordon, with great scholarship, argued for accepting as authentic the inscription that it was a message left by the captain of a Phoenician ship, separated by a storm from its sister ships, that had sailed from the Near East circa 534 B.C.

What is common to all these studies is, first, that the "discovery" of America was accidental, a result of a shipwreck or an off-course diversion by ocean currents; and second, that its time was in the first millennium B.C. and most probably in the second half of that millennium.

But we are discussing a much earlier time, almost two thousand years earlier; and we are claiming that the exchange of goods and people between the Old and New World was not accidental, but the result of the deliberate intervention of the "gods," the Anunnaki.

It is certain that the Cassites were not Britishers in disguise. Near Eastern records place them to the east of Sumer, in what is nowadays Iran. They were related to the Hittites of Asia Minor as well as to the Hurrians (the biblical *Horites,* "People of the Shafts") who acted as a geographical and cultural link between Sumer in southern Mesopotamia and the Indo-European peoples to the north. They and their predecessors, including the Sumerians, could have reached South America by sailing westward, around the tip of Africa and across the Atlantic to Brazil; or eastward, around the tip of Indochina and the island archipelago and across the Pacific to Ecuador and Peru. Each route would have required navigational feats and maps of sea routes.

Such maps, it must be concluded, did exist.

The suspicion that early maps were available to European

navigators begins with Columbus himself. It is now generally believed that he knew where he was going because he had obtained from Paolo del Pozzo Toscanelli, an astronomer, mathematician and geographer from Florence, Italy, copies of the letter and maps Toscanelli had sent in 1474 to the Church and Court in Lisbon wherein Toscanelli had urged the Portuguese to attempt a *westward* passage to India rather than by circumnavigating Africa. Abandoning centuries of petrified geographic dogma based on the works of Ptolemy of Alexandria (second century A.D.), Toscanelli picked up the ideas of pre-Christian Greek scholars such as Hipparchus and Eudoxus that the Earth was a sphere, and its measurements and size from Greek savants of earlier centuries. He found confirmation for these ideas in the Bible itself, such as in the prophetic book Esdras II that was part of the Bible in its first Latin translation, which clearly spoke of a "round world." Toscanelli accepted all that but miscalculated the width of the Atlantic; he also believed that the land lying some 3,900 miles west of the Canary Islands was the tip of Asia. This was where Columbus encountered land, the islands he believed were the "West Indies"—a misnomer that has remained to this day.

Modern researchers are convinced that the King of Portugal even possessed maps that delineated the Atlantic coast of South America, jutting more than a thousand miles eastward than the islands discovered by Columbus. They find confirmation of this belief in the compromise ordered by the Pope in May 1493 that drew a line of demarcation between the Spanish-discovered lands west of the line and unknown lands, if any, east of it. This north–south line 370 leagues west of the Cape Verde Islands, demanded by the Portuguese, gave them Brazil and the greater part of South America—to the eventual surprise of the Spaniards, but not of the Portuguese, who are believed to have known beforehand of this continent.

Indeed, by now a surprisingly large number of maps from pre-Columbian times have been found; some (as the Medicean map of 1351, the Pizingi map of 1367, and others) show Japan as a large island in the western Atlantic and, significantly, an island named "Brasil" midway to Japan. Others contain outlines of the Americas as well as of Antarctica—a continent whose features have been obscured by the ice covering it, suggesting that, incredibly, these maps were drawn based on data available when the icecap was gone—a state of affairs that existed right after the Deluge circa 11,000 B.C. and for a while thereafter.

The best known of these improbable yet extant maps is that of Piri Re'is, a Turkish admiral, bearing a Moslem date equivalent to A.D. 1513. The admiral's notation on it stated that it was partly based on maps used by Columbus. For a long time it was assumed that European maps from the Middle Ages as well as Arab maps were based on the geography of Ptolemy; but it was shown by studies at the turn of the century that very accurate fourteenth-century European maps were based on Phoenician cartography, and especially that of Marinus of Tyre (second century A.D.). But where did he obtain his data? C. H. Hapgood, in one of the best studies on the Piri Re'is map and its antecedents (*Maps of the Ancient Sea Kings*), has concluded that "the evidence presented by the ancient maps appears to suggest the existence in remote times ... of a true civilization of an advanced kind"; more advanced than Greece or Rome, and in nautical sciences ahead of eighteenth-century Europe. He recognized that before them all was the Mesopotamian civilization, extending back at least 6,000 years; but certain features on the maps, such as Antarctica, made him wonder who had preceded the Mesopotamians.

While most studies of these maps concentrate on their Atlantic features, the studies by Hapgood and his team established that the Piri Re'is map also depicts correctly the Andean mountains, the rivers including the Amazon that flow from them eastward, and the South American *Pacific* coast from about 4 degrees south to about 40 degrees south—i.e., from Ecuador through Peru to midway in Chile. Amazingly, the team found that "the drawing of the mountains indicates that they were observed from the sea, from coastwise shipping, and not imagined." The coasts were drawn in such detail that the Paracas Peninsula could be discerned.

Stuart Piggott (*Aux portes de l'histoire*) was one of the first to note that that stretch of Pacific coast of South America also appeared on the European copies of Ptolemy's Map of the World. It was shown, however, not as a continent beyond a vast ocean, but as a *Tierra Mitica,* mythical land, extending from the tip of southern China beyond a peninsula called *Quersoneso de Oro,* the Peninsula of Gold, all the way southward to a continent we now call Antarctica.

This observation prompted the noted South American archaeologist D. E. Ibarra Grasso to launch an extensive study of ancient maps; his conclusions were published in his *La Representacion de America en mapas Romanos de tiempos de Cristo.* As other researchers he concluded that the European maps leading to the Age of Discovery were based on the work of Ptolemy, which in turn was based on the cartography and geography of Marinus of Tyre and even earlier information.

a   b

Figure 126

Ibarra Grasso's study shows convincingly that the outline of the western coast of this "appendix" called Tierra Mitica conforms to the shape of the western coast of South America where it juts out into the Pacific. This is where legends placed the prehistoric landings all along!

The European copies of Ptolemy's maps included a name for a place in the midst of that mythical land, *Cattigara;* the location, Ibarra Grasso wrote, is "where in fact Lambayeque is situated, the principal center of gold metallurgy in the whole American continent." Not surprisingly, it is where Chavin de Huantar, the prehistoric gold processing center, was established, where the African Olmecs, the bearded Semites, and the Indo-Europeans had met.

Did the Cassites also land there, or in the Bay of Paracas, nearer Tiahuanacu?

The Cassites have left a rich legacy of metallurgical craftsmanship spanning the third and second millennia B.C. Their artifacts include numerous objects made of gold, silver, even iron; but their metal of preference was bronze, making the "Bronzes of Luristan" a renowned term among art historians and archaeologists. They decorated their artifacts, as often as not, with images of their gods (Fig. 126a) and of their legendary heroes, among whom a favorite was that of Gilgamesh wrestling with the lions (Fig. 126b).

Incredibly, we find identical themes and artistic forms in the Andes. In a study titled *La Religion en el Antiguo Peru* Rebecca Carnon-Cachet de Girard illustrated gods worshiped by Peruvians from depictions on earthenware vessels found in central and northern coastal areas; the similarity to the Cassite bronzes is astounding (Fig. 127a). At Chavin de Hauntar, it will be recalled, where statues depicted Hittite-like types, we also saw depictions of the Gilgamesh-and-the-lions scene. Whoever had come from the Old World to tell and depict the tale there, did so also at Tiahuanacu: among the bronze objects found there, a

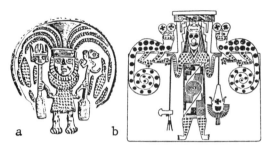

Figure 127

bronze plaque, as at Luristan of the Cassites, clearly depicted the Near Eastern hero in the same scene (Fig. 127b)!

Depictions of "angels," the winged "messenger gods" (the biblical *Mal'achim,* literally "emissaries") have been included in the art of all the ancient peoples; those of the Hittites (Fig. 128a) resemble most the winged messengers flanking the princi-

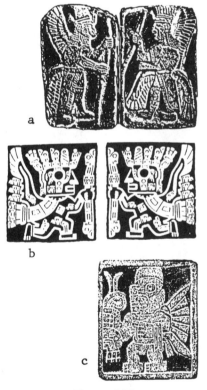

Figure 128

pal deity on the Gate of the Sun (Fig. 128b). It is significant, for reconstructing the events in American antiquity, that at Chavin de Huantar, where we believe the realms of the Teotihuacan and Tiahuanacu gods met, Olmec features replaced the Mesopotamian ones in the winged-god panels (Fig. 128c).

At Chavin de Huantar the Indo-European deity was the Bull God, a mythical animal for the other sculptors there. But although the bull was not present in South America until some were brought over by the Spaniards, scholars have been surprised to find that some Indian communities near Puno on Lake Titicaca and even at Pucara (a legendary stop on the route of Viracocha from the lake to Cuzco) worship the bull in ceremonies that originated in pre-Hispanic times (viz. J. C. Spahni, "Lieux de culte precolombiens" in *Zeitschrift für Ethnologie,* 1971). At Tiahuanacu and the southern Andes, this god was depicted armed with a lightning bolt and holding a metal wand —an image carved on stone, depicted on ceramics and on textiles. It is a combination of symbols well known from the ancient Near East, where the god called *Ramman* ("The Thun-

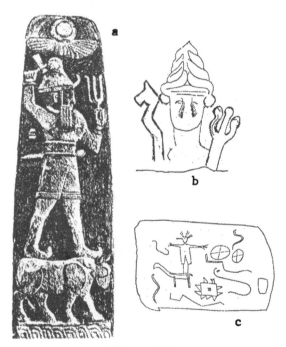

Figure 129

derer") by the Babylonians and Assyrians, *Hadad* ("Rolling Echo") by the West Semites, and *Teshub* ("Wind Blower") by the Hittites and Cassites, was depicted standing upon a bull, his cult animal, holding the metal tool in one hand and a forked lightning in the other (Fig. 129a).

The Sumerians, where the Old World pantheons originated, called this god Adad or ISH.KUR ("He of the Far Mountains"), and depicted him with the metal tool and forked lightning (Fig. 129b). One of their epithets for him was ZABAR DIB.BA—"He who bronze obtains and divides"—an illuminating clue.

Was he not Rimac of the southern coasts of Peru, Viracocha of the Andean highlands, whose image with the metal tool and forked lightning appeared all over, whose symbol of a lightning appeared by itself on many monuments? He may have even been shown standing upon a bull in a stone carving, found southwest of Lake Titicaca by Ribero and von Tschudi (Fig. 129c). Scholars who have studied the name *Viracocha* in its diverse variants agree that its components mean "Lord/Supreme" who of "Rain/Storm/Lightning" is "Maker/Creator." An Inca hymn described him as the god "who comes in the thunder and in the storm clouds." This is almost word for word the way this

Aerial photo from 2000 feet

Figure 130

deity, the God of Storms, was lauded in Mesopotamia; and the golden disk from Cuzco (Fig. 85b) depicts a deity with the tell-tale symbol of the forked lightning.

Some time in those remote days Ishkur/Teshub/Viracocha placed his symbol of the forked lightning, for all to see from the air and from the ocean, on a mountainside in the Bay of Paracas (Fig. 130)—the very bay the Hapgood team identified on the Piri Re'is map, the bay that was probably the anchorage harbor for the ships carrying the tin and bronze of Tiahuanacu to the Old World. It was a symbol proclaiming to gods and men alike:

THIS IS THE REALM OF THE STORM GOD!

For, as the Book of Job had stated, there was indeed a land of which the ingots come, whose underground is upheavaled as with fire . . . A place so high among the peaks that "even a vulture knows not the way thereto, and a falcon's eye has not discerned it." It was there that the god who provided the vital metals "set his hand to the granite . . . overturned mountains at their roots . . . cut galleries through the rocks."

12

GODS OF THE
GOLDEN TEARS

Some time after 4000 B.C. the great Anu, ruler of Nibiru, came to Earth on a state visit.

It was not the first time he had made the arduous space journey. Some 440,000 Earth-years earlier—a mere 122 years in terms of Nibiru—his firstborn son, Enki, had led the first group of fifty Anunnaki to Earth to obtain the gold with which this seventh planet was blessed. On Nibiru, nature and technological usages had combined to thin out and damage the planet's atmosphere, an atmosphere needed not only for breathing but that also had acted to envelop the planet into a greenhouse, preventing its inner-generated heat from dissipating. And only by suspending gold particles high above Nibiru, its scientists concluded, could Nibiru be saved from becoming a frozen and lifeless globe.

Enki, the brilliant scientist that he was, splashed down in the Persian Gulf and established his base, Eridu, on its shores. His plan was to obtain the gold by extracting it from the gulf's waters; but not enough was attained that way, and the crisis on Nibiru deepened. Tired of Enki's assurances that he would make the project a success, Anu came to Earth to see things for himself. He had with him his heir apparent, Enlil: though not the firstborn, Enlil was entitled to the succession because his mother, Antu, was a half sister of Anu. He lacked the scientific brilliance of Enki, but was an excellent administrator; not fascinated with the mysteries of nature, but one believing in taking charge and getting things done. And the thing to do, all the studies indicated, was to get the gold by mining it where it was abundant: in southern Africa.

Bitter arguments broke out not only regarding the project itself, but also between the rival half brothers. Anu even thought of staying on Earth and letting one of his sons act as regent on Nibiru; but the idea only caused more discord. Finally they drew lots. Enki was to go to Africa and organize the mining; Enlil was to stay in the E.DIN (Mesopotamia), build the necessary facilities for refining the ores and for shipping the gold back to Nibiru. And Anu returned to the planet of the Anunnaki. That was the first visit.

And then there was the second visit, brought about by another emergency. Forty Nibiru-years after the first landing, the Anunnaki who were assigned to work in the gold mines mutinied. How much was really caused by their arduous toil in the deep mines and how much reflected the envy and friction between the two half brothers and their contingents, one can only guess. The fact was that the Anunnaki supervised by Enki in southern Africa mutinied, refused to continue mining, and held Enlil hostage after he was there to defuse the crisis.

All those events were recorded; they were, millennia later, told to the Earthlings that they might know how it all began. A Council of the Gods was convened. Enlil insisted that Anu come to Earth and preside, to pass judgment against Enki. In the presence of the gathered leaders Enlil described the chain of events, accused Enki of leading the mutiny. But when the mutineers told their story, Anu sympathized with them. They were spacemen, not miners; and their toil had indeed become unbearable.

But did not the job need doing? How would life on Nibiru survive without this mined gold? Enki had a solution: we will create Primitive Workers, he said, who will take over the hard toil! To the astounded gathering he related that he had been conducting experiments, with the aid of the chief medical officer, Ninti/Ninharsag. There already exists on Earth, in East Africa, a primitive being—an Apeman. This being must have evolved on Earth from Nibiru's own Seed of Life, passed from Nibiru to Earth during the primeval celestial collision with Tiamat. There is genetic compatibility; what is needed is to upgrade this being, by giving it some of the Anunnaki's own genes. It will then be a creature in the likeness and in the image of the Anunnaki, able to hold tools, intelligent enough to carry out orders.

And so it was that LULU AMELU, the "Mixtured Worker," was created, out of genetic manipulation and the fertilization of an Apewoman's egg in a laboratory flask. The hybrids could not procreate; female Anunnaki had to act each time as birth-goddesses. But Enki and Ninharsag perfected them through trial and error until the perfect model was achieved. They named him *Adam*, "He Of Earth"—Earthling. With fertile servants, gold was produced in abundance, the seven settlements became cities, the Anunnaki—600 on Earth, 300 on orbiting stations—became used to a leisurely life. Some, over the objections of Enlil, took the Daughters of Man as wives, even had children by them. For the Anunnaki, obtaining the gold was now a task without tears; but to Enlil it all began to look like a mission perverted.

It all came to an end with the Deluge. For a long time the scientific observations had warned that the ice cap that was building up on the Antarctic continent became unstable; the next time Nibiru passed in Earth's vicinity, between Mars and Jupiter, its gravitational pull might cause this tremendous ice mass to slip off its continent, creating a worldwide tidal wave, abruptly changing the oceans' and Earth's temperatures, causing unparalleled storms. Consulting Anu, Enlil gave the order: prepare the spacecraft, be ready to abandon Earth!

But what about Mankind, its creators, Enki and Ninharsag, asked. Let Mankind perish, Enlil said. He made all the Anunnaki swear to secrecy, lest the desperate Earthlings interfere with the Anunnaki's departure preparations. Enki, reluctant, swore too; but pretending to speak to a wall, he instructed his faithful follower Ziusudra to build a *Tibatu,* a submersible ship, in which he and his family and enough animals could survive the avalanche of water, so that life on Earth should not perish. And he provided Ziusudra with a navigator to bring the ship to Mount Ararat, the Near East's most conspicuous double-peaked mountain.

The Creation and Deluge texts dictated by the Anunnaki to the Sumerians relate tales much more detailed and specific than the familiar biblical concise and edited versions. By the time the catastrophe occurred, there had been on Earth not only demigods. Some of the principal deities, members of the sacred circle of Twelve, were themselves in a way Earthlings: Nannar/Sin and Ishkur/Adad, Enlil's younger sons, were born on Earth; so were of course Sin's twin children, Utu/Shamash and Inanna/Ishtar. Enki and Ninharsag (with whom he may have shared his secret "Operation Noah") joined the others in suggesting that the Anunnaki not leave Earth for good, but remain in Earth orbit for a while to see what would happen. And indeed, after the immense tidal wave had come and gone and the rains had stopped, the peaks of Earth began to show and the Sun's rays, shining through the clouds, painted rainbows in the skies.

Enlil, discovering that Mankind had survived, was enraged at first. But then he relented. The Anunnaki, he realized, could still stay on Earth; but if they were to rebuild their centers and

resume the production of gold, Man must be enabled to prolif-
erate and prosper and be treated no longer as a slave but as a
partner.

In antediluvial times the spaceport, for the coming and going
of the Anunnaki and their supplies and for shipping out the
gold, was in Mesopotamia, at Sippar. But that whole fertile valley between the Euphrates and Tigris was now covered with
billions of tons of mud. Still using the twin-peaked Ararat as the
focal point on which to anchor the apex of the Landing Corridor, they erected twin artificial mountains at the thirtieth parallel on the bank of the Nile—the two great pyramids of Giza, to
serve as landing beacons for a postdiluvial spaceport in the Sinai
peninsula. It was as near, even somewhat nearer, to the African
gold sources as the spaceport in Mesopotamia had been.

So that the Earthlings could survive, multiply, and be helpful
to the Anunnaki, Mankind was granted civilization in three
states. Seeds for vital crops were brought over from Nibiru, wild
strains of grains and animals were domesticated, clay and metal
technologies taught. The latter was of great importance, for it
touched on the Anunnaki's own success in resuming the supply
of gold, now that the old mines were clogged with mud and
water.

Since the Deluge, Nibiru had come once again near Earth,
and vital materials had been received from it; but little of value
was sent back. In the olden gold sources it was now necessary to
locate hidden lodes, tunnel into mountainsides, cut shafts into
the earth, blast the rocks. Mankind had to be provided with
tools—hard tools—to be able to extract what the Anunnaki
could locate and blast with their ray guns. Fortunately, the avalanche of water had also done some good, for it had exposed
lodes, washed them out, filled riverbeds with golden nuggets
mixed with mud and gravel. Getting hold of this gold could
open up new sources—easier to work but more difficult to
reach and transport; for the place where this kind of nugget gold
was plentiful was on the other side of Earth: there, along mountain chains that face the great ocean, untold golden riches had
been exposed. It was just there for the taking—if the Anunnaki
would go there, if a way could be found to ship that gold.

And now that Nibiru had neared Earth again, the great Anu
with his spouse Antu had come to Earth for a state visit, to see
for himself where matters stood. What had been achieved by
granting Mankind the two divine metals, AN.NA and AN.BAR
with which to make the hard tools? What had been achieved by
expanding the operations to the other side of the world? Were

the storages filled with gold, as had been reported, ready to be shipped to Nibiru?

"After the Flood had swept over the Earth, when Kingship was brought down from Heaven, Kingship was first in Kish." So begins the recitation, in the Sumerian King Lists, of the various dynasties and capitals of the first Near Eastern civilization. Archaeology has indeed confirmed the preeminent antiquity of that Sumerian city. Of its twenty-three rulers, one bore a name-epithet that can be understood to mean that he was a metallurgist; it is clearly stated that the twenty-second ruler, Enmenbaragsi, was the "one who carried away as spoil the cast weapon of Elam." Elam, in the highlands east and southeast of Sumer, was indeed one of the places where metallurgy had begun; and the mention of the prize booty, a cast weapon, confirms the archaeological evidence of a fully developed metallurgy in the ancient Near East soon after 4000 B.C.

But "Kish was smitten with weapons," perhaps by the very same Elamites whose land had been invaded; and Kingship, the capital, was transferred to a brand-new city called Uruk (the biblical Erech). Of its twelve kings the best known has been Gilgamesh, of heroic fame. His name meant "to Gibil, god of Smelting/Casting [dedicated]." Metalworking, it appears, was important to the rulers of Uruk. One of them had the word *smith* describe that for which he was renowned. The very first ruler, whose reign began when Uruk was no more than a sacred precinct, had the prefix MES—"Casting Master"—as part of his name. Of him the inscription was unusually long:

Mes-kiag-gasher, son of divine Utu,
became high priest of Eanna as well as king . . .
Meskiaggasher went into the Western Sea
and came forth toward the Mountains.

This is, by the very fact that it is a lengthy statement where usually only the king's name and the length of his reign are listed, very important information, recording a renowned feat. Which sea Meskiaggasher, the Casting Master, crossed and at what mountain range he arrived, we shall never know for sure; but the wording does suggest the other side of the world.

We can understand the urgency of bringing metallurgy at Uruk to perfection: it had to do with Anu's forthcoming state visit. Perhaps to impress on him that all was going well, that very city, Uruk, was built in his honor, and metallurgical achievements were shown off. At the center of the sacred precinct a many-staged temple was built, its corners made of cast metal. Its name, E.ANNA, is generally taken to mean "House of Anu"; but it could also mean "House of Tin." The detailed texts that recorded the protocol and program of the royal visit to Uruk reveal a place lavished with gold.

Tablets found in the archieves of Uruk that, according to their scribe's notation were copies of earlier Sumerian texts, are legible only from a midpoint. Anu and Antu are already seated in the temple's courtyard, reviewing a procession of gods carrying in the golden scepter. Meanwhile, goddesses prepare the visitors' sleeping quarters in the E.NIR—"House of Brightness"—that was covered with the "handiwork of Lower World gold." As the skies darkened, a priest ascended the ziggurat's topmost stage to observe the expected appearance of Nibiru, "Great Planet of Anu of Heaven." After appropriate hymns were recited, the visitors washed their hands from golden basins and were served an evening meal from seven golden trays; beer and wine were poured from golden vessels. After more hymns hailing "the Creator's Planet, the Planet that is Heaven's Hero" had been recited, the visitors were led by a procession of torch-carrying gods to their "golden enclosure" for the night.

In the morning, golden censers were filled by priests during sacrifices as the gods were awakened for an elaborate breakfast served from golden dishes. When it was time to depart, the visiting deities were led in a procession of gods, accompanied by hymn-singing priests, to the quay where their boat was moored. They left the city through the Exalted Gate, proceeded down the Avenue of the Gods, and arrived at "The Holy Quay, the Dike of the Ship of Anu" that was to take them on "The Path of the Gods." At a chapel called House of *Akitu,* Anu and Antu joined the Gods of Earth in prayers, reciting blessings seven times. And then, "grasping hands," the gods departed.

If, by the time of this state visit, the Anunnaki had already been seeking gold in the New World, would Anu and Antu have sought to include the new lands of gold in their itinerary? Would the Anunnaki on Earth seek to impress them with their new achievements, the new prospects, the promise of providing Nibiru with the vital metal in sufficient quantities, once and for all?

If the answer is yes, then the existence of Tiahuanacu and much else about it could be explained. For if, in Sumer, a special city with a brand-new sacred precinct, with a golden enclosure, and an Avenue of the Gods and Holy Quays was established for the visit to the Olden Land, we could presume the similar establishment of a new city with a brand-new golden enclosure and a sacred avenue and sacred quays in the heart of the New Lands. And, as at Uruk, we would expect to find an observatory for determining the moment of the appearance of Nibiru in the evening skies, followed by the rising of the other planets.

Only such a parallelism, we feel, can explain the need for the observatory that the Kalasasaya had been, for its precision, and for its date: circa 4000 B.C. Only such a state visit, we suggest, can explain the elaborate architecture of Puma-Punku, its royallike piers, and, yes, its gold-plated enclosure. For that is precisely what archaeologists had found at Puma-Punku: incontrovertible evidence that gold plates covered not only portions of gates (as were the back panels of the Gate of the Sun at Tiahuanacu), but that whole walls, entrances and cornices were plated with gold. Posnansky found and photographed rows of small round holes in many polished and dressed stone blocks that "served to support golden plates which covered them by means of nails, also of gold." When he delivered a lecture on the subject to the Geographic Society in April 1943, he presented one of these blocks with five golden nails still sticking in it (the other nails having been pulled out by gold seekers when they removed the golden plates).

The possibility that at Puma-Punku there had been erected, at the earliest time, an edifice whose walls, ceiling, and cornices were covered with gold just as the E.NIR had been in Uruk becomes even more significant when we find that the bas-reliefs decorating the ceremonial gates at Puma-Punku, as well as some of the gigantic statues of the Great God at Tiahuanacu, were inlaid with gold. Posnansky discovered and photographed the attachment holes, "some two millimeters in diameter, round about the reliefs." A principal gate at Puma-Punku that he named Gate of the Moon had its relief of Viracocha as well as the god's face in the meander under it "inlaid with gold... which made the principal hieroglyphs stand out with great brilliance."

No less significant was the discovery of Posnansky that where these figures depicted the god's eyes, the gold inlay and nails "secured into the slits of the eyes small round plates of turquoise. We have found," Posnansky reported, "many of these pieces of turquoise perforated in the center, in the cultural strata of Tiahuanacu"—a fact that led him to believe that not only the reliefs on the gates, but also the gigantic stone statues of gods that have been found at Tiahuanacu, were inlaid with gold on their faces and their eyes inlaid with turquoise.

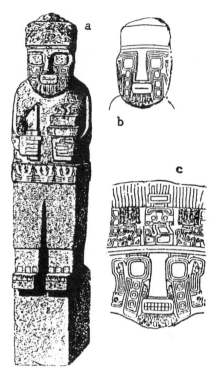

Figure 131

This discovery is most remarkable, for there is no turquoise
—a semiprecious blue-green stone—anywhere in South America. It is a mineral whose earliest mining, at the end of the fifth
millennium B.C., is believed to have taken place in the Sinai
peninsula and in Iran. All told, these inlaying techniques were
purely Near Eastern and are found nowhere else in the Americas—certainly not at those early times.

Virtually all the statues found at Tiahuanacu depict the gods
shedding three tears from each eye. The tears were inlaid with
gold, as can still be seen on some of the statues now on display
at the Museo del Oro in La Paz. A famous large statue that has
been nicknamed El Fraile (Fig. 131a), which is about ten feet
high, has been carved, as other gigantic Tiahuanacu statues
have been, of sandstone; this suggests that they all belong to the
earliest Tiahuanacu period. The deity holds a serrated tool in
his right hand; the three stylized teardrops from each eye, which
were undoubtedly inlaid with gold, can be clearly seen (as in the
sketch, Fig. 131b). Similar three teardrops can be seen on the
face called the Gigantic Head (Fig. 131c) that treasure hunters

broke off a colossal statue because of the local belief that Tia-huanacu's builders "possessed the secret of compounding stone" and that the statues were not carved from stone but were cast by a magical process that enabled the hiding of gold inside the statues.

This belief may have been sustained by the inlaying of the god's tears with gold, a practice that may explain why the Andean people (like the Aztecs) called gold nuggets "tears of the gods." Since all these statues depicted the same deity as on the Gate of the Sun, where he is also shown shedding tears, he has come to be called "The Weeping God." In view of our evidence, we feel justified calling him "God of the Golden Tears." A gigantic carved monolith found at a satellite site (Wancai) depicts the deity with a conical and horned headdress—the typical headdress of Mesopotamian gods—and with lightning bolts instead of tears (Fig. 132), clearly identifying him as the Storm God.

Figure 132

One of the gold-plated stone blocks at Puma-Punku with "mysterious cavities" and a deep channel within it was cut at a corner to hold a funnel, and Posnansky surmised it was part of a sacrificial altar. However, one of the several satellite sites near Tiahuanacu, where stone remains make them a mini Puma-Punku and where golden artifacts have been found, is called *Chuqui-Pajcha,* which in Aymara means "where the liquid gold is funneled," suggesting a gold producing process rather than sacrificial libations.

That gold was available and plentiful at Tiahuanacu and its satellites is evident not only from legends, tales, or place names, but also from archaeological remains. Many golden objects classified by scholars as Classical Tiahuanacu because of their shape or decorations (stylized images of the God of the Golden Tears, staircases, crosses) have been found at nearby land sites as well as islands in the course of excavations in the 1930s, 1940s, and 1950s. Especially noteworthy were the archaeological missions sponsored by the American Museum of Natural History (under William C. Bennett), the Peabody Museum of American Archaeology and Ethnology (under Alfred Kidder II), and the Ethnological Museum of Sweden (under Stig Rydén, together with Max Portugal, then curator of the Archaeological Museum in La Paz.)

The objects included cups, vases, disks, tubes, and pins (one of the latter, some six inches long, had a head in the shape of a three-branched plume). Golden objects found during earlier excavations on the two sacred islands, Titicaca (Island of the Sun) and Coati (Island of the Moon), were described by Posnansky in his *Guia General* to Tiahuanacu and its environs, and even more so by A. F. Bandelier (*The Islands of Titicaca and Koati*). The finds on Titicaca have been mostly in unidentifiable ruins in the vicinity of the Sacred Rock and its cavern; scholars cannot agree whether the artifacts belong to the early periods of Tiahuanacu, or (as some hold) stem from Inca times, for it is known that the Incas came to this island to worship and to erect shrines in the reign of Mayta Capac, the fourth Inca ruler.

The finds at and around Tiahuanacu of golden and bronze artifacts leave no doubt that gold preceded bronze (i.e., tin) in that area. Posnansky was emphatic in relegating bronze to the third period of Tiahuanacu, and showed incidences where bronze clamps were used to repair structures from the golden era. Since the mines in the nearby mountains show clear evidence that tin ores and gold were obtained at the same sites, it was probably the discovery of gold followed by its placer mining in the Titicaca region that brought out the existence of cassiterite: the two are found intermingled in the same riverbeds and streams. At the Tipuani river and at the river that flows from Mount Illampu, an official Bolivian report (titled *Bolivia and the Opening of the Panama Canal,* 1912) stated that in addition to the tin ores, "both rivers are famous for the presence of gravels containing immense quantities of gold"; at depths of 300 feet, rock bottom could not be found. Remarkably, "the proportion of gold increases with the depth of the gravel." The report pointed out that Tipuani river gold was 22–23½ carat fine—almost purest gold. The list of Bolivian sites of placer gold is almost inexhaustible, even after all the centuries of exploitation since the Conquest. The Spaniards alone, between 1540 and 1750, extracted from Bolivian sources over 100,000,000 ounces of gold.

Before the land now called "Bolivia" became independent in the nineteenth century, it was known as Upper Peru and was part of the Spaniards' Peruvian domains. The mineral resources certainly knew no political borders, and we have already described in earlier chapters the riches in gold, silver, and copper that the Spaniards encountered in Peru proper and the European belief that the "mother lode" of all gold in the western Americas, north and south, lay within the Peruvian Andes.

A look at a map of South America mineral resources provides a clear picture. Three bands of varying widths of gold, silver, and copper lodes snake their way along the Andean ranges in the northwestern–southeastern slant, all the way from Colombia in the north to Chile and Argentina in the south. Dotted along the way are some of the world's most renowned sources for these metals, some regarded as almost pure mountains of the minerals. The slow forces of nature, and no doubt the immense avalanche of water of the Deluge, have forced the metals and their ores out of their rock-embedded lodes—exposing them, washing them down mountainsides and into riverbeds. Since most of the mightiest rivers of South America flow off the Andean ranges eastward, through the vast plains of Brazil to the Atlantic Ocean, it is no wonder that gold and copper have also been plentiful on this side of the continent.

But it is the lodes within the Andean ranges that are the ultimate source of all the placer and mined metals; and as one looks at these interwined bands of lodes, differently colored on a map for identification, the image bears a resemblance to color drawings of the double-helix structure of DNA, entwined within itself and with its counterpart RNA, the genetic chains of life and heredity of everything that lives on Earth. Within these bands there are scattered other valuable, even rare minerals—platinum, bismuth, manganese, wolfram, iron, mercury, sulphur, antimony, asbestos, cobalt, arsenic, lead, zinc; and, quite important for modern and ancient smelting and refining, coal and petroleum.

Some of the richest lodes of gold, partly washed down riverbeds, lie east and north of Lake Titicaca. It is there, in the Cordillera Real that embraces the lake from its northeast to its southeast that a fourth band joins the others: a band of tin in the form of cassiterite. It becomes prominent on the lake's eastern shore, bends westward along the Tiahuanacu basin, then runs southward almost parallel to the Desaguandero river. It joins the other three bands near Oruro and Lake Poopo, and vanishes there.

When Anu and his spouse arrived to see all the mineral

Figure 133

riches, the sacred precinct of Tiahuanacu, its golden enclosure, its quays, were all in place. Whom did the Anunnaki enlist and bring over, at about 4000 B.C., to build all that? By then, the highland peoples around Sumer had already a tradition of rudimentary metallurgy and stoneworking, and they could have been among the artisans brought over. But the true metallurgical technology including that of casting, of high-rise construction, of building according to architectural plans, and following stellar orientations, was in the hands of the Sumerians.

The central effigy in the semisubterranean sacred enclosure is bearded, as are many of the stone heads attached to the enclosure's wall that portray unknown dignitaries. Many are turbaned, as Sumerian dignitaries had been (Fig. 133).

One must wonder where and how the Incas, continuing the custom of the Ancient Empire, acquired the Sumerian (i.e., Anunnaki-given) rules of succession. Why was it that in their incantations the Inca priests invoked Heaven by uttering the magical words *Zi-Ana* and Earth by the words *Zi-ki-a*—totally meaningless terms in either Quechua or Aymara (according to S. A. Lafone Quevado, *Ensayo Mitologico*)—but words that in Sumerian mean "Heavenly Life" (ZI.ANA) and "Life of Earth and Water" (ZI.KI.A). And why did the Incas retain from ancient empire times the term *Anta* for metals in general and copper in particular—a term that is Sumerian, as AN.TA, would have been of a class with AN.NA (tin) and AN.BAR (iron)?

These relics of Sumerian metallurgical terms (which were borrowed by their successors) are augmented by the discovery of Sumerian mining pictographs. German archaeologists led by A. Bastian have found such symbols incised on rocks on the banks of the Manizales river in Colombia's central gold region (Fig. 134a); and a French governmental mission under E. André, exploring riverbeds in the eastern region, found similar

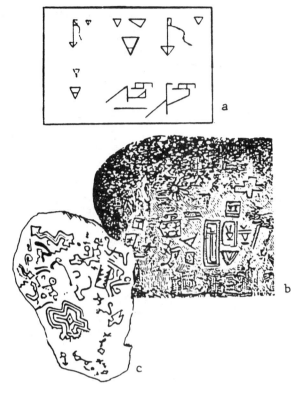

Figure 134

symbols (Fig. 134b) carved on rocks above caves that have been artificially deepened. Many petroglyphs in the Andean gold centers, the routes to them, or at places where the term *Uru* appears as a name-component include symbols that resemble Sumerian cuneiform script or pictographs, such as the radiating cross (Fig. 134c) found among petroglyphs northwest of Lake Titicaca—a symbol that the Sumerians had used to represent the planet Nibiru.

Add to all that the possibility that some of the Sumerians brought over to Lake Titicaca may have survived to present times. Nowadays only a few hundred of them are left; they live on some islands in the lake, sailing upon it in reed boats. The Aymara and Kholla tribesmen that now make up most of the area's inhabitants consider them remnants of the area's earliest dwellers, aliens from another land, whom they call *Uru*. The name is taken to mean "the Olden Ones"; but have they been so called because they came from the Sumerian capital Ur?

According to Posnansky, the Urus named five deities or *Samptni:* Pacani-Malku, meaning Olden or Great Lord; Malku, meaning Lord; and the gods of the Earth, the Waters, and the Sun. The term *malku* is of obvious Near Eastern origin, where it meant (as it still does in Hebrew and Arabic) "king." One of the few studies on the Urus, by W. La Barre (*American Anthropologist* vol. 43), reports that Uru "myths" relate that "we, the people of the lake, are the oldest on this Earth. A long time we are here, from before the time when the Sun was hidden ... Before the Sun hid himself we were already a long time in this place. Then the Kollas came ... They used our bodies for sacrifices when they laid the foundations for their temples ... Tiahuanaco was built before the time of the darkness."

We have already established that the Day of Darkness, "when the Sun was hidden," occurred circa 1400 B.C. It was, we have shown, a global event that left its mark in the writings and recollections of people on both sides of the Earth. This Uru legend, or collective memory, affirms that Tiahuanacu was built before that event, and that the Urus had been there also for a long time before.

To this very day, the lake's Aymara tribesmen sail upon it in reed boats that, they say, they had learned to make from the Urus. The remarkable similarity of these boats to the reed boats of the Sumerians prompted Thor Heyerdahl to replicate the boat and embark on the Kon-Tiki (an epithet of Viracocha) voyages, to prove that the ancient Sumerians could have crossed the oceans.

The extent of Sumerian/Uru-rian presence in the Andes can be gleaned by such other imprints as the fact that *uru* means "day" in all the Andean languages, both in Aymara and Quechua, the same meaning ("daylight") that it had in Mesopotamia. Such other Andean terms as *uma/mayu* for water, *khun* for red, *kap* for hand, *enu/ienu* for eye, *makai* for blow are so clearly of Mesopotamian origin that Pablo Patron (*Nouvelles etudes sur les langues americaines*) concluded that "it is clearly demonstrated that the Quechua and Aymara languages of indigenous Peru had a Sumerian-Assyrian origin."

The term *uru* appears as a component of many geographical names in Bolivia and Peru, such as the important mining center Oruru, the Sacred Valley of the Incas Urubamba ("Plain/valley of the Uru") and its famed river, and many many more. Indeed, in the center of the Sacred Valley there still live in caves the remnants of a tribe that consider themselves descendants of the Urus of Lake Titicaca; they refuse to move from the caves to houses because, they claim, the mountains would collapse if they leave their insides, causing the world's end.

There are other apparent links between the civilization of Mesopotamia and that of the Andes. How explain, for example, the fact that, as in the case of Tiahuanacu, the Sumerian capital Ur was surrounded by a canal with a northern harbor and a southwestern one (leading to the Euphrates river and beyond)? And how explain the Golden Enclosure of the main temple of Cuzco, where the walls were covered with gold plates—just as the ones at Puma-Punku *and Uruk?* And the "Bible in Pictures" in the Coricancha, depicting Nibiru and its orbit?

There were the many customs that led the arriving Spaniards to see in the Indians descendants of the Ten Tribes of Israel. There were the coastal cities and their temples that brought to explorers' minds the sacred precincts and ziggurats of Sumer. And how account for the incredibly ornate textiles of the coastal people near Tiahuanacu, unique in the Americas, except by comparison with the Sumerian textiles, especially those of Ur, that were renowned in antiquity for their exquisite designs and colors? Why the portrayal of gods with conical headdresses, and a goddess with the Umbilical Cutter of Ninti? Why a calendar as in Mesopotamia, and a zodiac as in Sumer, with Precession and twelve houses?

Without rehashing all the evidence that has filled the previous chapters, it seems to us that all the pieces of the puzzle of Andean beginnings fall into place if we acknowledge the hand of the Anunnaki and the presence of Sumerians (alone or with their neighbors) in this region circa 4000 B.C. The legends of the ascent heavenward of the Creator and his two sons, the Moon and the Sun, from the sacred rock on the Island of the Sun (Titicaca Island) may well be recollections of the departure of Anu, his son Shamash and his grandson Sin: having made a short trip by boat from Puma-Punku to a waiting airborne-craft of the Anunnaki.

On that memorable night at Uruk, as soon as Nibiru had been sighted, the priests lit torches that were a signal to nearby villages. There bonfires were lit, as signals to the neighboring settlements; and soon the whole land of Sumer was aglow, celebrating the presence of Anu and Antu and the sighting of the Planet of the Gods.

Whether or not people then realized that they were viewing a celestial sight that occurs once in 3,600 Earth-years, they certainly knew it was a phenomenon once in their lifetimes. Mankind has not ceased to yearn for the return of that planet, and it justly recalls that era as a Golden Age: not only because it was physically so, but also because it culminated a period of peace and unparalleled progress for Mankind.

But no sooner (in Anunnaki terms) had Anu and Antu returned to Nibiru than the peaceful division of Earth among the Anunnaki clans was disturbed. It was circa 3450 B.C., according to our calculations, when the incident of the Tower of Babel took place: an attempt by Marduk/Ra to obtain primacy for his city Babylon in Mesopotamia. Though frustrated by Enlil and Ninurta, the attempt to involve Mankind in building a launch tower brought about the decision of the gods to disperse Mankind and confuse its languages. The sole civilization and its language were now to be split up; and after a chaotic period that lasted some 350 years, the civilization of the Nile, with its own language and rudimentary writing, was formed. It happened, Egyptologists tell us, circa 3100 B.C.

Frustrated in his effort to assume supremacy in civilized Sumer, Marduk/Ra seized upon the granting of civilization to the Egyptians to return to that land and reclaim its lordship from his brother Thoth. Now Thoth found himself a god without a people; and it is our suggestion that accompanied by some of his faithful followers he chose an abode in the New Realms —in Mesoamerica.

And we further suggest that it happened not just "circa 3100 B.C." but exactly in 3113 B.C.—the time, the year, and even the day from which the Mesoamericans began their Long Count.

Counting the passage of time by anchoring the calendar to a major event is not unusual at all. The Western Christian calendar counts the years from the birth of Christ. The Moslem calendar begins with the *Hegira,* the migration of Mohammed from Mecca to Medina. Skipping over the many examples from various preceding lands and monarchies, we shall mention the Jewish Calendar, which is in effect the ancient (and first-ever) Calendar of Nippur, the Sumerian city dedicated to Enlil. Contrary to the common assumption that the Jewish count of years (5,748 in 1988) is from the "beginning of the world," it is actually from the beginning of the Nippurian calendar in 3760 B.C.— the time, we assume, of Anu's state visit to Earth.

Why not then accept our suggestion that the arrival of Quetzalcoatl, i.e., the Winged Serpent, in his new realm was the occasion for starting the Long Count of the Mesoamerican calendar—especially since it was this very god who had introduced the calendar to these lands?

Figure 135

Having been overthrown by his own brother, Thoth (known in Sumerian texts as *Ningishzidda*—Lord of the Tree of Life) was a natural ally of his brother's adversaries, the Enlilite gods and their Chief Warrior, Ninurta. It is recorded that when Ninurta desired that a ziggurat-temple be built for him by Gudea, it was Ningishzidda/Thoth who had drawn the building plans; he may have also specified the rare materials for it, and had a hand in assuring the supplies. As a friend of the Enlilites, he had to be friendly with Ishkur/Adad and the Andean realm that was put under his control in the Titicaca region; he was probably even a welcome guest there.

Indeed, we can discern evidence that a Serpent God and his African followers probably lent a hand in developing some of the satellite metal-processing sites around Tiahuanacu. Some stone stelae and sculptures from a time in between Periods I and II of Tiahuanacu are decorated with serpent symbols—a symbol otherwise rare and unknown in Tiahuanacu; and some of the sculptures of people found at nearby sites (Fig. 135) as well as two colossal busts that have been moved and put up by the natives as a decoration at the entrance to the Tiahuanacu village church (Fig. 136) reveal, even in their eroded state, negroid features.

Posnansky, stung by criticism of his "fantastic" antiquity, did not attempt to date the transition from Period I, when sandstone was used for construction and statuary, to the more sophisticated Period II when hard andesite stone began to be used. But the fact that the changeover also marked the shifting

Figure 136

of Tiahuanacu's focus from gold to tin suggests to us the 2500 B.C. period. If, as we surmise, the Enlilite gods in charge of Near Eastern highland domains (Adad, Ninurta) were away in the New Realm, busy establishing the Cassite colony, it explains why, at about that time, Inanna/Ishtar usurped the power in the Near East and launched a bloody offensive against Marduk/Ra to avenge the death of her beloved spouse Dumuzi (caused, she claimed, by Marduk).

It was at that time, and probably as a consequence of the instability in the Old Realms, that the concerned gods decided to create a new civilization away from it all—in the Andes. While Tiahuanacu was to focus on supplying tin, there were almost inexhaustible sources of gold all along the Andean slopes. All that was needed was to give Andean Man the necessary know-how and tools to go after the gold.

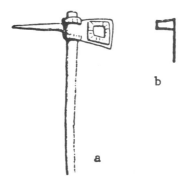

Figure 137

And so it was, circa 2400 B.C.—just as Montesinos had concluded—that Manco Capac was given the golden wand at Titicaca and sent to the gold region of Cuzco.

What was the shape and purpose of this magical wand? One of the most thorough studies on the subject is *Corona Incaica* by Juan Larrea. Analyzing artifacts, legends, and pictorial depictions of Inca rulers, he concluded that it was an axe, an object called *Yuari* that when first given to Manco Capac was named *Tupa-Yuari*, Royal Axe (Fig. 137a). But was it a weapon or a tool?

To find an answer, we go to ancient Egypt. The Egyptian term for "gods, divine" was *Neteru*, "Guardians." That however was exactly the term by which Sumer (actually, Shumer) was called—"Land of the Guardians"; and in early translations of biblical and pseudo-biblical texts into Greek, the term *Nefilim* (alias Anunnaki) was rendered "Guardians." The hieroglyph for this term was an axe (Fig. 137b); E. A. Wallis Budge (*The Gods of the Egyptians*) in a special chapter titled "The Axe As a Symbol of God" concluded that it was made of metal. He mentioned that the symbol (as the term *Neter*) was probably borrowed from the Sumerians. That it was indeed so can be gleaned from Fig. 133.

Thus was Andean civilization launched: by giving Andean Man an axe with which to mine the gods' gold.

The tales of Manco Capac and the Ayar brothers in all probability also mark the end of the Mesopotamian and gold phases of Tiahuanacu. A hiatus followed; it lasted until the place came back to life as the world's tin capital. The Cassites arrived and moved the tin or ready bronze via the transpacific route. In time other routes developed. The existence of settlements with an astonishing abundance of bronzes points to a route along the Beni River eastward to Brazil's Atlantic coast, thence with the help of ocean currents all the way to the Arabian Sea, the Red Sea to Egypt, or the Persian Gulf to Mesopotamia. There could be and probably was a route via the Ancient Empire and the Urubamba river, as suggested by the megalithic sites and the discovery of a lump of pure tin at Machu Picchu. This route led to the Amazon and the northeastern tip of South America, thence across the Atlantic to West Africa and the Mediterranean.

And then, once Mesoamerica attained a modicum of civilized settlements, a third and quicker alternative was offered by its narrow neck that provided a virtual land-bridge between the Pacific Ocean and the Atlantic via the Caribbean Sea—a route essentially followed, in reverse, by the conquistadores.

This third route, that of the Olmec civilization, must have become the preferred route after 2000 B.C., as evidenced by the presence of Mediterraneans; for, in 2024 B.C. the Anunnaki led by Ninurta, fearing that the spaceport in the Sinai would be overrun by followers of Marduk, destroyed it with nuclear weapons.

Unstoppable, the deadly nuclear cloud drifted eastward toward southern Mesopotamia, devastating Sumer and its last capital, Ur. As though fate had decreed it, the cloud drifted southward, sparing Babylon; and losing no time, Marduk marched in with an army of Canaanite and Amorite followers, declaring kingship in Babylon.

It was then, we believe, that the decision was made to grant the African followers of Thoth/Quetzalcoatl civilization in his Mesoamerican realm.

One of the rare academic studies admitting that the Olmecs were negroid Africans was *Africa and the Discovery of America* by Leo Wiener, professor of Slavic and other languages at Harvard University. Based on racial features and other considerations but mostly on linguistic analysis, he concluded that the Olmec tongue belonged to the Mande group of languages that originated in West Africa, between the Niger and Congo river. But writing in 1920, before the true age of Olmec remains became known, he attributed their presence in Mesoamerica to Arab seafarers and slave traders in the Middle Ages.

More than half a century had to pass before another major academic study, *Unexpected Faces in Ancient America* by Alexander von Wuthenau, tackled the problem head on. Enriched with a profusion of photographs of Semitic and Negroid portraits from Mesoamerica's art heritage, he surmised that the first links between the Old and New World developed during the reign of the Egyptian Pharaoh Ramses III (twelfth century B.C.) and that the Olmecs were Kushites from Nubia (Egypt's principal source of gold). Some other black Africans, he felt, could have come over on "Phoenician and Jewish ships" between 500 B.C. and A.D. 200. Ivan van Sertima, whose study *They Came Before Columbus* set out to bridge the half-century gap between the two previous academic works, tended toward the Kushite solution: it was when the black kings of Kush ascended the throne of Egypt as its twenty-fifth dynasty in the eighth century B.C., trading in silver and bronze, that they—probably as a result of shipwrecks—also held sway in Mesoamerica.

This conclusion was prompted by the notion that the giant Olmec heads were from about that time; but now we know that Olmec beginnings go back to circa 2000 B.C. Who, then, were these Africans?

We hold that Leo Wiener's linguistic studies have been correct, but not so his time frame. When one compares the faces on the colossal Olmec heads (Fig. 138a) with those of West Africans (as this one of Nigeria's leader, General I. B. Banagida—Fig. 138b), the gap of thousands of years is bridged by the obvious similarity. It is from that part of Africa that Thoth could have brought over his followers expert in mining, for it is there that gold *and tin,* and copper to alloy bronze with, have been abundant. Nigeria has been renowned for its bronze figurines—cast in the telltale Lost Wax process—for millennia; recent research has carbon-dated some of the sites, in which the most ancient ones have been found to date to about 2100 B.C.

It is there, in West Africa, that the country now called Ghana bore for centuries the name *Gold Coast,* for that is what it

Figure 138

Figure 139

was—a source of gold known even to the Phoenicians. And then we have the area's Ashanti people, renowned throughout the continent for their goldsmithing skills; among their handiwork are weights made of gold whose shape is frequently that of miniature step-pyramids (Fig. 139)—in lands where no such structures exist.

It was, we believe, when the Old World order was upheavaled, that Thoth undertook the task of bringing his expert followers over: to start a new life, a new civilization, and new mining operations.

In time, as we have shown, these operations and the miners, the Olmecs, moved south, first to Mexico's Pacific shores, then across the isthmus into northern South America. Their ultimate destination was the Chavin area; there they met the gold miners of Adad, the people of the golden wand.

The golden age of the New Realms did not last forever. Olmec sites in Mexico underwent destruction; the Olmecs themselves and their bearded companions met a brutal end. Mochica pottery depicts enslaving giants and winged gods warring with metal blades. The Ancient Empire witnessed tribal clashes and invasions. And in the highlands of Titicaca, Aymara legends recalled invaders who marched up the mountains from the seacoast and slew the white men who were still there.

Were these reflections of the conflicts among the Anunnaki, in which they increasingly involved Mankind? Or did it all begin to happen after the gods had left—sailing off upon the sea, ascending heavenward?

Whichever way it happened, it is certain that in time the links between the Old Realms and the New Realms were broken off. In the Old World the Americas became only a dim memory—hints by this or that classical writer, tales of Atlantis heard from Egyptian priests, even perplexing maps that trace unknown continents. Was it all myth, were there really lands of gold and tin beyond the Pillars of Hercules? In time, the New Realms became the Lost Realms as far as Westerners were concerned.

In the New Realms themselves, the golden past became only a legendary memory as the centuries rolled on. But the memories would not die, and the tales persisted—of how it all began and where, of Quetzalcoatl and Viracocha, of how they will one day return.

As we now find colossal heads, megalithic walls, abandoned sites, a lonely gate with its Weeping God, we must wonder: Were the American peoples right in telling us that these gods were among them, in expecting them to return?

For until white man came again and only wrought havoc, the people of the Andes, where it all began, could only look at the empty golden enclosures and hope against hope to see once again their winged God of the Golden Tears.

Figure 140

SOURCES

In addition to specific references in the text, the following periodicals, scholarly studies and individual works were among sources consulted:

I. Studies, articles and reports in various issues of the following periodicals and scholarly series:

Academia Colombiana de Historia: Biblioteca de Antropologia (Bogotá)
Acta Antropologica (Mexico City)
American Anthropological Association, Memoirs (Menasha, Wisc.)
American Anthropologist (Menasha, Wisc.)
American Antiquity (Salt Lake City)
American Journal of Anthropology (Baltimore)
American Museum of Natural History: Anthropological Papers (New York)
American Philosophical Society: Transactions (Philadelphia)
Anales del Instituto Nacional de Antropologia e Historia (Mexico City)
Anales del Museo Nacional de Arqueologia, Historia y Etnologia (Mexico City)
Annals of the New York Academy of Sciences (New York)
Anthropological Journal of Canada (Ottawa)
Anthropology (Berkeley)
Archaeoastronomy (College Park)
Archaeology (New York)
Arqueologia Mexicana (Mexico City)
Arqueologicas (Lima)
Atlantis (Berlin and Zurich)
Baessler Archiv (Berlin and Leipzig)

Biblical Archaeology Review (Washington, D.C.)

Biblioteca Boliviana (La Paz)

Bureau of American Ethnology: Bulletin (Washington, D.C.)

California University, Archaeological Research Facility: Contributions (Berkeley)

Carnegie Institution of Washington, Publications: Contributions to American Archaeology (Washington, D.C.)

Carnegie Institution of Washington, Department of Archaeology: Notes on Middle American Archaeology and Ethnology (Cambridge, Mass.)

Connecticut Academy of Arts and Sciences: Memoirs (New Haven)

Cuadernos Americanos (Mexico City)

Cuzco (Cuzco)

El Mexico Antiguo (Mexico City)

Ethnographical Museum of Sweden: Monograph Series (Stockholm)

Harvard University, Peabody Museum of American Archaeology and Ethnology: Memoirs and *Papers* (Cambridge, Mass.)

Inca (Lima)

Instituto Nacional de Antropologia e Historia: Memorias and *Boletin* (Mexico City)

International Congresses of Americanists: Proceedings (Various cities)

Journal of the Ethnological Society of London (London)

Journal of the Manchester Egyptian and Oriental Society (Manchester)

Journal of the Royal Anthropological Institute (London)

Liverpool University Centre for Latin American Studies: Monograph Series (Liverpool)

Museum für Volkerkunde im Hamburg: Mitteilungen (Hamburg)

Museum of the American Indian, Heye Foundation: Contributions and *Leaflets* and *Indian Notes and Monographs* (New York)

National Geographic Magazine (Washington, D.C.)

National Geographic Society, Technical Papers: Mexican Archaeology Series (Washington, D.C.)

Natural History (New York)

New World Archaeological Foundation: Papers (Provo)

Revista del Museo de La Plata (Buenos Aires)

Revista del Museo Nacional (Lima)

Revista do Instituto Historico e Geografico Brasiliero (Rio de Janeiro)

Revista Historica (Lima)
Revista Mexicana de Estudios Antropologicos (Mexico City)
Revista Mexicana de Estudios Historicos (Mexico City)
Revista Universitaria (Lima)
Revue Anthropologique (Paris)
Revue d'Ethnographie (Paris)
Scientific American (New York)
Smithsonian Institution, Bureau of American Ethnology: Bulletin (Washington, D.C.)
Studies in Pre-Columbian Art and Archaeology (Dumbarton Oaks)
University of California Anthropological Records (Berkeley)
University of California: Publications in American Archaeology and Ethnology (Berkeley)
University of Pennsylvania, the University Museum: The Museum Journal (Philadelphia)
Wira-Kocha (Lima)

II. Individual Works and Studies:

Allen, G. *Gold!* 1964.
America Pintoresca: Descripcion de viajes al Nuevo Continente. 1884.
Anders, F. *Das Pantheon der Maya.* 1963.
Andree, R. *Die Metalle bei den Naturvölkern.* 1884.
Antiguo Peru: espacio y tiempo. 1960.
Anton, F. *Alt-Peru und seine Kunst.* 1962.
Arnold, J. R. and W. F. Libby. *Radiocarbon Dates.* 1950.
Arte Prehispanico de Mexico. 1933.
Aveni, A. F. (ed.) *Archaeostronomy in Pre-Columbian America.* 1975.
——. (ed.) *Native American Astronomy.* 1977.
——. (ed.) *Archaeoastronomy in the New World.* 1982.

Batres, L. *Teotihuacan o la Ciudad Sagrada de los Toltecas.* 1889.
——. *Civilizacion Prehistorica (Estado de Veracruz).* 1908.
Baudin, L. *La Vie Quotidienne au Temps des Derniers Incas.* 1955.
Baudin, L., C. Troll and C. D. Gibson. *Los origines del Indio-Americano.* 1937.
Belli, P. L. *La Civilizacion Nazca.* 1960.
Beltran-Kropp, M. *Cuzco—Window on Peru.* 1956, 1970.
Bennett, W. C. *Excavations at Tiahuanaco.* 1934.

——. *Excavations in Bolivia.* 1936.
——. *The Ancient Arts of the Andes.* 1954.
Bennett, W. C. and J. B. Bird. *Andean Culture History.* 1964.
Benson, E. P. *The Maya World.* 1967.
——. (ed.) *The Dumbarton Oaks Conference on the Olmecs.* 1968.
Bernal, I. *Ancient Mexico in Color.* 1968.
——. *El Mundo Olmeca.* 1968.
——. *Stone Reliefs in the Dainzu Area.* 1973.
Bernal, I., R. Piña-Chan and F. Camara Barbachano. *3000 Years of Art and Life in Mexico.* 1968.
Bird, J. *Paracas Fabrics and Nazca Needlework.* 1954.
Bird, J. (ed.) *Art and Life in Old Peru.* 1962.
Blom, F. and O. La Farge. *Tribes and Temples.* 1926.
Bollaert, W. *Antiquarian, Ethnological and Other Researches in New Granada, Eqador, Peru and Chile.* 1860.
Braessler, A. *Ancient Peruvian Art.* 1902/1903.
——. *Altperuanische Metallgeräte.* 1906.
Brinton, D. G. *The Books of Chilam Balam.* 1892.
British Academy, The. *The Place of Astronomy in the Ancient World.* 1974.
Buck, F. *El Calendario Maya en la Cultura Tiahuanacu.* 1937.
Burland, C. A. *Peoples of the Sun.* 1976.
Buse, H. *Huaras y Chavin.* 1957.
——. *Guia Arqueologica de Lima.* 1960.
——. *Machu Picchu.* 1961.
——. *Peru 10,000 años.* 1962.
Bushnell, G.H.S. *Peru.* 1957.
——. *Ancient Arts of the Americas.* 1965.

Cabello de Balboa, M. *Historia del Peru.* 1920.
Carnero Albarran, N. *Minas e Indios del Peru.* 1981.
Caso A. *La religion de los Aztecas.* 1936.
——. *Thirteen Masterpieces of Mexican Archaeology.* 1936.
——. *El Complejo Arquelogico de Tula.* 1941.
——. *Calendario y Escritura de las Antiguas Culturas de Monte Alban.* 1947.
——. *The Aztecs—People of the Sun.* 1958.
——. *Los Calendarios Prehispanicos.* 1967.
——. *Reyes y reinos de la Mixteca.* 1977.
Centro de Investigaciones Antropologias de Mexico. *Esplendor del Mexico Antiguo.* 1959.
Chapman, W. *The Search for El Dorado.* 1967.
——. *The Golden Dream.* 1967.

Coe, M. D. *Mexico*. 1962.
——. *The Maya*. 1966.
Coe, M. D. and R. Diehl. *In the Land of the Olmec*. 1980.
Cornell, J. *The First Stargazers*. 1981.
Corson, C. *Maya Anthropomorphic Figurines from Jaina Island*. 1976.
Cottrell, A. (ed.) *The Encyclopedia of Ancient Civilizations*. 1980.
Crequi-Montfort, G. de. *Fouilles de la mission scientifique française à Tiahuanaco*. 1906.

D'Amato, J. and J. H. del Mazo. *Machu Picchu*. 1975.
Dennis, W. H. *Metallurgy in the Service of Man*. 1961.
Diccionario Porrua de Historia, Biografia y Geografia de Mexico. 1971.
Dihl, R. A. *Tula—The Capital of Ancient Mexico*. 1983.
Disseldorf, E. P. *Kunst und Religion der Maya Völker*. 1926, 1931.
Disselhoff, H. D. *Gott Muss Peruaner Sein*. 1956.
——. *Kinder der Erdgöttin*. 1960.
——. *Les Grandes Civilizations de l'Amerique Ancienne*. 1963.
——. *Geschichte der Altamerikanischen Kulturen*. 1967.
——. *Oasenstadte und Zaubersteine im Land der Inka*. 1968.
——. *El Imperio de los Incas*. 1973.
——. *Incaica*. 1982.
Doering, H. *Old Peruvian Art*. 1926.
Dubelaar, C. N. *The Petroglyphs in the Guianas and Adjacent Areas of Brazil and Venezuela*. 1986.
Duran, Fray D. *Historia de las Indias de Nueva España*. 1867. (English translation by Heyden D. and F. Horacasitas, 1964).

Emmerich, A. *Sweat of the Sun and Tears of the Moon*. 1965.
——. *Gods and Men in Precolumbian Art*. 1967.
Engel, F. *Elementos de Prehistoria Peruana*. 1962.
——. *Le Monde Précolumbien des Andes*. 1972.

Fage, J. D. *A History of West Africa*. 1969.
Falb, R. *Das Land der Inca*. 1883.
Fernandez, A. *Pre-Hispanic Gods of Mexico*. 1984.
Festschrift Eduard Seler. 1922.
Fisher, J. R. *Silver Mines and Silver Miners in Colonial Peru*. 1977.
Flornoy, B. *Découverte des Sources des Andes a la Forêt Amazonienne*. 1946.
——. *The World of the Inca*. 1956.

——. *Amazone—Terres et Hommes.* 1969.
Forbes, D. *On the Aymara Indians of Bolivia and Peru.* 1870.
Forbes, R.J. *Metallurgy in Antiquity.* 1950.
Furst, J.L. and P.T. Furst. *Pre-Columbian Art of Mexico.* 1980.
Furst, P.T. *Gold Before Columbus.* 1964.

Garcia Rosell, C. *Los Monumentos Arqueologicos del Peru.* 1942.
Garcilaso de la Vega, el Inca. *Royal Commentaries of the Incas* (translated into English by Livermore, H.V.) 1966.
Gates, W. *An Outline Dictionary of Maya Glyphs.* 1931.
Giesecke, A.A. *Guide to Cuzco.* 1924.
Gonzalez de la Rosa, M. *Les deux Tiahuanacos.* 1910.
Gordon, G.B. *Prehistoric Ruins of Copan, Honduras,* 1896.

Haberland, W. *Die Kulturen Meso—und Zentralamerika.* 1969.
Harlow, W.T. (ed.) *Voyages of Great Pioneers.* 1929.
Hawkins, G.S. *Beyond Stonehenge.* 1973.
Hedges, E.S. *Tin and Its Alloys.* 1959.
Heggie, D.C. (ed.) *Archaeoastronomy in the Old World.* 1982.
Heim, A. *Wunderland Peru.* 1948.
Heizer, R.E., P. Drucker, and J.A. Graham. *Investigations at La Venta.* 1968.
Helfritz, H. *Mexican Cities of the Gods.* 1970.
Heyerdahl, T. *The Kon-Tiki Expedition.* 1951.
——. *The Ra Expeditions.* 1971.
Homenaje al Profesor Paul Rivet. 1955.

Ibarra Grasso, D.E. *Tiahuanaco.* 1956.
——. *Prehistoria de Bolivia.* 1965.
——. *Cosmogonia y Mitologia Indigena Americana.* 1980.
——. *Ciencia en Tihuanaku y el Incario.* 1982.
——. *Ciencia Astronomica y Sociologia.* 1984.
——. *Pueblos Indigenos de Bolivia.* 1985.
Illescas Cook, G. *El Candelabro de Paracas y la Cruz del Sur.* 1981.
Inwards, R. *The Temple of the Andes.* 1884.
Ixtlilxochitl, F. de Alva. *Historia Chichimeca* (Translated and edited by Bonte, H.G. : *Das Buch der Könige von Tezuco.* 1930).

Jenness, D. (ed.) *The American Aborigines and Their Origin and Antiquity.* 1933.
Joyce, T.A. *South American Archaeology.* 1912.
——. *The Weeping God.* 1913.

——. *Mexican Archaeology*. 1920.
——. *Maya and Mexican Art*. 1927.

Katz, F. *The Ancient American Civilizations*. 1972.
Kaufmann-Doig, F. *Arqueologia Peruana*. 1971.
——. *Tiahuanaco a la luz de la Arqueologia*. 1965.
Keating, R.W. (ed.) *Peruvian Prehistory*. 1986.
Krickberg, W. *Altmexikanische Kulturen*. 1956.
——. *Felsplastik und Felsbilder bei den Kulturvolkern Altamer-iker*. 1969.
Krickberg, W., H. Trimborn, W. Müller, and O. Zerris, *Pre-Columbian American Religions*. 1968.
Kroeber, A. L. *Archaeological Explorations in Peru*. 1926 and 1931.
Krupp, E. C. *Echoes of Ancient Skies: The Astromomies of Lost Civilizations*. 1983.
——. (ed.) *In Search of Ancient Astronomies*. 1978.
——. (ed.) *Archaeoastronomy and the Roots of Science*. 1983.
Kubler, G. *The Art and Archaeology of Ancient America*. 1962.
Kutscher. G. *Chimu, Eine altindianische Hochkultur*. 1950.

Lafone Quevedo, S. A. *Tres Relaciones de Antiquedades Peruanas*. 1950.
Landa, Diego de. *Relacion de las cosas de Yucatan*. 1956 (English translation by W. Gates: *Yucatan Before and After the Conquest*. 1937).
Larrea, J. *Del Surrealismo a Machupicchu*. 1967.
Lathrap, D. W. *The Upper Amazon*. 1970.
Lawrence, A. W. and J. Young. (eds.) *Narratives of the Discovery of America*. 1931.
Leicht, H. *Pre-Inca Art and Culture*. 1960.
Lehmann, W. *Einige probleme centralamerikanische kalenders*. 1912.
——. *The History of Ancient Mexican Archaeology*. 1922.
Lehmann, W. and H. Doering, *Kunstgeshichte des alten Peru*. 1924.
Leon-Portilla, M. *Pre-Columbian Literature of Mexico*. 1969.
Lothrop, S. K. *Zacaulpa: A Study of Ancient Quiche Artifacts*. 1936.
——. *Metals from the Cenote of Sacrifice, Chichen Itza, Yucatan*. 1952.
——. *Treasures of Ancient America*. 1964.
Lothrop, S. K., W. F. Foshag, and J. Mahler, *Pre-Columbian Art: The Robert Woods Bliss Collection*. 1957.

Ludendorff, H. *Über die Entstehung der Tzolkin-Periode im Kalendar der Maya.* 1930.
——. *Das Mondalter in der Inschriften des Maya.* 1931.

Maguina, J.E. *Lima Guide Book.* 1957.
Maler, T. *Explorations in the Department of Peten, Guatemala.* 1911.
Mantell, C.L. *Tin, Its Mining, Production, Technology and Application.* 1929.
Markham, C.R. *Peru.* 1880.
——. *Narratives of the Rites and Laws of the Yncas.* 1883.
——. *The Travels of Pedro de Cieza de Leon.* 1884.
——. *The Incas of Peru.* 1912.
Marquina, I. *Arquitectura Prehispanica.* 1951.
Martinez Hernandez, J. *La creacion del mundo segun los Mayas.* 1912.
Mason, J.A. *The Ancient Civilizations of Peru.* 1957, 1968.
Maspero, G. *Popular Stories of Ancient Egypt.* 1915.
Maudsley, A.P. *Explorations in Guatemala.* 1883.
——. *Archaeology.* 1889–1902.
Mead, C. *Prehistoric Bronzes in South America.* 1915.
Means, P.A. *Ancient Civilizations of the Andes.* 1931.
Meggers, B.J. *Ecuador.* 1966.
Metropolitan Museum of Art, New York *The Iconography of Middle American Sculpture.* 1973.
Meyer, C. and C. Gallenkamp. *The Mystery of the Ancient Maya.* 1985.
Middendorf, E.W. *Wörterbuch des Runa Simi oder der Keshua-Sprache.* 1890.
——. *Las Civilizaciones Aborigines del Peru.* 1959.
Miller, M.E. *The Arts of Mesoamerica.* 1986.
Mitre, B. *Las Ruinas de Tiahuanaco.* 1955.
Montell, G. *Dress and Ornaments in Ancient Peru.* 1929.
Morley, S.G. *The Inscriptions at Copan.* 1920.
——. *The Inscriptions of Peten.* 1937–1938.
Morris, A.A. *Digging in Yucatan.* 1931.
Morris, C. and D.E. Thompson. *Huanaco Pampa.* 1985.
Morris, E.H., J. Charlot, and A.A. Morris. *The Temple of the Warriors at Chichen Itza.* 1931.
Mosley, M.E. *The Maritime Foundations of Andean Civilization.* 1975.
Myers, B.S. *Art and Civilization.* 1967.

Neruda, P. *Alturas de Machu Picchu.* 1972.

O'Neil, W.M. Time and the Calendars. 1975.

Pardo, L.A. *La Metropoli de los Incas*. 1937.
——. *Los Grandes Monolitos de Sayhuiti*. 1945.
——. *Ruinas del Santurio de Huiracocha*. 1946.
——. *Historia y Arqueologia del Cuzco*. 1957.
Paredes, R. *Tiahuanaco y la Provincia de Ingavi*. 1956.
——. *Mitos y supersticiones de Bolivia*. 1963.
Patron, P. *Nouvelles Etudes sur les Langues Américaines*. 1907.
Piña-Chan, R. *El pueblo del jaguar*. 1964.
——. *Jaina, La casa en el agua*. 1968.
——. *Chichen-Itza*. 1980.
Ponce Sangines, C. *Ceramica Tiwanacota*. 1948.
——. *Tunupa y Ekako*. 1969.
——. *Tiwanaku: Espacio, Tiempo y Cultura*. 1977.
——. *La cultura nativa en Bolivia*. 1979.
Portugal, M. and D. Ibarra Grasso. *Copacabana*. 1957.
Posnansky, A. *Guia para el Visitante de los Monumentos Prehistoricos de Tihuanacu e Islas del Sol y la Luna*. 1910.
——. *El Clima del Altiplano y la Extension del Lago Titicaca*. 1911.
——. *Tihuanacu y la civilizacion prehispanica en el Altiplano Andino*. 1911.
——. *Templos y Viviendes prehispanicas*. 1921.
Prescott, W.H. *History of the Conquest of Mexico*. 1843.
——. *History of the Conquest of Peru*. 1847.
Prieto, C. *Mining in the New World*. 1973.
Proskouriakoff, T. *An Album of Maya Architecture*. 1946.
——. *A Study of Classical Maya Sculpture*. 1950.
Raimondi, A. *El Peru*. 1874.
——. *Minerales del Peru*. 1878.
Ravines R. and J.J. Alvarez Sauri. *Fechas Radiocarbonicas Para el Peru*. 1967.
Reiss, W. and A. Stübel. *Das Totenfeld von Ancon in Peru*. 1880–1887.
Rice, C. *La Civilizacion Preincaica y el Problema Sumerologico*. 1926.
Rivet, P. *Los origines del hombre Americano*. 1943.
Roeder, G. *Altaegyptische Erzählungen und Märchen*. 1927.
Romero, E. *Geografia Economica del Peru*. 1961.
Roys, R.L. *The Book of Chilam Balam of Chumayel*. 1967.
Rozas, E.A. *Cuzco*. 1954.
Ruppert, K. *The Caracol at Chichen Itza*. 1933.
Ruz-Lhuillier, A. *Campeche en la arqueologia Maya*. 1945.
——. *Guia arqueologica de Tula*. 1945.

Rydén, S. *Archaeological Researches in the Highlands of Bolivia.* 1947.
——. *Andean Excavations.* Vol. I 1957, vol. II 1959.

Saville, M.H. *Contributions to South American Archaeology.* 1907.
Scholten de D'Ebneth, M. *Chavin de Huantar.* 1980.
Schmidt, M. *Kunst und Kultur von Peru.* 1929.
Seler, E. *Peruanische Alterthümer.* 1893.
——. *Gesammelte Abhandlungen zur Amerikanischen Sprach— und Alterthumkunde.* 1902–03.
Shook. E.M. *Explorations in the Ruins of Oxkintok, Yucatan.* 1940.
Shook, E.M. and T. Proskouriakoff. *Yucatan.* 1951.
Sivirichi, A. *Pre-Historia Peruana.* 1930.
——. *Historia de la Cultura Peruana.* 1953.
Smith, A.L. *Archaeological Reconnaissance in Central Guatemala.* 1955.
Smith, G.E. *Ships as Evidence of the Migrations of Early Cultures.* 1917.
Spinden, H.J. *A Study of Maya Art.* 1913.
——. *The Reduction of Maya Dates.* 1924.
——. *New World Correlations.* 1926.
——. *Origin of Civilizations in Central America and Mexico.* 1933.
Squier, E.G. *The Primeval Monuments of Peru.* 1853, 1879.
——. *Tiahuanaco—Baalbek del Nuevo Mundo.* 1909.
Steward, J.H. (ed.) *Handbook of South American Indians.* 1946.
Stirling, M. *An Initial Series from Tres Zapotes, Veracruz, Mexico.* 1939.
——. *Stone Monuments of Southern Mexico.* 1943.
Stoepel, K.T. *Südamerikanische Prähistorische Tempel und Gottheiten.* 1912.
——. *Discoveries in Ecuador and Southern Colombia.* 1912.
Strebel, H. *Alt-Mexico.* 1885–1889.

Tello, J.C. *Antiguo Peru: Primera epoca.* 1929.
——. *Arte Antiguo Peruana.* 1938.
——. *Origen y Desarrollo de las Civilizaciones Prehistoricas Andinas.* 1942.
——. *Paracas.* 1959.
Temple, J.E. *Maya Astronomy.* 1930.
Thompson, J.E.S. *Maya Hieroglyphic Writing.* 1950.
——. *A Catalog of Maya Hieroglyphs.* 1962.

——. *The Rise and Fall of Maya Civilization.* 1964.
——. *Maya History and Religion.* 1970.
Tozzer, A.M. *Chichen Itza and its Cenote of Sacrifices.* 1957.
Tres Relaciones de Antiguedades Peruanas. 1879, 1950.
Trimborn, H. *Das Alte Amerika.* 1959.
——. *Die Indianischen Hochkulturen des Alten Amerika.* 1963.
——. *Alte Hochkulturen Südamerikas.* 1964.
Tylecote, R.F. *A History of Metallurgy.* 1976.

Ubbelohde-Doering, H. *Old Peruvian Art.* 1936.
——. *The Art of Ancient Peru.* 1952.
——. *Alt-Mexicanische und Peruanische Mallerei.* 1959.
Uhle, M. *Kultur and Industrie Südamerikanischer Völker.* 1889.
——. *Pachacamac.* 1903.
——. *The Nazca Pottery of Ancient Peru.* 1912.
——. *Wesen und Ordnung der altperuanischen Kulturen.* 1959.
Uzielli, G. *Toscanelli, Colombo e Vespucci.* 1902.

Valcarcel, L.E. *Arte antiguo Peruana.* 1932.
——. *The Latest Archaeological Discoveries in Peru.* 1938.
——. *Muestrari de Arte Peruana Precolombino.* 1938.
——. *Etnohistoria del Peru.* 1959.
——. *Machu Picchu.* 1964.
Vargas, V.A. *Machu Picchu—enigmatica ciudad Inka.* 1972.
von Hagen, V.F. *The Ancient Sun Kingdoms of the Americas.* 1963.
——. *The Desert Kingdoms of Peru.* 1964.
von Tschudi, J.J. *Die Kechua-Sprache.* 1853.

Westheim, P. *The Sculpture of Ancient Mexico.* 1963
——. *The Art of Ancient Mexico.* 1965.
Willard, T.A. *The City of the Sacred Well.* 1926.
——. *The Lost Empires of the Itzaes and Maya.* 1933.
Willey, G.R. *An Introduction to American Archaeology.* 1966.
Willey, G.R. (ed.) *Archaeology of Southern Mesoamerica.* 1965.
Williamson, R.A. (ed.) *Archaeoastronomy in the Americas.* 1978.
Wiener, C. *Pérou et Bolivie.* 1880.
——. *Viaje al Yucatan.* 1884.

Zahm, J.A. *The Quest of El Dorado.* 1917.

INDEX

287